THE RIGHT TO WIN

CYRIL FARRELL
with
MARTIN BREHENY

BLACKWATER PRESS

Printed in Ireland at the press of the publishers 1994

© 1994 Blackwater Press,
Broomhill Road,
Tallaght,
Dublin 24.

ISBN 0 86 121 5397

Editor
Deirdre Greenan

Design & Layout
Edward Callan

Front Cover
Philip Ryan

All rights reserved. No part of this publication may be reproduced, stored in a retrieval system, or transmitted in any form, or by any means, electronic, mechanical, photocopying, recording, or otherwise, without prior written permission of the publishers.

This book is sold subject to the conditions that it shall not, by way of trade or otherwise, be lent, resold, hired out or otherwise circulated without the publisher's prior consent in any form of binding or cover other than that in which it is published and without a similar condition including this condition being imposed on the subsequent purchaser.

Dedication

For my mother, Lucy and my late father, Vincent.

The support and generosity of AIB Bank in the publication of this book is greatly appreciated by the authors.

AIB's enthusiasm and interest in the project was very helpful in bringing it to fruition.

Acknowledgements

It's only when you become involved in a project like this that you realise how many people are required to guide it through the various stages. The success, or otherwise, depends greatly on those around you.

I was lucky to have a first class squad whose support, in many and varied ways, was central to this publication. Martin Breheny, using his own special methods of persuasion, helped me to recollect what was relevant and discard what was not and then sifted, sorted and collated my memories, before arranging them in book form.

He did it with an unrelenting zeal and enthusiasm and I thank him sincerely for all his efforts. I am also grateful to John O'Connor and his Blackwater Press team, Deirdre Greenan, Edward Callan, Philip Ryan and Anna O'Donovan for their great work in bringing this book to fruition.

It was most encouraging to get the backing of AIB Bank. Right from the start, AIB's Pat O'Mahony and Adrienne Murray did more than represent the sponsors, they were also very enthusiastic backers of the project. That was much appreciated. I am grateful to the *Irish Press* Group, *Tuam Herald* and *Connacht Tribune* for the use of pictures and to Sportsfile for providing the cover shot.

Thanks to my family, my friends and to all in Galway hurling who provided me with so much support over the years. I was lucky too in making a great many friends through hurling outside of Galway. I treasure them all and hope that they will enjoy my book.

Cyril Farrell - October 1994

While my role in this book was purely as a conduit to assist Cyril Farrell's thoughts, memories and experiences flow into print, there are several people to whom I owe a debt of gratitude for their support with my end of the project.

My family felt the brunt of the demands on my time more than anybody this year, but Rosemary, Alan and Linda bore my regular absences cheerfully while always offering encouragement. I am also indebted to my sister Maureen, to Roger and Beth O'Shea, John Redmond, Liam Hayes, Jim Carney and to Phelim and Nellie Murphy, all of whom contributed more in terms of support and practical help than they will ever know. My editors and colleagues in the *Irish Press* Group were also very helpful. Thanks too to Cyril's mother, Lucy for her hospitality.

I offer my sincere appreciation to Cyril Farrell for making my job a lot easier than it might otherwise have been. His recall of events and people, his honesty and patience and his availability (often at short notice) all helped to lighten my load.

Finally, I dedicate my contribution to this book to the memory of the late Jarleth P Burke, former Editor of the *Tuam Herald*, the best journalist I ever knew and the man who taught me most of what I know about writing.

Martin Breheny - October 1994

Contents

1. Home are the Heroes 1
2. Westside Glory 9
3. Growing up On Sport 21
4. Coping with Loss 29
5. New Beginnings 37
6. One Step Forward, Two Steps Back 47
7. New Highs and Old Lows 55
8. This is The Start –
   There's A Lot More To Come. 68
9. Hot August Afternoon. 75
10. Burning The Midnight Oil 82
11. 'There's Got To Be a Better Way' 89
12. Doing It My Way 94
13. Winners, But Not All Right. 102
14. Mind Over Matter. 107
15. 'People of Galway, We Love You' 113
16. Tall Stories From a Non-Champagne
    Performance. 119
17. Sowing the Seeds 126
18. Serving My Apprenticeship. 131
19. The Shape of Things To Come 137

20.	'Now For The Two-in-a-Row'................	142
21.	'Save Your Excuses for Others'............	147
22.	The Psyching Game	154
23.	Through A New Frontier	162
24.	The Keady Affair	169
25.	Chaos in Croke Park	177
26.	Could This Season End, Please?............	185
27.	'A Good Team Should Never Lose a Seven-Point Lead'	191
28.	'If You Had Your Mouth Open, You'd Have Caught the Ball'................	198
29.	Mission Improbable	213
30.	Sticks and Stones.........................	221
31.	The Pick of The Pack......................	226
32.	Planning For The Future	236

Prologue

Could there be a more satisfying feeling in the world? A warm August evening with the sun slanting in on Kenny Park, Athenry… a group of thirty fit, young hurlers training for an All-Ireland final… a few hundred fans watching intently from the terraces.

I felt at home there. There was a sense of togetherness about it, an expression of identity felt in any county which ever reached an All-Ireland final. Of course, you don't have to be involved in All-Ireland finals to enjoy the true value of GAA life.

More than any other sport, Gaelic Games represent a sense of place. My parish against yours, my county against yours. There is nothing artificial, nothing contrived, about it. It's real and substantial.

Don't get me wrong. I love all sports and have no time for those who cocoon themselves mentally in one sport and refuse to look over the fence. I certainly looked over the fence as I sought new ways of improving team preparation over the years.

I looked at soccer, particularly at the old Liverpool teams, whose greatest asset was their detailed simplicity. I looked at rugby too, especially the All-Blacks, the masters of invention and cohesion.

But all the time, my abiding love was (and is) for Gaelic Games, especially hurling. I grew up at a time when Galway hurling was seen by the big powers as no more than a support act, one which could spend its life warming up but which would never be hot enough to melt down the traditional walls.

Thankfully, that has all changed now. I would like to think I played my part in that process, just as hundreds of others did. Galway's revival shows what can be achieved when the will is there. Offaly's emergence took it a step further.

The GAA remains one of this country's great strengths. Yes, it has its faults, but the core concept is very sound indeed. I recall former Taoiseach, Dr Garret FitzGerald, once commenting that as a young politician he had the idea that, for local government purposes, it would be appropriate to redraw county boundaries. But he quickly dropped the notion when it was pointed out that it would cause a riot among GAA supporters. Imagine redrawing Gort into Clare, Johnstown into Tipperary or Kilmallock into Cork.

I have tried to be as honest as possible in this book. It was a policy which I always found best as a coach and I see no reason to change now.

Hurling has always been a huge part of my life. I love the game, the people, the atmosphere. Essentially this book is a celebration of the great game in all its forms. Yes, I have dealt the odd critical hand too but, as a GAA man all my life, it's done with the best of constructive intentions.

CHAPTER 1
HOME ARE THE HEROES

This is the life. It has been a long, tiring forty-eight hours, physically and emotionally, but nobody feels drained. We are on a high and, with the adrenalin still pumping, the exhausting demands of an All-Ireland weekend are ignored.

It is the Monday night after the 1988 All-Ireland final and we are making good progress on the journey back home to Galway. Our driver, Miko Donoghue, is an expert at making up time, even in the heaviest traffic. Later, he will show even greater expertise as he noses his coach through packed streets, inches away from thousands of toes.

We have passed Kilbeggan and are heading on towards Moate. There is a strange sense of calm aboard. The boisterous good humour which filled the coach for most of the journey from Dublin has subsided, apart from the irrepressible few at the back who always did think that a moment's silence was a monstrous insult to any occasion. For the rest, though, it's as if they want a brief period to recharge themselves for the glorious hours ahead.

Most of them have been through it before, some several times. Men like Conor Hayes, Sylvie Linnane, Noel Lane and Steve Mahon have seen both sides through two different eras. There were the awful nights when Galway returned home after losing, trying to put a brave face on it. There were great nights too. This would be another one and was there to be savoured.

It was a brand new experience for Michael Coleman, who was in his first championship season. Not only that but he had been hoisted from obscurity and given a midfield position for the final. Now he was returning home a hero after a very sound performance. It was only his second championship game and he had won an All-Ireland medal. It really was a matter of being in the right place at the right time.

My thoughts turn to Tipperary. Why, I don't know. They should be the furthest thing from my mind. But they just won't go away. I suppose it's because they have occupied my every waking moment for the previous four weeks. I close my eyes and imagine them pulling into Thurles, empty-handed and disappointed. There will be a big crowd there and 'Babs' Keating will thank them for their support and promise to be back with the McCarthy Cup next year.

We all do that. I did it more often than most, looking down on 20,000 expectant faces in Eyre Square, telling them that we would be back with the Cup next year. It's unconvincing but it's something to say, a way of sending the supporters home with a feeling of hope. But when the formal home-coming is over and players and mentors drift away, that's when the doubts set in. Up to then the disappointment has been diluted by the sense of togetherness and the general buzz which prevails after an All-Ireland final.

But when you wake up on the Tuesday morning as a losing All-Ireland finalist, the following year seems an awful long way off. It's as if you have camped for weeks just below the mountain summit, only to be swept to the bottom in a massive landslide the moment you tried to press on to the top. Now, as you look back up, the peak is invisible through the clouds.

I walked up the hill to my home in Woodford in 1986, feeling that every pair of eyes in the community were on my back. Galway had been two-time All-Ireland losers and, as manager, I became the focus of attention. People blamed me for the 1986 defeat, claiming that the tactics used in the final were at best, naïve, at worst downright stupid. A show of hands would have shown a comfortable majority in favour of the 'stupid' theory. A year earlier, Offaly had beaten us and we returned home on a wet, miserable night with our spirits in perfect keeping with the conditions. We had beaten Cork, who were the defending All-Ireland champions, in the semi-final and were favourites to win the final too. The disappointment was all the more acute for that.

We were told that we could, and should, have won both finals. Perhaps, but then we could have lost both the 1987 and 1988 finals. Whoever is responsible for distributing luck is a rather eccentric character, not given to following any logical pattern. We were a luck-free zone in 1985-86 while it took a distinct liking to us in 1987-88.

Luck remains the wild card in all sports; more so in hurling than most others, where the merest touch can change the course of a game. We were convinced in 1985 that Joe Cooney's second-half shot had crossed the goal line before Offaly goalie, Jim Troy, knocked the ball out for a '65'. We were equally certain that Tomas Mulcahy over-carried before scoring a crucial second-half goal for Cork in the 1986 final.

Luck was allergic to the maroon and white on both days.

That had changed in 1987. Kilkenny's Liam Fennelly was the deadliest finisher around and you would have backed him every time to beat a goalie in a one-to-one situation, but he missed from a few yards in the final. In 1988, Galway got some very fortunate breaks too as Tipperary pressed in the second-half of the final. Over a period of time, luck tends to even itself out. The odd thing is that it almost invariably sides with the more experienced team. Maybe that's no accident. Experience teaches and, very often, produces a calmness of mind which translates into greater resolve in tight situations.

As the whine of the coach engine rises in volume as Miko accelerates on towards Moate, a feeling of total serenity sets in. The lonely, gut-wrenching sensation of double defeat in 1985-86 is as remote as a long-forgotten toothache. It's just over two days since we travelled this road in the opposite direction, yet so much has changed. We have crossed that elusive line between 'good' and 'great'. Good teams win All-Ireland finals, great teams retain them.

I had thought about that on my way to Dublin on Saturday. Galway had gone through two frontiers in 1980 and 1987. This was yet another. It was a different sort of challenge. We were no longer underdogs. Or if we were, it was only because of the massive publicity surrounding Tipperary. We were champions, riding into town to defend our title. Tipperary were approaching from another direction, accompanied by incredible hype. Deep down though, they were feeling a lot more insecure than they were letting on. If we were positive enough we would win. I was convinced of that.

Now, on this Monday night, my thoughts drift back to Tipperary and their homecoming. Their script had never included the possibility of returning home without the McCarthy Cup. They were on a euphoric march, ever since captain, Richard Stakelum had formally declared that the famine was over, following their Munster final win over Cork a year earlier. It was their first Munster title win for sixteen years. We had halted them in the All-Ireland semi-final but they saw that as no more than a temporary interruption. By the summer of 1988 they were acting as if God had personally ordained that they should win the All-Ireland final.

That's the thing about counties like Tipperary. They always expect to win finals. That very definitely included this one. After all, they were only playing Galway! When Tipperary signed off from the hurling big-time after the 1971 All-Ireland win, Galway were no more than ambitious triers. Seventeen years later, we were a real power, although it took the 1988 All-Ireland final to convince Tipperary of that. We were the nouveau riche of hurling but, in Tipperary eyes, old money was better than new money.

Why the hell should I even consider them as we return home with the two-in-a-row? They certainly wouldn't have had much sympathy for us if we had been beaten. They will feel sick tonight.

The countryside is zooming past on a balmy September night as we head towards Athlone and my mind rewinds to the night in 1980 when Galway were travelling this very same road, fuelled by a cocktail of euphoria and relief after winning the All-Ireland final for the first time since 1923. Nothing could ever compare with that for sheer emotion, just as the 1987 success over Kilkenny was unrivalled in terms of personal satisfaction for me. They were both special landmarks, but 1988 was different. It was the product of consistent excellence, of a type never previously achieved in Galway hurling.

Soon we will be heading across the bridge of Athlone, traditionally our first major stop on the triumphant route home. We always had great support from the Athlone area. Westmeath people felt a special affinity with us, possibly because, like Galway, their team colours are maroon and white, while the hurling centres of Roscommon took a great pride in seeing the McCarthy Cup coming West. I always got a special tingle as the coach crossed the bridge. We were now in the West, back among our own people. We were there as winners who had taken on the rest of the country and won.

The shiny waters of the Shannon have been a dividing line for generations. 'To Hell Or To Connacht' may have been a phrase from an age gone past but it still has a certain truth in the national psyche. Worse still, Connacht people are inclined to accept it, as if they are second-class citizens, lucky to be accepted by the rest of the country. We tend to be apologetic even when we are good. And if we are being wronged, we don't shout about it, almost as if it's our role in life to be subservient. No, I'm not being paranoid. It's a simple fact of economic life in particular, that the West has always got shabbier treatment than the rest of the country. In the circumstances, it takes a great deal of inner strength to fight off an inferiority complex. For years that negative attitude had undermined Galway hurling teams. Not anymore. We now had complete belief in ourselves.

The cheering masses in Athlone salute the new heroes. Very soon we will be crossing the Roscommon boundary into Galway. A quick pit-stop for a drink and a welcome in Connaughtons' Bar and then it's time for the real homecoming. From there the bonfire procession starts, like a long colourful snake of light and heat. The heat from the welcoming fires bounces off the coach in a magnificent symbol of warmth and affection. The squad can sense both as they press their faces to the windows, lapping up that special feeling of returning to their own people as winners. Supporters have stood for hours to see the team coach as it speeds past, trying desperately to time the light-up properly so that the blazes are at their most powerful at the crucial second. By now, they have become expert at it.

The coach will pass the cheering crowds, leaving them with a glimpse of their heroes, followed by a feeling of contentment. 'I was there the night Conor Hayes and the lads came home with the two-in-a-row.' There can hardly be a more satisfying feeling in sport than that experienced by a team returning home with an All-Ireland title. It is more than just a celebration of sporting success. It is a definitive expression of a county's identity and sense of togetherness.

Into Ballinasloe and the cavalcade slows to a crawl. We are back in Galway with the two-in-a-row! Conor Hayes, who works in Ballinasloe and who lives a short distance away in Kiltormer, waves the Cup and the town erupts in ecstasy. As Hayes gives yet another speech, I glance down and spot one particular man who is hoarse from shouting. A few days earlier, he had trapped me for at least five minutes in a doorway in Loughrea, lecturing me in serious tones on the folly of playing Hayes.

'English will destroy him. Could ye not have come up with somebody else. God, what are are we going to do? Hayes is finished. Finished, I'm telling you. He'll cost us the All-Ireland.'

I told him not to worry about it and that Hayes would be fine, just as he was against Kilkenny in 1987. He looked at me as if I had publicly removed what common sense I had and dumped it on the street. 'Finished, I'm telling you, finished. Can you not see it?' he lamented sadly before walking on, clearly convinced that the selectors had made a pig's ear of choosing the team.

Now here he was at the front of the crowd in fits of delight. Quite probably, he had bored all around him for hours about what a great full-back and captain Hayes was. The winner really does take it all. Had Hayes played badly, his one-time detractor would, no doubt, have been perched on a high stool, announcing to all-comers that he had 'told Farrell only last week that Hayes was finished but he wouldn't listen.' He wasn't the only one who questioned the selectors' sanity.

Had we lost, the best I could have hoped for was a few days' grace before the critics arrived with the extermination equipment. There was another reason that the win over Tipperary pleased me so much. Together with my co-selectors, Phelim Murphy and Bernie O'Connor, we had gambled big-time for that final, leaving out Noel Lane. Not only that but we had brought in a championship rookie in Michael Coleman, who had never previously played at this level. Had it backfired, we would have been classified as complete fools. Past triumphs would have been as useless as a losing Lotto slip once the knockers got loose on that one. As it was, Coleman played well and Lane came on and scored the game's only goal.

The 'mad' selectors had been vindicated. We had sat for hours over many nights in Phelim's kitchen in Turloughmore drinking tea, trying to get the balance right for the final. Once or twice, it was dawn when we broke up, still not totally convinced which way to go. Eventually we settled on a team which probably not one Galway supporter would have chosen.

Lane would never understand why he was omitted from the starting line-up. At the All-Ireland celebration the night before, he told me that had he been in from the start he would have scored four or five goals. Perhaps, or maybe he would have finished the game with the same sense of frustration which he experienced after the 1985 and 1986 finals.

As it was, he was the hero this time, the man who had come on in the second-half and teased the resistance out of the Tipperary defence before stinging them with the winning goal. He would always regret not being in the winning team photographs in 1987 and 1988 but, as far as I was concerned, he was. No team rides to glory on fifteen wheels. It needs at least eighteen. Lane could be as proud of his contribution as any of the players who started in the two-in-a-row finals.

On through Kilrickle and into Loughrea. Through the thronged masses in Loughrea, I spot the sign for my hometown, 'Woodford – 23 kilometres'. I grew up when distances were measured in miles and Galway was always miles away from big hurling honours. My mind flicked back to the first time I saw Galway playing a championship match in 1959. They were beaten out of sight by Waterford in Limerick.

My father had brought me to the game and I got to see men like Joe Salmon, Jimmy Duggan and Tim Sweeney. They were heroes in my ten year-old eyes, men who stood at least nine feet tall and who could hit the ball two hundred yards with a flick of their wrists. They had been in the All-Ireland final a year earlier where they lost to Tipperary. Yet, here they were being hammered by Waterford which, at the time, was a dim and distant land as far as I was concerned. It seemed so unfair. The fact that Waterford had a very good team which went on to win that year's All-Ireland final was irrelevant. All I could see were my heroes getting an unmerciful beating.

My father bought me pears as we left the ground. That eased the disappointment. Boyish disappointments don't last long, especially when under attack from the soothing influence of soft, succulent pears. He would have been a proud man tonight watching me returning home as a successful team manager. But sadly, he was tragically killed in a tractor accident in 1968, leaving a gap in all our lives which could never be filled. My mind went back to my childhood and days when my father brought me to hurling and rugby matches, instilling a love of sport in me. It was to become a passion which has lasted to this very day. It seemed so horribly unfair that he should be taken away in his prime. The transience of it all hit me as we eased through Loughrea on that special night. Life, with all its mysterious twists, will always remain unfathomable. Today, glory and success, tomorrow – who knows?

It's the same in life as in sport. Tomorrow's great uncertainty will always be a mystery. Who would have thought in 1984 after Offaly had destroyed Galway in the All-Ireland semi-final that we would appear in the next four finals, winning two? Who would have thought that we would have beaten Kilkenny and Tipperary in successive finals? As we reached Galway City, Phelim Murphy said to me: 'We'll bring the three-in-a-row back next year, you know.' I told him they would have to do it without me. I had no intention of continuing as manager. I had had enough. Phelim just laughed. I knew he didn't believe me even if I was deadly serious. I felt it was time to get out. I would later have my mind changed for me by the persuasive powers of Phelim and Bernie, plus the dream of the three-in-a-row.

The ocean of faces awaiting us in Eyre Square was an awesome sight. It was as if all of County Galway had banged their doors behind them and headed for the city to be part of the great occasion. Those who are not involved in the GAA have no idea what it means for their county to win an All-Ireland title. They are missing a great deal because hurling and Gaelic football are the only two sports which are organised on such a strict county level. Nothing touches the soul of the people as much as an All-Ireland success.

I heard afterwards that quite a few people travelled up from Clare to join in the celebrations. They always had a special bond with us. Far from being jealous of our success, they were pleased for us. We represented a break with tradition, something which Clare always found a heavy weight on their shoulders. Of course, Clare was represented on our back-up team. Colm Flynn, a man who had worked tirelessly for years in Clare hurling, was our excellent physio.

As the night drifts on, the talk turns to the three-in-a-row. I keep a good distance from that, but the optimism tide is high and at last Galway hurling people are thinking like winners. I feel proud of my contribution to that metamorphosis. I think back to 1979 when I was appointed coach, weeks after the defeat by Kilkenny in the All-Ireland final. I knew that some of the senior players thought it was pure madness. What could Cyril Farrell, a man whose hurling career rarely poked its head above the club scene with Tommy Larkins, achieve where other, more experienced coaches had failed?

At face value, not a lot perhaps. But I could inject into the squad a passionate belief in the benefits of self-belief, proper planning and total fitness. Frankly, I never had believed in the 'divine right' attitude. There was absolutely no reason why Galway hurlers could not be as successful as Kilkenny, Cork or Tipperary. Yet, somehow, that ludicrous theory had settled over the county like a winter fog and had even restricted the vision of some of our best hurlers, who lost their self-confidence once they saw the black and amber of Kilkenny, in particular.

That was now a thing of the past. The new Galway was self-confident and mature. Not only had we beaten Kilkenny and Tipperary in successive All-Ireland finals, we had done it in a systematic, controlled and confident way. The taming of Tipperary was all the talk as the welcome home party continued towards the dawn hour, but I couldn't help glancing back to the previous year's breakthrough.

It was a final throw of the dice for many of us. A third consecutive All-Ireland final defeat in 1987 would have been a disaster. Our winning margin of six points over Kilkenny may look very comfortable in the record books, but it was a much different story on the pitch. In fact, it all hinged on the final ten minutes of a tense and tough game, which changed the course of Galway hurling.

CHAPTER 2
WESTSIDE GLORY

I had a feeling something was about to break. The game had sat there all afternoon, waiting to be taken by the hand and led one way or the other. Instead, Galway and Kilkenny had thrashed about in a furious cauldron, as if so engrossed in each other that the ultimate prize was almost peripheral to the struggle for individual and collective superiority.

Both sides had chances to make a serious charge for the winning line, but as the 1987 All-Ireland final ticked into its sixty-second minute, the destination of the McCarthy Cup was still very much undecided. Galway were leading by two points but it was a game which always seemed certain to be settled by a goal. It was a question of who would blink first.

'Move up, Eanna, this one is going to break for you. Quick, quick.' Eanna Ryan galloped back into the Galway half. Ger Fennelly was preparing to take a line-ball in front of the Cusack Stand, up near the Canal End goal. It was a dangerous situation for us. Fennelly's striking had not been particularly good earlier on, which was most unusual, but would this be the time he connected properly? After all, he was a proven marksman and a sideline cut into your square is very difficult to defend against.

I noticed that Fennelly's midfield partner had also moved forward, leaving a huge tract of unmanned pitch in the centre of the field. Our defence and midfield were massed back in a concentrated funnel in front of goalie, John Commins. Fennelly hoisted the ball across in a carefully angled arc, inviting forwards to run onto it. Our midfielder, Steve Mahon, met it first, batted it down and doubled on it. It flew straight to Eanna Ryan who dodged past Sean Fennelly and sprinted off on a solo run into open space.

As his run ended, he almost lost possession but managed to scoop the ball to Joe Cooney who wriggled around three or four defenders. He hand-passed to the right where Ryan and Noel Lane were converging. Ryan missed the catch, but Lane whipped on the ball as it went to ground. Kilkenny goalie, Kevin Fennelly half-blocked it, but the ball squirmed agonisingly over the line. Lane had scored a goal. The winning goal! The same Noel Lane who only five days earlier had been dealt the disappointing news that he was being left out of the team.

We have them! We have them! There were still some minutes to go, but we had a good feeling now. It was as if we had been tossed and battered on the high seas for years and now we had sailed into quiet, tranquil waters.

We were five points up on Kilkenny in an All-Ireland final. And there wasn't a damn thing they could do about it. We have them! So much for all the rubbish about Kilkenny having some sort of hoodoo over Galway in All-Ireland finals. So much for their contention that they had under-estimated us in the previous year's semi-final. So much for the whispering campaign which claimed we were losers. There were still a few minutes to go, but they were there to be enjoyed. The misery of the two previous years was a million miles away. Could these delightful few minutes go on forever?

The Galway crowd behind me in the Cusack Stand couldn't wait. They climbed over the wire in droves. One fan left the seat of his trousers dangling on the barbed wire. But he didn't care. It was no time for false modesty. Suddenly, an awful thought set in. What if the crowd came in on the pitch and referee, Terence Murray, called the game off? It wasn't a very rational consideration, but then it wasn't a very rational moment.

'Will ye stay where ye are and let them hurl,' I screamed at nobody in particular. Tony Keady hoisted another long range point and it was all over. Galway 1-12 Kilkenny 0-9. Stuff the begrudgers who said our 1980 All-Ireland success was flawed because it had been achieved without beating one of the super-powers. Now, we had beaten Tipperary and Kilkenny in a semi-final and final. Our pedigree was proven.

Of all my years in hurling, the 1987 All-Ireland final provided the sweetest moments. For sheer emotion, it could not compare with the 1980 win over Limerick which ended a fifty-seven year barren run by Galway. But in terms of personal satisfaction, 1987 was far more rewarding.

I had inherited the 1980 team to a large degree. They were seasoned campaigners, who had been through the All-Ireland mill before. Admittedly, they hadn't won it, but they had come very close. The 1987 squad was different. Together with Phelim Murphy and Bernie

O'Connor, I had moulded them. It was a mixture of new and old. It was a team born of that awful All-Ireland semi-final defeat by Offaly in 1984, a team which suffered two successive All-Ireland defeats and a team which knew quite well that another final defeat would have classified them as hurling's all-time great losers.

My own coaching career would have sunk with them. There is a limit to how wide you can allow the credibility gap to become. Losing three All-Ireland finals in a row might just be too much.

I found the build-up to the '87 final very demanding. Almost stressful, in fact. After two All-Ireland nightmares, I felt as if every pair of eyes in the county were on my back. I knew well that some people were blaming me personally for the 1986 defeat, in particular. I was an easy scapegoat.

'Farrell's tactics were all wrong. How the hell could he play Conor Hayes at corner-back? And did you ever see anything as stupid as using tactics which left Johnny Crowley clearing ball after ball unmarked from corner-back?'

I couldn't blame the critics. As far as they were concerned, Galway had lost two consecutive finals and somebody had to take responsibility. I was the obvious choice. Such is life for a present-day GAA manager. The safety net has long since been removed. In fact, it probably never did exist for a manager who lost two finals in a row.

This was very much the last chance. Besides, it was the final year of the three year term we had been given in the autumn of 1984. It was time to deliver or get out. There could be no half-measures.

With Tipperary out of the way in 1987, our focus zoomed in on Kilkenny, who were still reigning in Leinster and who had survived a scare in the All-Ireland semi-final before finally beating Antrim by 2-18 to 2-11 in Dundalk. For some strange reason, the semi-finals were played at different venues then. They were even played on different Sundays. Thankfully, that fixture madness has since been ended.

Kilkenny were fired with a real obsession to win the 1987 final. They not only wanted to take another title but were also determined to bury us in the process. They had been badly stung by the hammering we gave them in the 1986 All-Ireland semi-final. The 1987 final was to have been their day of revenge.

We knew it was going to be a very tough game in every sense. Kilkenny believed that we had conned them in 1986. They had watched videos of that game over and over and had reached the conclusion that if they sat tight on our forwards, they would win. It would be man-to-man marking in the strictest sense. Their instructions were to stay with our forwards even if they went over to the sideline for a drink of water. The space which our attackers had enjoyed in the 1986 semi-final was to be cut down and eventually cut off completely.

Our first dilemma centred on the type of game we would play. We decided that there would be no return to the unorthodox line-up we used against Kilkenny a year earlier. There were a few reasons for that. Our circumstances had changed so that we no longer needed to improvise with tactical complications. In short, our panel had been strengthened. Also, the 1986 plan was unlikely to work as well against Kilkenny second time around. They would be better prepared to counteract it this time.

We now had Eanna Ryan and 'Hopper' McGrath playing in attack, which gave us a very potent right-wing combination. Joe Cooney and Brendan Lynskey would man the centre and we opted for Martin Naughton and Anthony Cunningham on the left.

That meant no place for Noel Lane, who had come on and scored a great goal against Tipperary, or Tony Kilkenny, who had been replaced by Pat Malone in the semi-final. Those were two of the hardest decisions we ever had to make.

Most people thought that both Lane and Kilkenny would be on for the final. The general view was that Kilkenny would beat Malone for the second midfield position alongside Mahon and that Lane would squeeze out Anthony Cunningham at left corner-forward. But we had made up our minds earlier on that Lane's benefit to the team – for that year at least (although it was also to be the case in 1988) – was as a substitute. Tactically, we reckoned he would be great in the super-sub role, coming on in the second-half to bring experience and cunning, not to mention skill, to the mixture.

Tony Kilkenny's case was different. He had done everything we had ever asked of him and was always one of the best readers of a game, but we felt that Malone was that little bit stronger and more flexible at midfield. We also believed he would dovetail better with Mahon.

Telling a player that he has been left off an All-Ireland final team is the nastiest job a team manager can have. All the players are your friends, lads who work with you three or four times a week, so it is very difficult to walk up to a player and say: 'Sorry, but you are not on the team.' Still, it has to be done and while I always hated it, I never once took the easy way out by releasing the team to the papers before letting the squad know it first. A player is entitled to be told in person why he is not being selected.

I think Lane was half-expecting it that year (although not in 1988), but it came as a surprise to Kilkenny. I couldn't blame him. When I told him the bad news he asked me what was the problem. I couldn't tell him because there wasn't any. He had not done anything wrong. It was just we had a hunch for Malone and, all things being equal, you have to go with your hunches. It must be said that Lane and Kilkenny took their omissions like real men and both contributed handsomely to Galway's cause for a long time afterwards. Privately, they were devastated and probably hated the selectors' guts for dropping them but that was a very natural reaction.

Manliness was a central part of that squad. There were no whingers or cry-babies. There were several times when players had to endure deep, personal disappointment, but they took it as part of the game. It wasn't easy on the selectors either, but if we were to do our job properly we had to put the team's welfare above personal considerations. Any selector who does not do that is a disgrace to himself and his county.

Kilkenny's team selection for the 1987 final underlined exactly the extent to which they disregarded the 1986 semi-final defeat. They came back with virtually the same fifteen, as if to say: 'Last year was a freak, let's settle it this time.' They had made a fair number of positional adjustments, but in terms of personnel, there was only one change, Liam Walsh for Frank Holohan in defence. We had played them in a challenge game earlier that summer and I knew for a fact that they were not impressed by us. Word filtered back to me that they were convinced they had been the victims of a freak in 1986 and that they felt there was no chance that we would beat them again. Frankly, I think they saw us as chokers. If we couldn't beat Offaly and Cork in finals over the previous two years, what right did we have to believe we would beat Kilkenny?

Every right, as far as I was concerned. I kept telling the lads that the reason Kilkenny had not made many changes from 1986 was because no new talent had come through. That was true, in fact, as a glance at their subs' bench proved. They were nowhere near as well off as we were. We had got better, so really that final was in our own hands. Unlike 1985, when we lacked experience, or 1986 when Cork played better than us, it was all in our favour in 1987.

Normally, Kilkenny would have been disappointed to see us beat Tipperary in the semi-final. Such feelings are not based on any great love of their neighbours but rather on the basis that if Tipperary are to be beaten in an All-Ireland final then Kilkenny should be doing it. But after what happened in 1986, Kilkenny badly wanted another shot at us.

A week before the final, I announced that win or lose, I would be stepping down as team manager afterwards. I was contributing a column to the *Sunday Press* and I deliberately chose the Sunday before the game to make the announcement. It might have seemed an odd thing to do but there was a certain logic behind it.

I did it for a few reasons. Firstly, because I meant it. If we lost, I would have had no option but to go anyway, but even if we won, I was planning to quit. Hurling was taking up every waking moment and there were days when I felt that there must be more to life than that.

Some coaches may be able to divide their lives into compartments which don't overlap. Not me. It's either all or nothing. My retirement announcement was a sort of safety valve in the period before the final. It was also designed to bring home to the players the importance of this final. It wasn't just another final but a test of everybody concerned.

If we lost, I would have gone. So would many of the players. After all, what new coach would want three-time losers? I have always been a great believer in giving people responsibility. In a team situation, a player can sometimes hide. It may not be always obvious to the untrained eye but inevitably you will get players who will take the easy option when things get tough and those who won't. Going into the 1987 final, I wanted every squad member to look into his own heart and be prepared to take individual responsibility. I reckoned that my retirement announcement would encourage that process.

The announcement stunned Galway fans, many of whom believed it was a bad idea to declare it before the final. It was wrongly interpreted as a defeatist attitude when, in fact, it was the opposite. I wanted to use it as a rallying point and certainly the players saw it that way. We didn't talk a whole lot about it in the week before the final but it was there in the background, not as a threat but as a reminder that defeat would spark off a break-up of a squad which had been together through thick and thin for three years.

Although we had beaten Kilkenny in the rain in 1986, we were hoping for a dry day for the final. Some chance! Sunday morning dawned dark and depressing. Inside a couple of hours, great sheets of rain were sweeping down from a spiteful sky. It was a bloody awful day. The only consolation was that the wind was not very strong.

I took a quick glance at the Sunday papers, which were mixed in their predictions for the final. However, one item of interest caught my eye in the *Sunday Press*. Cork coach, Johnny Clifford, who was rating the players individually, had singled out Gerry McInerney as a possible weak link on the Galway team. 'Had a poor semi-final and will have to show a huge improvement if Galway are not to find themselves in trouble in this area. Kilkenny may well choose to pressurise him because he is vulnerable,' said Johnny. His comments on McInerney's direct opponent, Kieran Brennan, added more fuel to the fire. 'If he hits form, he could go to town on McInerney. Wouldn't surprise me if he ended up man-of-the-match.'

I showed it to Mac. 'See what they're saying about you. They don't rate you at all. Imagine that Mac. It says here that Kieran Brennan will be man-of-the-match. How about that?' He just grunted but I could see the gathering intent in his eyes. Kieran Brennan, man-of-the-match indeed!

At that stage, McInerney barely knew any hurlers outside Galway. He was home from New York only for a few months each year and wasn't in tune with what was happening. In fact, he must have been the only man in the history of the game to win two All-Ireland medals before playing a League game. Quite honestly, he probably would not have known who Kieran Brennan was if he met him in the street.

Still, I was quite happy to use Johnny Clifford's comments to my own ends. Mac might not have known much about Kieran Brennan up to then, but you could sense his annoyance at the suggestion that he would be wiped out in this particular duel.

Brennan was going well that year. He was a fine hurler and I knew a lot about him from his days playing with UCG. He always liked to get the ball into his hand and run at defences, so I instructed McInerney to stay on top of him all the time. I reckoned too that Mac was stronger, so the plan was that every time he got the ball he would burst through Brennan's tackle and try to break his spirit. There is nothing worse for a forward than a defender who sees himself as much more than a stopper. It worked well. Brennan made no impact and McInerney ended up man-of-the-match.

Johnny Clifford also helped me to get Martin Naughton psyched up for the game. Johnny said that 'Nocko' wasn't his type of player and that he was inclined to lose touch with his colleagues. Martin was a quiet sort but I knew that those comments stung him. Good! We would take any help we could get.

We were staying in the Ashling Hotel that weekend and I had a policy of taking the panel up to the nearby Phoenix Park for a noon puckaround. We used to travel to Dublin on the Saturday afternoon and I felt it important for the players to get the feel of their hurls before going to Croke Park. It was a routine sort of thing, designed to refocus their thoughts on the match, while also having a leisurely tap around. It also got them away from the fans.

We went to the Park as usual that day but gave it up as a bad job. It was so wet and miserable that I decided not to proceed. We got out of the coach just to stretch our legs and stood for a while sheltering under a huge tree.

It was a most eerie experience. There wasn't a single person in that particular area of the park. It was as if we were away in a remote hide-out, a million miles from Croke Park and an All-Ireland final. A mile away, traffic was backed up in a long, meandering snake as Galway fans poured in through Lucan and Chapelizod. The lads got back on the bus and I felt I had to say something. Deep down, I knew that they were cursing the conditions. So was I. Hand-passing at speed was a major feature of our game plan and it's difficult to control a wet ball.

There was only one thing to do. Try to pick something positive from the gloomy weather. I reminded them that two of their best performances had been produced on wet days, against Cork in 1985 and against Kilkenny in 1986. That's right, against Kilkenny. Imagine them right now. They're hating the rain even more than us because it reminds them of Thurles last year.

I wasn't at all convinced that what I was saying was true, but I said it anyway. When we got back to the Ashling I got a friend to ring the Met Office to see what the forecast for the day was. 'Rain clearing from the west by evening.' Thanks a lot, but we want the clearance now. During a light lunch some of the lads were reflecting ruefully how we never seemed to get the sort of day we wanted. Pete Finnerty took a more light-hearted but practical approach. 'Don't mind all that stuff, just tuck into the sandwiches. It will be a long time before we eat again and the McCarthy Cup is heavy.' Typical Finnerty. Always up-beat, always positive.

The weather did improve somewhat but it was still dark and drizzly as the team bus set off for Croke Park. On our way we met another coach, full to capacity with a happy party going to the Phoenix Park, where there was a big race meeting. I almost envied them. A few bets, a nice day out and not a care in the world.

By an odd coincidence our coach arrived at Croke Park at exactly the same time as Kilkenny's. You don't want to see your opponents at a time like that. They are the only people who can spoil the day for you, so the further you can keep them from your mind the better. I'm sure they felt the same.

There is a mystique about what is said in dressing-rooms before big games. Quite honestly, there is not a whole lot to be said, other than to get the players focused and to remind them of everything you have practised and planned. Rousing speeches may sound good, but if they are not controlled they may do more harm than good.

I had a feeling that Kilkenny, who had a strong team physically, would try to assert themselves straightaway. We had a big, powerful team too so I suppose that a shuddering collision was inevitable. There was absolutely no way that we were going to be intimidated. The tone was set early on when McInerney and Brennan clashed as the ball came between them. Both needed attention but Brennan seemed to come off worst and did no damage for the rest of the day.

From there on it was a battle of wills, expressed both mentally and physically. Some critics had a field day afterwards, decrying it as a dirty match. I think that was an over-reaction. Yes, it was tough, but much of the unfavourable media comment was passed by people who were watching it on TV and who have absolutely no idea of what is involved in hurling.

Ger Henderson, one of the most committed hurlers I ever saw, got a nasty cut in his hand in the first-half, which sent blood spurting all over the place. It looked terrible and it gave the critics an opportunity to depict the final as a violent brawl, which it wasn't. Typically, Ger battled on and played extremely well.

Unquestionably though, it was a fiercely competitive game. Seven players were booked by referee, Terence Murray, who gave a vintage performance in calmness and common sense. A less experienced, impressionable referee might have sent players off, which would have been totally unnecessary. Indeed, he only awarded thirty-one frees in the entire seventy minutes.

There was a time when Galway hurling would not have stood up to a test like that. Previously, most of our best performances came in high-scoring games. Put Galway in a low-scoring, dour type of game and our record was poor. Now we were tough enough and seasoned enough to stand up to anything.

That was another reason I got great satisfaction from winning that final. It underlined the degree to which we had matured. We knew Kilkenny would try to horse us out of the fluent rhythm we established against Tipperary in the semi-final and we were determined not to allow them. In a sense, then, we had all angles covered.

We also enjoyed a fair share of luck, although God knows we deserved it. Ger Fennelly, who was normally so deadly from frees, had an off-day and we were very lucky not to concede a second-half goal when John Commins made a great stop from Liam Fennelly's hand-passed effort.

Many people claim that was the turning point. Neither side had got a real grip on the game and there was never more than a point or two in it after we surrendered a first-half lead of 0-4 to 0-1. We led 0-5 to 0-4 at the interval. Despite our misses, I was happy enough at the break. We hadn't played especially well, yet we were leading. Only by a point admittedly, but a lead is a lead. I told the lads that if they believed in themselves nothing could stop them. I encouraged them to take on their men in one-to-one situations because I felt that we had a lot of individual advantages which we were not exploiting.

We brought on Noel Lane five minutes into the second-half and ten minutes later PJ Molloy was sent in. Both did very well. Their craft and experience were invaluable in such a high-tension game. Also it was a great lift to be able to bring in two campaigners of such vast experience. With respect to the two Kilkenny subs who came in, Tommy Lennon and Liam McCarthy, they could hardly be expected to exert the same influence as Molloy, who was playing in his seventh All-Ireland final and Lane, who was playing in his sixth.

Kilkenny took the lead briefly ten minutes into the second-half but we never panicked. Confidence was high and a point deficit was not going to upset us. I'm not sure though what impact Liam Fennelly's miss (or more Commins' great save) had. A goal would have given Kilkenny a point lead with fifteen minutes left which was exactly what happened against Tipperary in the semi-final, but we had held our resolve and won. Kilkenny were adamant that if Fennelly had goaled it would have changed everything, just as Lane's goal did for us. We will never know. I doubt if we would have fallen apart had Fennelly scored, but a goal at that stage for Kilkenny could have given them an extra dimension which might have been difficult to counteract.

We eventually won by 1-12 to 0-9. Odd isn't it? We scored 2-15 against Cork a year earlier and lost. Three years later we would score 2-21 and still lose to Cork. A final score of 1-12 would not have won any final since 1954 when Cork beat Wexford by 1-9 to 1-6. That was over an hour so, minute-for-minute, the 1987 final had one of the lowest scoring rates this century. Black and Amber fans had to live with the disappointment of watching their side score just nine points, the lowest recorded in a final by a Kilkenny team since 1937 when they scored just 0-3 against Tipperary.

Personally, I couldn't have cared less about the score. I would have been happy with 0-2 to 0-1, provided we had the 0-2. It surprises me to hear people talking about winning games in style. It's great if you can achieve that but winning always has to be the first priority.

That's why it irritated me to read some commentators criticising Galway because they used the hand-pass so much for a period in the 1980s. I'm not even sure that we used it that much more than other counties but yes, I was a fan of the hand-pass, largely because you can control the play with it.

Long sweeping shots are great to watch but, most of the time, they give the opposition a 50-50 chance of getting possession. A well-controlled hand-passing movement reduces the risk of losing possession. So to those sanctimonious dinosaurs who are living in a hurling time-warp, where only Cork, Kilkenny and Tipperary should ever win anything, I say: 'Lock up your prejudices, hurling is a game which offers a lot more tactical variations than are being currently used.'

Besides, if I thought that the hand-pass offered us a greater chance of success, were we not right to use it? We weren't spending four and five evenings a week in training and locking ourselves into a discipline which some professionals would even find tough, simply to please commentators. We were doing it to win. The days of pleasing others and losing were over.

The palpable feeling of relief after the win over Kilkenny was unreal. It was as if a great load had been lifted. We had done it the hard way against a county with a fantastic record in finals. They had put a huge effort into that game, but we had matched them in every single department.

This time the journey home would be so different. We got a Garda escort all the way from the Burlington Hotel to Eyre Square on Monday evening and I recall remarking as we sped out through Dublin's rush hour traffic with two Garda outriders clearing our path: 'This is the difference between winning and losing.'

That win justified everything which had happened over the previous three years. Losing an All-Ireland final is always a painful experience but it also tests a team's character. Real winners recover. Losing two consecutive finals demanded even greater powers of recovery, but we had enough players on that panel to do that. And, when Galway fans analyse where hurling in the county stood after the 1984 championship, they would have to admit that it was a near-miracle that the wagon got back on the road so quickly.

The 1987 defeat signalled the end of that Kilkenny team. They did not win another Leinster title until 1991 and by the time they reached that year's All-Ireland final against Tipperary only five of the players who lined out in 1987 were in action. That is the difference an All-Ireland defeat can make. Had Kilkenny won the 1987 final, their confidence would have soared and they might well have gone on to dominate for a few seasons. Instead, it was our turn to take our place at the top.

CHAPTER 3

GROWING UP ON SPORT

On a clear day I can see across into Clare and Tipperary from the front window of my home in Woodford. I love this place. Nestled in the shadow of the Slieve Aughty mountains in the South-Eastern tip of County Galway, there is a beautiful peace and serenity about it.

There is space to breathe and reflect and be yourself. I always loved coming back here after the hectic bustle of big match days. Crowded cities don't encourage people to think. Life seems like a never-ending noisy gallop where people don't stop to check where they are going. I wouldn't like that. Give me the country every time. It's more real, more substantial, more natural. Probably more healthy too. I lived in Dublin for a few years in the early 1980s when I was teaching in St Joseph's CBS, Fairview, and while I quite enjoyed it at the time, I never saw it as more than a temporary measure. I still go to Dublin quite a lot and I enjoy that too but, like all big cities, Dublin is more a place to visit, rather than to live in, as far as I am concerned.

I was brought up in Woodford, where my parents owned a pub in the town and some land outside the village. I was fourth in the family line, behind Elsie, Ann and Eddie and ahead of Dolores and Vinny. It was a busy household. My parents ran the pub and the farm as well as rearing six lively youngsters.

Growing up around a pub environment brings you into contact with a great many different characters. It had one lasting effect on me. It turned me into a sports' fanatic. Pubs always have been the headquarters of sporting discussion in Ireland and, from the day I could walk, I was listening to stories of sporting heroes and villains, depending on who was doing the talking. I heard of sad and great days, of great goals and awful misses, of the dogs which were beaten by a whisker and the horses which weren't even trying.

Hurling was the prime topic of discussion, although it was by no means the only one. Gaelic football, horses, dogs and rugby also figured prominently in the endless chat about sport. It seemed to dominate so much of people's thinking. I marvelled about how animated people could become about what appeared to be rather minor issues. Of course, they weren't minor at all when tossed into the debating pot in Farrell's Bar.

My father was interested in all sports, although hurling was his favourite. He had been a good player himself in his younger days and, later on, had been a Galway minor selector. He was also very taken by rugby. In fact, the high points of my early sporting memories in the late 1950s-early 1960s are of trips to Lansdowne Road for international rugby matches. I saw my first international rugby game in Lansdowne Road when I was eleven years old. It might have been the 'Ban' era as far as the GAA were concerned, but that meant nothing to an eager youngster who couldn't wait for the 6 am call on the Saturday morning of a rugby match.

Frank Mullen, Mick McMahon and Larry Gohery were my father's travelling companions and the routine was that we would have a full and wholesome breakfast in our place around 6.30, prior to setting off to catch the train from Cloughjordan. It was like going to heaven.

There was a great sense of wonder to life as the train sped through the countryside on crisp winter mornings. I was exploring new frontiers, looking out beyond my own small world back in Woodford. Dublin, with its rows of houses all packed neatly together, fascinated and confused me. I wondered how the hell people found their way home through the maze of streets and roads. Fear of getting lost in such a strange place ensured that I was never more than a foot behind my father and his friends. We would have lunch somewhere near the railway station in Dublin, before taking the bus across to Lansdowne Road. I loved that part of the journey and I could feel the rising excitement with every passing yard as we came nearer to the ground. At that stage, I had never been to Croke Park. Galway hurling was in a trough, having aligned itself with Munster after losing the 1958 All-Ireland final to Tipperary, so Croke Park was not on our agenda.

No, Lansdowne Road was the place to be as far as I was concerned. The sight of the ground always brought a special sense of excitement and I couldn't wait for the first clash between the rival forwards. I always found that especially memorable, as sixteen massive men thundered towards each other for an inevitable collision. I marvelled how they never seemed to hurt each other, irrespective of how many of them fell in an untidy heap, scuffling for possession. The finer points of the game were lost on me but it didn't matter. The whole thing was a great adventure, something to talk about and be remembered for ages.

Once Mike Gibson arrived on the scene the memories became extra special. He was capable of doing magical things. I adopted him as my hero and took a very dim view of any opponent who even tackled him. I was convinced that they were all out to get him (they probably were!) and felt downright aggrieved that the referees did not afford him more protection.

My abiding memory of him was of the amount of time and space he seemed to have by comparison with the others. There was always time to check, time to move and time to kick. He looked so beautifully elegant in everything he did. A truly great player and very definitely one of my great heroes. The capacity to make room is, of course, the hallmark of class players in all codes, but Gibson was the first one whom I actually recall doing it with such aplomb.

Rugby brought me my first major sporting disappointment. A match against Wales was postponed in the spring of 1962 because of an outbreak of smallpox in Wales, leaving a young Woodford lad in a deep depression for days. It had been vaguely mentioned that the match might be postponed but I took no notice until I arrived home from school one evening to be told that there would be no trip to Lansdowne Road. Not for the foreseeable future, anyway. It was a bombshell. Consoling words, promising that we would travel if, and when, the game was eventually played, brought little relief. It never occurred to me to ask what smallpox was or what effect it was having in Wales. As far as I was concerned, it had robbed me of a day out! The game was eventually played in the following November.

Apart from the expeditions for international games, my father used to also bring me into Galway to watch the Connacht rugby teams playing in the inter-provincials. They nearly always lost and we came to expect it. The funny thing was that the margins of defeat were often quite small, but Connacht invariably seemed to be on the wrong side of close calls. Even then, I kept thinking to myself: 'Why are Connacht teams not as good as the rest? It's only fifteen against fifteen.' It was a dilemma to which I would devote a great deal of thought in a hurling context many years later.

Apart from Mike Gibson, another player who always took my fancy in the inter-pros was Ulsterman, Dave Hewitt, who played as a centre with Queen's University and Instonians. He played several times for Ireland in the 1960s, but I remember him most for his darting runs through the Connacht defence in Galway. When he got the ball, I felt a sense of anticipation even if I knew that it probably meant another defensive emergency for Connacht. There was something incisive about him which marked him ahead of most of his rivals.

My interest in rugby was heightened by the fact that two Woodford men, Dick Roche and Mick Leahy, played for Ireland. Dick won a few caps in the 1950s while Mick won one cap against Wales in Lansdowne Road in 1964. The Welsh were always very conscious of the need to establish physical dominance early on and were not averse to the odd sneaky punch, as Noel Murphy could testify after his Cardiff 'welcome' from Brian Price one year.

Mick Leahy was a big forward with lots of heart and there was no way he was going to be intimidated by the Welsh. A bit of a punch-up developed and Mick ploughed in with a degree of determination which even took the Welsh aback. Mick's Woodford supporters were infuriated by the lack of support he got from some of his forward colleagues. Here was our Mick, battling bravely for Ireland's cause, without any support from what we regarded as the wimps from the toffee-nosed clubs in the other Provinces. They eventually did arrive at the scene of the dust-up but, as far as we were concerned, they didn't show much stomach for action then either. I suspect that the scenario was not quite so unbalanced but it looked that way to us at the time. Mick had been left to scrap it out on his own. He was all the more our hero for that. We were even more angry when he lost his place on the team and saw it as a deliberate snub to Connacht. We felt that the other Provinces carved up the positions for themselves and threw Connacht the odd consolation cap for being good, obedient boys out West.

Rugby always fascinated me, for a number of reasons. There was a real manliness about it and, despite the hard knocks, the players had a great sense of discipline. To this day that impresses me. You rarely get a player dissenting against a referee's decision, even if he has a penalty awarded against him and his side are two points down with a minute to go. GAA players are far less disciplined in this regard, while in soccer you can virtually man-handle the referee and get away with it.

Accepting a referee's decisions is part of the rugby ethos, but then maybe the players have more faith in the referees' judgements than GAA and soccer players have. In other words, the standard of refereeing may be better in rugby. Either that or nobody has a clue what is going on in rugby, so there is scarcely any point in complaining about a bad decision!

While the big rugby occasions played a great part in my childhood, there was never any chance that I might actually take up the game seriously, although I later played for Loughrea. Woodford was hurling country, with Gaelic football as the second choice.

That was inevitable. Apart from being at the hurling end of Galway, we were also within a few miles of Tipperary and Clare. The hurling affairs of all three counties were regular sources of discussion in the pub and my ears were always open for tales of what was happening in Tipperary, in particular. They were a major power and seemed to be playing in All-Ireland finals virtually every second year. I couldn't understand how they never seemed to lose a big game while Clare and Galway rarely won one. Certainly that was Galway's bitter experience through the 1960s.

Living next door to a big, domineering neighbour inevitably creates some jealousy and while we knew a great many Tipperary people, we still took something of a delight when they were beaten. It wasn't that we had anything personal against Tipperary. Far from it, they were our near-neighbours and deep down, I suppose, we were happy to be so close to such great hurling names. Nonetheless, it was nice to see them beaten now and then, just to keep them in check. It was a feeling which was to be very close to our hearts in the 1980s when we finally managed to master them on a consistent basis.

One particular Tipperary defeat stands out. It was in the 1960 All-Ireland final. Tipperary had not lost an All-Ireland final for almost forty years and were confident of beating Wexford, but they never got into the game and were well beaten at the finish. A group of Wexford people were in our pub that evening and they were in great spirits. Winning an All-Ireland title was sweet, but beating Tipperary so convincingly was a real cause for celebration.

Our pub was a sort of sporting HQ and we came into contact with a lot of people from outside our own area. Long-term that was helpful in broadening horizons, but some of my fondest memories of growing up are of the fair day in Woodford.

The town had a fair green but much of the important business of selling and buying cattle took place on the narrow street. That was the norm in country towns in those days, as farmers drove their cattle in darkness to the local fair. Selling animals was more than just a business transaction. It was a test of nerve, skill and wit between buyer and seller. The modern-day mart has removed that aspect of farming. Nowadays, it is much easier to sell a beast at the local mart. There is no real skill involved, unlike the old-fashioned fairs where it took a great deal of cunning and know-how to ferret out the best price.

If you didn't know your trade, you would be cleaned out by the cattle 'jobbers'. They were the buyers who drove from fair to fair. They were seen as mysterious men with rolls of banknotes and every farmer's aim was to use his bargaining skills to lighten their pockets by as much as possible. Listening to the dealing was fascinating for a youngster. Both sides knew their trade inside out and when the bargain was finally struck with a spit on the palm and a handshake, it was generally taken that the market value of the animal had been established with a degree of accuracy which even the most sophisticated computer could never hope to match.

Private enterprise prospered among the young lads too. We saw fair day as an opportunity to earn a few shillings, minding cattle for farmers who took a break from serious business to have a drink. As often as not they went into our pub, so the Farrells were making on the double! The trick was to stand as close as possible when a deal was at the point of being finalised. If it was a good fair and prices were high, the happy seller would adjourn for refreshments the moment the price was settled. Meantime, the cattle had to be minded for an hour or two until such time as the buyers had completed their day's activities. If things went really well, a young minder might be paid on the spot, even before he had begun his guarding stint.

Despite being raised in a pub atmosphere, I always stayed away from alcohol. It wasn't a conscious decision or anything like that. I tried most drinks but could never find one I really liked and it seemed rather pointless drinking something which tasted horrible.

I'm not sure whether or not the pub scene generated a sub-conscious rebellion against drink. I saw what it could do to people and I never did think it very funny to see a grown man getting drunk. In fact, I found it profoundly sad. Don't get me wrong. I'm not one of those people who preaches about the evils of drink. I probably spend as much time in pubs as regular drinkers because I like the crack and the sociability. It's just that the thought of drinking, or getting even mildly drunk, does nothing for me. Especially so, since I don't even like the taste of drink in the first place.

Despite my own attitude to drinking, I never found it difficult to cope with drinkers. Many team managers adopt a strict policy on drinking and try to impose it on their players. It is very easy to lay down a rule which states that drinking is out in the run-up to the championship but how are you going to enforce it? Start going into pubs to see are players there? Besides, is it really necessary?

I have always held that discipline cannot be imposed on teams. It must come from within. Yes, the management can lay down guidelines, but you are going to win nothing with a team which has to have discipline hoisted on it. So if a player wants to take a few drinks, that's fine, provided he has the inner discipline to decide when enough is enough. If he hasn't, the chances are that he is no use to you anyway.

Football was the big sport in Galway in the 1960s. The Sean Purcell-Frank Stockwell era of the mid 1950s had passed, but was replaced by an even better team, which reached four consecutive All-Ireland finals, winning three. It might have been four, but Dublin beat them by two points in 1963. It was a desperately close call and, to this day, there are Galway people who claim that midfielder, Mick Garrett, should have been awarded a penalty in the last minute as he bore down on the Dublin goal. Still, Galway learned from that defeat and came back to win three-in-a-row in 1964-65-66 without conceding a single goal.

There is something special about the three-in-a-row. It marks a team as being apart from the rest. While most of the Galway side were from football strongholds in the north of the county like Tuam, Dunmore, Mountbellew, Moylough, Kilkerrin and Ballygar we felt we knew them in the south as if they were our own. There was a similar feeling about the Galway hurling sides of the 1980s. The hurling frontier does not extend much beyond Turloughmore and Abbeyknockmoy in the north of the county – certainly not at the highest level anyway – but the support for hurling from North Galway has been fantastic. In fact, when the Hurling Board holds a church gate collection around All-Ireland time, the take from the north is as good as from the hurling strongholds in the south.

Despite living in out-and-out hurling territory, I was introduced to other sports very quickly. Apart from my father's interest in rugby, I also came under the influence of a man from Donegal, who had a passionate interest in soccer.

Pat Gallagher was the teacher at the local school and he was soccer-mad. He was into all sports but soccer was his first love, so much of our school-yard activities were devoted to it. I was handy enough at it, without ever threatening to be a George Best. I liked running too and won a few Connacht cross-country titles, but lost interest later on when I discovered that my younger brother, Vinny, was a lot better than me! He went on to be a very good cross-country runner and won quite a few Connacht titles.

It was almost inevitable that hurling would be my prime interest, however. It wasn't nearly as well organised in Galway then as it is now and it was quite common for youngsters to be playing with hurleys which were a few sizes too big. It hardly encouraged the active development of skill but it was the way of the time and nobody took any notice of it.

Nor were there many activities for minor players. The championship started on Easter Sunday and if you were unlucky enough to be knocked out in the first round it meant that you had no more organised activity for the Summer.

It was not exactly helpful in promoting hurling or in improving standards, but it was a fact of life and nobody complained. Besides, we organised games among ourselves and quite probably had hurleys in our hands a lot more often than youngsters do nowadays. Later, the structures were improved dramatically and I would say that Galway's underage set-up is now as good as, if not better than, anywhere else in the country. Galway's success at Féile na nGael and at underage level provides clear proof of how times have changed.

I grew into Galway hurling at a time when the senior side was trapped in Munster. The championship was a one-match endurance test. More often than not, the only discussion on the way to the game was of how much Galway were going to lose by. It seemed to be something that happened naturally. Winning big championship matches was for other counties. Our heroes had to come from the Galway club scene.

Living so close to Munster meant that we saw most of their hurling championship games. Leinster's big games were played in Croke Park, while a lot of Munster activity took place in Ennis, Limerick and Thurles, which were within striking distance of Woodford. I loved the excitement of big match days but, like so many other young Galway lads, it was distant and remote from us. Cork and Tipperary were giants from a different planet. Galway had no right to even think about being in the same class. I couldn't understand that and nobody could explain it to me. It was just the way things were.

In a sense, that is the essence of tradition. Some counties think in a certain way and are conditioned by the past. The danger is that negative conditioning, caused by on-going defeats, develops into an inferiority complex which undermines players at crucial moments. Meanwhile, players from counties with a history of winning think positive, even when they are not as good as the opposition.

Chapter 4

COPING WITH LOSS

My father died tragically in July 1968. He was killed in a fall from a tractor at a place called Upper Forge about a mile from home. We were on our way to the bog to bring home turf at the time.

I was in the trailer with my uncle Brian. Mick Regan was driving the tractor and my father was sitting on the mudguard alongside him. They were passing a cigarette to each other when the tractor jolted over a little hump on the road and my father slipped down in front of the back wheel. It was all over in a split second. One minute we were motoring along without a care in the world, the next minute my father was dying before my eyes. The back wheel had run over him, breaking his neck. He died almost instantly. I was nineteen years old at the time.

I ran back to the village to raise the alarm. I was in a state of shock, confusion and panic. But above all else, I didn't want my younger brother, Vinny, to see Dad. I knew that his injuries were very, very serious. But as a I raced back, I kept convincing myself that everything would be OK. It wasn't.

What happened after that is a blur. People cope with death in different ways. For me, it was a question of shutting it out, I suppose. I can remember very little about the funeral or the days afterwards. A huge number of people came and went. Our house was constantly packed but it all passed in a daze. Nothing can prepare you for such a shock. Nor can you explain it afterwards. Somehow, you find the inner strength to cope with it. From where, I don't know.

The sad irony was that, nine times out of ten, we would never have been bringing home turf on the day the accident happened. It was the Wednesday of Galway Race week, which was a great attraction even then and my father would normally be in Ballybrit. For some reason, there was a change of plan that year.

It's at times like that you realise how much we all take for granted. My father was a strong, healthy man, full of life and vigour. He was only fifty-three years old when he died. Had he been ill, it might have been easier to cope with his death. But it's very difficult to come to terms with the sudden loss of somebody who is in the prime of life. Especially, when it happens in such a freak way.

I was working at the Kinsealy Research Centre in Dublin at the time. After my father's death, I set about getting a job nearer home and eventually I was lucky enough to get one in McLysaght's Nurseries in Scarriff. It was close enough to Woodford for me to live at home.

Our pub had been in the Farrell family for a long time but, after my father's death, running it became too much for my mother. The shock of his death, allied to the daily grind of pub life, put terrible pressure on her. Family-wise, I was the only one who was available to take over the running of the pub, but I didn't see it as a way of life I wanted to pursue.

As time passed, the strain was beginning to show on my mother, so we decided it was time to make a break. We sold the pub and built a house just outside Woodford. It was the right thing to do. In fact, it was the only thing to do. There are times when a person's health and well-being must come above all other considerations. Especially when that person is your mother. She perked up straightaway and is still in good health today, thank God.

It's amazing how one's life is tied into events which can never be anticipated. Were it not for my father's death, I would probably not have come back home. I was enjoying life in Dublin, even if I wasn't exactly earning a fortune.

In fact, I was earning £5.2.6 per week, of which £3 went to my landlady, Mrs Douglas, for digs. I paid £1 per week in the canteen at the Kinsealy Research Centre, which left me with the princely total of £1.2.6 a week to spend on myself. It wasn't a whole lot, even in 1968. But I was young and carefree and money didn't matter a whole lot.

Once I returned home, I began reflecting on other things. I hadn't thought a whole lot about going to University when I left secondary school in Woodford. Some years later, the prospect seemed more appealing, so I signed on as a mature student, studying English, History, Geography and Economics in University College, Galway.

Going to UCG was a great eye-opener for me. Apart from the obvious benefits of furthering my education, it broadened my horizons on several different levels, not least in hurling. Like all youngsters in a hurling-mad area, I always dreamed of being a star player; perhaps even playing for Galway if I was good enough. There was a special sense of honour reserved for players who were elevated to county status. They were different to the rest. They had crossed a frontier reserved for relatively few, certainly relatively few by comparison with the thousands of club players who line out Sunday after Sunday.

Meath footballer, Liam Hayes, dealt with it excellently in his book *Out Of Our Skins,* explaining the sense of achievement he experienced when he first became a 'countyman'. At the end of a great career, he saw it from a different perspective to those of us who never made the top grade as players.

I would have given anything to be a great hurler and to have played for Galway in an All-Ireland final in Croke Park. But it wasn't to be, simply because I never reached the necessary standard with the consistency required to make the top grade.

No, my endeavours were confined to the bedrock activity of the GAA, the club scene. Winning a county senior title is the pinnacle of club achievements (the All-Ireland club championship is a great concept, but winning it can never match a county triumph) and I was lucky to achieve that.

In the mid-'60s, neighbouring parishes, Woodford and Ballinakill, had merged to form the Tommy Larkin's Club. By 1971, we were county senior champions! It was quite an achievement for a new club. Woodford had won county titles back in 1913 and 1917, but by the mid-60s a merger with Ballinakill was seen as the most sensible option. The new club was called Tommy Larkin's, in honour of two men of that name. The first Tommy Larkin was a young Woodford man who died in jail after the Clanrickard evictions of the post-Famine era, while the second Tommy Larkin had been parish priest in Ballinakill back in the 1930s and had done a great deal for hurling, and indeed sport in general, in the area.

Although team preparation was not as high-powered in the 1970s as it is now, our new club showed a lot of initiative by inviting Johnny Geraghty to train the team. Johnny, a Kilkerrin man who was then living and teaching in Galway City, had been the star goalkeeper during Galway's three-in-a-row football success in the 1960s and was also an accomplished trainer. Conor Hogan, Jimmy Shiel, Eamonn Harte, Brian Cosgrove and the late Josie Darcy were in charge of the team. Geraghty's arrival gave us that extra impetus we required. He was a proven winner with Galway footballers, so we reckoned he could be the same with us.

I usually played in the half-forwards. I also had very definite views on how the team should be run. Some people are interested in that angle of things while others couldn't care less, provided they are getting a game themselves. I was forever suggesting changes, either in personnel or in pattern, and generally poked my nose in whether it was welcome or not.

We made good progress through the 1971 championship, reaching the final with a 6-8 to 5-4 win over Turloughmore in the semi-final. We went in as outsiders but played very well against a club which had dominated the Galway scene for a long time in the 1960s. I scored 1-2 in the semi-final. I had scored fairly regularly right through the year and felt confident enough of my place for the final against Carnmore, even allowing for the fact that we would have some players back from America for the game. I had a shock in store. Paddy Donoghue, who was a fine player, was back for the final and had to be accommodated. C Farrell was dropped! People claimed in 1988 that I had no idea how Noel Lane felt when he was left off for the All-Ireland final, but that wasn't strictly true. Believe me, I probably felt just as upset when I wasn't in the starting line-up for the 1971 county final.

Disappointment is relative. A county final or an All-Ireland final, disappointment knows no boundaries. I thought I was very hard done by to be dropped, but then every player does. Maybe I had said too much about how things should be run! Carnmore were favourites to win a final between two clubs which, up to then, had never won a county senior title. Once again, we upset the odds and we won by 5-2 to 1-12. It was an extraordinary game really. We wore the Thurles Sarsfield's Club jerseys to avoid a clash of colours and I'm not sure whether or not they mesmerised Carnmore because they leaked goals at an incredible rate. We didn't score a single point in the first-half but still went in level at 3-0 to 0-9 at half-time.

Padraig Fahy and Sean Murphy were Carnmore's 'big two' around then but we coped well with them. John 'Stack' Finn did a great marking job on Fahy, which proved most influential. Fahy was a magnificent hurler – in fact I believe that he was let go too soon by Galway – but Finn stayed with him all the way that day and never gave him space to operate. Still, I suppose you would have to say that Carnmore were unlucky not to win the game. Not that we cared, we took whatever good fortune was going.

Going off memory, the Tommy Larkin's team which started that day was: Colm Dervan; Tom Fahy, Mike Fahy, Brendan Dixon; John 'Stack' Finn, Frank Donoghue, Tony Brehony; Sam Stanley, Paddy Kelly; Pat Madden, Cathal Stanley, Eddie Donoghue; Tom Donoghue, Paddy Donoghue, Mick Fogarty.

The following week's *Connacht Tribune* made interesting reading, not least that, according to the report, I had started the game when, in fact, I only came on as a sub. Looking back now, some other comments in the *Tribune* were even more interesting.

Noting the changing attitudes towards hurling in the county, it reported: 'The new attitude was typified by the atmosphere after the win, with the almost Wembley-like cheer the crowd gave the lap of honour of the stadium as the Cup was held aloft. It was then that many people realised that hurling in Galway is on the way back and that it is no longer the poor relation of sport in the county.'

Those in Galway hurling who expect success almost by right nowadays, will find those comments interesting. Back then, football was the dominant sport. Galway had won three All-Ireland finals since 1964 and had also played in the 1971 final, losing to Offaly. Hurling wasn't so much the poor relation, but rather the weak child who needed lots of attention and nourishment. Thankfully, there were enough far-seeing people in the county to provide both.

It's interesting to note that the *Tuam Herald* gave county hurling championship games more coverage in those days than did the Galway-city based *Connacht Tribune*. Although the *Herald* was circulating mainly in North Galway, it always showed a great interest in hurling affairs. That was down to the late Jarlath P Burke, the then editor. Although football was his first love, he was also deeply interested in hurling. He was a man of great vision in every sense and his opinions and comments on all sports were widely respected. Jim Carney, who is now sports editor of the *Herald*, was a young reporter there in the early 1970s and he too showed a great zeal for hurling. It was encouraging to see that at a time when football was very much the heavyweight force in the county. Nowadays, the *Connacht* gives blanket coverage to hurling.

As Galway champions, Tommy Larkin's played in the 1971-72 All-Ireland club championship. We lost the semi-final to Cork champions, Blackrock, by a few points after conceding a late goal. Blackrock, who had Cork stars, John Horgan, Ray and Brendan Cummins and Pat Moylan and Kilkenny's Frank Cummins on their side, went on to win the All-Ireland final, beating Rathnure (Wexford) by a point.

Our team broke up after that. Several lads emigrated and we never again reached the same heights. It was a pity because it was a fine team. Sam Stanley was the only regular senior inter-county player but overall we had a great balance.

I was also playing some football around that time and was back in action the Sunday after we won the county hurling title, playing against Cortoon in a county junior semi-final. Tommy Larkin's had won the East Board title while Cortoon were North Board champions. We drew with them but lost the replay heavily. Cortoon were going well at the time. They were backboned by the Gilmore brothers, with Tommy Joe, who had played at centre-back for Galway in the All-Ireland final earlier that year, as the anchor man.

My football talents, such as they were, attracted attention outside Galway. Believe it or not, I am the proud holder of a Tipperary junior medal, having won it with Lorrha. As for the legality of it, well I'm not too sure about that! My uncle, Sonny Ryan was involved with Lorrha and he brought me across the border to play for them. I didn't ask any questions. Neither it seems did anybody else. The upshot is that I won a Tipperary championship medal as a wing-forward with Lorrha.

The story goes that a player with exceptionally long hair had played in the same position in the semi-final. I had much shorter hair and some suspicious glances were thrown my way, but nobody protested. Just as well or we could have had a 'Keady Affair' eighteen years early! Only this time, there would have been justifiable grounds for complaint against my participation in a Tipperary final.

My involvement with the Galway minor team as coach in 1973 pointed me in a sideline rather than playing role. Still, I was hopeful of squeezing into the Galway team at some stage. I was a middle-of-the-road hurler in terms of skills, but fitted fairly well into a pattern, provided there was one there. I always reckoned that you could create a pattern and that even players of modest talent could fit into it, provided they understood clearly what was required of them.

University hurling was ideal in this regard. We had plenty of time to work on things and had great fun seeing how they would develop in actual games. Hurling was very strong in the universities in the 1970s. There weren't as many third level colleges then, so you had quite a few inter-county players on the various teams. UCG had such well-known names as Joe McDonagh, Joe Connolly, Niall McInerney, Conor Hayes, Pat Fleury and Kieran Brennan while St Patrick's Maynooth were able to call on Iggy Clarke, Sean Silke and Sean Stack. We won the Fitzgibbon title in 1977, with yours truly at corner-forward. We beat Maynooth by two points in the final in Maynooth in a great game.

The Fitzgibbon and Sigerson Cups had a higher media profile in those days. The national newspapers always sent staff reporters to cover the finals, unlike nowadays, when even the finals get scant attention. The proliferation of third level colleges has changed the emphasis. You don't tend to get as many top players on the one team as was the case in the past and consequently the media are not as interested. That does not mean that the competitions are any less prestigious. Sigerson and Fitzgibbon are still greats events to win.

I was going pretty well in 1977 and the following season I got a run with Galway seniors in a challenge game against Cork in Charleville. It was on a Sunday evening and most of the players had dashed to Charleville after playing club games earlier in the day. I scored two goals off John Horgan and was quite pleased with myself, as John was one of the top corner-backs in the game at the time. Obviously it wasn't enough to convince the Galway selectors that I was good enough to be part of their plans. Not that I blame them. I wasn't up to the level required for top-class inter-county hurling. That is the blunt truth.

Obviously I always regretted that but there was not a whole lot I could do about it. Mind you, it might explain why I was – and still am – intolerant of players who have lots of ability but who cannot be bothered working at it. I have always regarded a waste of talent as virtually criminal, yet you see it happening all the time.

How many great minors have we seen losing their way afterwards, not because they lacked talent but because they could not be bothered working on improving their game? I find that very sad.

Captaining UCG was a big thrill for me and played a big part in my development as a coach. As captain, I had several responsibilities and I took them all very seriously. I also learned a lot about how to deal with others, which was important in later life. I read every book I could find on the psychology of dealing with other people and also studied the way things were being done in other sports, especially rugby. Every little bit helps.

Having completed university, I got a teaching job in St Joseph's, Fairview. I enjoyed my spell in Dublin, even if the travelling up and down to Galway in the 1979-81 period was very tough. Still, I had the advantage of being on holidays in June-July-August when the bulk of the championship training was being done.

I finished my first stint with Galway seniors in 1982 and, although I was back in 1983 as coach to the minors, it was a relatively short campaign and left me with time to pursue other challenges.

I enjoyed my spell with Skyrne footballers, even if they didn't win the Meath County title, but had better luck with Erin's Isle in Dublin. I coached them in 1983 when they won the Dublin hurling title. John Twomey, who is still going strong for Dublin, was starring for them at the time as was PJ Buckley, who won an All-Ireland football medal with Dublin the same year. Charlie Redmond was also on the squad. The physio was none other than Mick Byrne, who spends most of his time with the Irish soccer team these days.

I returned to live full-time in Galway in the Summer of 1984, having got a teaching job in St Raphael's, College, Loughrea. It meant that when the call came to take over Galway that autumn, I was able to respond, without having to endure 250 mile return runs from Dublin.

The truth is that had I still been in Dublin, I would not have taken the job. I knew that to do it properly, I would have to take it for a three-year term and there was no way I could have given the necessary commitment from 125 mile range.

Spending a few years outside Galway was a big help to me in a lot of ways. I came across different people and learned a lot of new things. Coaching Skryne was a real experience for me, as it was the first time that I had been involved in that capacity with a football team. It was a different sort of challenge and is one I would like to try again sometime.

Chapter 5
NEW BEGINNINGS

Had a bookmaker set up stall outside Semple Stadium, Thurles on the evening of 5 August 1984 and offered odds of 100/1 against Galway appearing in the next four All-Ireland finals, it is unlikely that he would have taken a single penny.

Galway fans streamed out of the famous stadium in various degrees of shock, disappointment and resignation. They had just seen Offaly beat Galway by fourteen points in the All-Ireland semi-final. Offaly 4-15...Galway 1-10! Could it really have happened? Yes it could. And it did.

It was the biggest thrashing Galway had suffered in a semi-final since 1972 when Kilkenny won by twenty-seven points. Back then, of course, Galway were accustomed to losing semi-finals. We had slid free of Munster's smothering clutches only a few seasons earlier, so the revival was a mere toddler. By 1984, that had changed. Galway were now regarded as genuine All-Ireland contenders every season.

They were far from that in Centenary year. The manner of the defeat by Offaly was alarming. Galway started well enough but when Offaly injected some pace and power into the game, Galway melted like a snowball in an oven. There was a terrible sense of gloom among Galway people afterwards. I remember thinking to myself as I returned home that evening, that whoever was in charge for the new League season would have to make wholesale changes. Too many of the team which flopped to Offaly were no more than shells dressed in maroon jerseys. Their hearts and spirits were gone. A year later only seven of them lined up against Cork in the All-Ireland semi-final.

When I was asked if I would be interested in taking over as team manager a few weeks later, I agreed to let my name go forward, but only if I got a three-year term. There could be no quick fix. The whole scene needed an overhaul. On the night of the appointment, I told the Hurling Board meeting in Loughrea that if there were people there who thought they could win an All-Ireland with the squad as it stood, they should take the job. There were no takers. The Thurles shambles had left nobody under any illusion. Major surgery was required. Even then there was no guarantee of success.

Choosing selectors wasn't difficult. Phelim Murphy and Bernie O'Connor were my immediate choices. Bernie had been a selector with myself and the late 'Inky' Flaherty in 1980 and I knew his form from then.

Phelim had been a selector with me when Galway won the All-Ireland U-21 final in 1978 and we thought on the same wavelength. He was also Hurling Board Secretary. He knew the clubs and the players well and would be a key figure in organising the club programme to fit in with the county team's requirements. That is a crucial matter in any county. With so many fixtures and strands of competition, it is vital to streamline the operation. Phelim was brilliant at that.

Drawing up a new panel was our first job and while we knew we had to go for sweeping changes, we were also conscious of the need for experience. We had plenty of that available in players like Conor Hayes, Sylvie Linnane, Michael Connolly, Steve Mahon, Noel Lane and PJ Molloy. They were to be the anchor men of the new side.

Whether or not we would be successful depended to a large extent on the quality of the new lads we brought in. We were lucky in that Galway had done very well at U-21 and minor level in 1983, winning both All-Ireland titles.

Good under-age teams don't guarantee success but both of those U-21 and minor teams proved themselves well above average. Tony Keady, Pete Finnerty, Ollie Kilkenny, Michael Coleman, 'Hopper' McGrath and Eanna Ryan were all on the 1983 U-21 squad, while John Commins, Sean Treacy, Pat Malone, Gerry McInerney, Tom Monaghan, Joe Cooney and Anthony Cunningham were minors that year. By 1988 eleven of the '83 minors and U-21s were on the team which beat Tipperary in the All-Ireland senior final. Significantly perhaps, Galway beat Tipperary at minor and U-21 level in 1983 so when they clashed as seniors, Galway had a psychological advantage. It's amazing how that sticks in a player's mind. We beat them once, we can do it again. Quite often it happens that way.

I coached the minor team in 1983 and, as always, we went into the All-Ireland semi-final without a clear idea of how good the team was. It didn't take long to find out. Galway drew with Tipperary in Croke Park and showed real steel to win the replay by two points in Ennis. We were very disappointed not to have won at the first attempt. We led by six points with ten minutes to go but Tipperary finished well to level it at 3-10 each. We got an early goal in the replay in Ennis and went on to win by 1-7 to 0-8.

Dublin produced a fine minor team that year, winning a great Leinster final against Wexford, having beaten Kilkenny earlier on in the championship. They had high hopes of taking their first All-Ireland minor title for eighteen years. All the talk going into the final was of Niall Quinn, a giant of a lad from the Robert Emmett's Club. He was Dublin's top scorer on 4-8 from three games and was seen as a possible match winner. Dublin played him at right corner-forward but he never got into the game against Sean Treacy. In fairness, he didn't get much good ball, as Gerry McInerney was in smashing form at left half-back. Quinn, of course, subsequently showed that he had a talent for more than hurling and has, of course, developed into an international soccer star. The Galway lads are still asking Sean Treacy where he went wrong!

Galway won the game 0-10 to 0-7 on a horrible, windy day. It was a significant breakthrough as it brought us our first-ever All-Ireland minor title. In fact, prior to that, Galway had lost all eleven minor finals we had contested since 1931. The win represented another strand in the development of Galway hurling. You can rest assured that anytime Galway win a minor title, we have a pretty special team. Otherwise, there is no way we could win it, since the All-Ireland semi-final is the lads' first competitive game together. Seniors can cope better with automatic entry to the semi-final every second year because they are playing together in the League earlier on and are usually around for several seasons, thus getting to know each other very well.

It's worth recalling the 1983 Galway minor team in full just to show how many of them progressed to senior level: John Commins; Martin Killeen, Pakie Dervan, Sean Treacy; Padraig Brehony, Pat Malone, Gerry McInerney; Declan Jennings, John Joe Broderick; Tom Monaghan, Tom Moloney, Joe Cooney, Sean Keane, Anthony Cunningham, Padraig Higgins. Quite a team!

Phelim, Bernie and myself spent long hours discussing how many of the 1983 minors we could bring into the senior panel a year later. One stood out straightaway. Joe Cooney had star quality from the first time I saw him. Everything about him was right and I am quite convinced that he would have been a star in any sport.

He had just turned nineteen when we took over in 1984. We debated whether or not he was too young to bring into the senior side. I felt that his great skill would insulate him against any attempts by older, stronger opponents to show him the harsh reality of life in the fast lane. Also, Joe was deceptively strong himself. He looked slight enough on the pitch but he was quite durable, even as a minor.

I went down to his house to talk the matter over with his parents and they were happy to let him take his chance with the seniors. A year later, he had won an All-Star award.

Moulding a new side is always an interesting experience. I had spotted Tony Keady playing for the Galway U-21s in a challenge game against the seniors in 1984 and marked him down as one for the future. He had good balance, was comfortable left or right and looked very, very confident. When Peter Finnerty came into the squad, he saw himself as a full-back, having played there at minor level, but he wasn't needed at No 3. We convinced him that he could make a wing-back and once he realised that there was an opening at No 5 he worked like hell to fit in. Tony Kilkenny had come back from England and settled in nicely on the other wing. I knew his brother Ollie from my previous spell in charge and felt that he had a lot to offer too.

We also brought Brendan Lynskey into the panel, something which surprised many people in Galway. Lynskey was one of those players who seemed to be around for ages, without ever actually winning a permanent place on the team. He had his critics, but we felt that he could play a central role in our attacking play over the coming seasons.

With runners like Cunningham, Cooney and Naughton, we wanted a strong anchor man, somebody who could win possession and throw the ball around. We never saw Lynskey as a scoring forward and neither did he. But he was a brilliant ball winner and forager and many of our attacking moves pivoted on him. He greatly appreciated the chance to extend his career at a time when many people saw him as being finished. He took a lot of pressure off the younger lads because, for some reason, the opposition seemed to take a delight in walloping him. He was utterly fearless, though, and the harder he was hit, the more determined he became.

We started our League programme with a win over Tipperary (little did we know that they would become such great rivals) in Ballinasloe in October and worked hard right through the Winter of 1984/85 in Loughrea. We played a lot of indoor football to break the monotony and also to bring the squad together, not just in terms of physical fitness, but to develop a sense of harmony. This is one aspect of team management which sometimes tends to be overlooked. When a new squad comes together, it is vitally important that they get to know each other as well as possible. Building a family-like spirit can take time, but it is crucial. It was to stand to us in later years.

We did well enough in the League, with one game in particular standing out. We beat Cork by 1-10 to 1-7 in Midleton early in February 1985. It might not have looked especially significant at the time, but it was an important statement from a new-look team against the reigning All-Ireland champions. It showed Cork were fallible and that was helpful when we next came to playing them in the All-Ireland semi-final. We lost to Offaly but went straight into the League semi-finals, where we were beaten by six points by an experienced Clare team, which was going well at the time.

We beat Leinster, but lost the Railway Cup final to Munster by a point. We had a good run in the open draw competition, even if we got easy games early on. Armagh were no match for us in Trim and Kerry were easily dismissed in Tralee, but we had a good tussle with Kilkenny in Limerick in the semi-final, before winning 0-13 to 0-7. We lost the final to Tipperary by 1-13 to 1-10. That didn't look all that important at the time, but losing those two finals started a trend which took a frustratingly long time to change.

Still, things were taking shape to some degree, but there was still a huge air of uncertainty about the team that summer. We didn't know how good we were and all we could do was work day and night to make sure that, whatever else, we would be oozing fitness for the All-Ireland semi-final. I would have loved to have had an All-Ireland quarter-final just to have a look at the team in a championship situation, but it wasn't our turn that year.

Our spring form had looked decent enough but there is no comparison between League and Championship hurling. For a start, we were taking a brand new team to Croke Park and we had no idea how they would cope with playing there. Some thrive on it while others freeze, but there is no test you can run in advance to give you any pointers.

The nearest we came to a decent warm-up for the All-Ireland semi-final was in a tournament game against Offaly in Dunshaughlin on 25 July . It was a miracle that it was played at all. A thunderstorm left the pitch water-logged but both sides squelched their way through it in a most competitive (Is there any other sort when Galway play Offaly?) match. Both sides were almost at full strength, so it was an excellent work-out. We didn't realise it at the time, but playing in those conditions was the best possible practice we could have had for the semi-final. We won by 3-9 to 2-10. Next time we met, Offaly had two points to spare in the All-Ireland final. Things were that finely balanced between us at that stage. Sadly for us, Offaly won the match which mattered!

Our preparations for the semi-final went ahead without any notice. We would normally have had a posse of journalists down to see us the week or two before the semi-final, but not this time. Cork had retained the Munster title with a fairly comfortable win over Tipperary and nobody saw any reason to suspect that a new-look Galway team would deviate from the script, which was hinting at a Cork-Offaly final.

In the week before the semi-final, I got several calls from journalists in the national papers, asking me about players like Tony Keady and Peter Finnerty. They were unknown outside Galway and remained very much mystery men as far as the national media were concerned.

When we headed into Croke Park on the first Sunday in August, it was a journey into the unknown. Only 8,200 spectators turned out for our game with Cork on a day when even ducks were running for shelter. The downpour might have had an impact on the size of the crowd but not to the degree many thought.

The truth was that nobody gave Galway any chance against a Cork team which had won the All-Ireland final a year earlier. Hardly anybody from Cork travelled and only the most loyal of Galway fans turned up. The great mass of the Galway following had been sickened by what had happened in Thurles a year earlier and remained to be convinced that the new-look side would do any better.

They weren't going to disrupt an August Bank Holiday weekend to travel to Croke Park and risk the sort of humiliation they had witnessed the year before. There is a lesson there for every county. Fans can be very, very fickle. Certainly, when we took a look around Croke Park that day, it hardly inspired confidence. Even our own didn't trust us. Still, in a dogged sort of way, it made us that bit more determined. The atmosphere in Croke Park was unreal. The heavy rain was swirling in on the stands, forcing the small crowd to congregate at the back. Down on the pitch, there was an impression of emptiness, almost as if nothing important was going on. It really was one of the most miserable days August ever threw up.

I have no doubt that Cork under-estimated us. They have always denied that but, deep down, I'm sure they felt that while we might play well, we would lose out in the final twenty minutes. I had the Galway lads programmed to go through the wall, if necessary. I reckoned that psychologically Cork would see the game as a sort of irritant between the Munster final and the All-Ireland final and would be all the more vulnerable for that. We had a surprise or two planned for them.

The foul weather helped us too. The more determined a team is, the better it copes with the conditions and there were a few occasions when some of the Cork players weren't keen on the hard graft necessary for survival on such a filthy day. Our lads seemed to relish it. Cork also had to line out without Jimmy Barry-Murphy, which gave us a big lift. His very presence would have been worth a score or two to them. He came on as a sub but, by then, we had the initiative (and the match) safely tucked away.

It was an amazing game. We conceded five goals but still won by four points. I couldn't help thinking back to it after we lost the 1990 final to Cork. We also conceded five goals that day too and took terrible stick. The selectors, in particular, shipped a lot of criticism from the know-all brigade, who claimed the wrong full-back line was chosen.

Amazing, isn't it? When you win a game it doesn't matter how many goals are conceded, but if you lose, somebody has to be blamed. More often than not, the selectors are fingered.

Our plan in the 1985 semi-final was to rattle Cork straightaway. It didn't quite work out. Cork won the toss and opted to play against the wind and rain so they must have been delighted at half-time when they trailed by just a point, 1-7 to 2-3. It was beginning to look like a formality for them, especially when a Kevin Hennessy goal put them 3-4 to 1-8 ahead early in the second-half. What happened in the next fifteen minutes will long be remembered by those who saw it. Galway exploded into life and goals by Lynskey, Cooney and Lane, plus a string of points, left us leading by an amazing ten points with ten minutes to go.

Inevitably, Cork rallied and John Fenton scored 2-1, but it wasn't enough. We had achieved a famous win, 4-12 to 5-5. The hurling world was stunned. To some degree, so were we. It wasn't that we didn't expect to win (you've got to be positive to have any chance) but we could never have envisaged the style and texture of our success. Had we been told in advance that we would concede five goals, we would have assumed that another big hammering was in prospect. After all, a poor Galway team had conceded only four goals against Offaly a year earlier. Meanwhile, up in Armagh, Offaly produced a routine performance to beat Antrim by fourteen points in the other semi-final.

Having beaten Cork, we were immediately installed as favourites to beat Offaly in the final. That worried me because, in a sense, we had reached the final almost as much by accident as design and well ahead of schedule. We were working to a three-year plan, yet here we were in the final after just one year.

The risks were obvious. Offaly had a very experienced team. Ten of them had played in the 1981 All-Ireland final against Galway, a game which held sweet memories for Offaly. Also, Offaly had been in the 1984 All-Ireland final and although they had lost fairly heavily to Cork in Thurles, they had still got the benefits of the big day experience. They had beaten Galway in the 1984 semi-final and had beaten our new-look team by seven points in the League in the previous February. They had hauled back a nine-point deficit against Kilkenny to snatch a draw in the Leinster semi-final, before winning the replay by six points. The Leinster final against Laois was a virtual walk-over, with Offaly winning by thirteen points. All in all, they were a very formidable and experienced outfit.

We had eight newcomers, five of them in defence, including a brand new half-back line, Peter Finnerty, Tony Keady and Tony Kilkenny. The old adage about there being no substitute for experience is perfectly true. It won't win matches on its own but, in a tight situation, it can make a crucial difference. It certainly did in 1985.

The final was best summed up by the late JP Burke, Editor of the *Tuam Herald*, who wrote: 'Galway did the hurling, Offaly did the scoring'. That was it in a nutshell.

We missed an awful lot of chances. We shot twenty wides, thirteen in the first-half alone. We were also guilty of some dreadful mis-hitting in great scoring positions, particularly in the first half. Then we made the mistake of trying to feed too much ball into the full-forward line. Bernie Forde, Noel Lane and PJ Molloy had done most of the scoring in the semi-final and our outside men were inclined to drop the ball in towards them rather than go for scores themselves. It was down to inexperience really. The Offaly full-back line, Aidan Fogarty, Eugene Coughlan and Pat Fleury did a great marking job on our full-forward line who, between them, scored just 1-1 from play.

Offaly led by 1-6 to 0-7 at half-time and struck for the vital breakthrough seconds after the re-start. I have always impressed on midfielders the absolute necessity of winning the pull from the throw-in. Failing that, they shouldn't lose it, even if that involves spoiling the opponent. There is nothing more heartening for a team than a quick pull from the middle of field from a throw-in.

Galway paid a heavy price for not getting it right from the throw-in at the start of the second-half. Offaly swept downfield and Pat Cleary knocked the ball into the net. Cleary was the hottest goal-shot around in those days. He scored two that day and went through a string of games where he always scored at least one goal.

Three minutes into the second-half and it was double scores, 2-8 to 0-7. Disaster, or so it seemed. In fairness, Galway buckled down to the daunting challenge and a smashing goal by PJ Molloy followed by a couple of quick points brought us right back into it. Offaly had only a point to spare with thirteen minutes left but it was from there on that their greater seasoning told. They had more experience on the subs' bench too and were able to call on Brendan Keeshan and Declan Fogarty. In later years that was one area where we were especially well-endowed. Paddy Corrigan and Padraig Horan put Offaly three points ahead and our last retort was a pointed free by Tony Keady.

The reality was that we blew it in the first quarter. We needed to build a decent platform but, instead, we found ourselves two points down after Cleary's first goal in the twenty-sixth minute. From there we were chasing the game.

Offaly deserved to win simply because they were more economical. As usual, they had to listen to the old familiar line that they wouldn't have beaten Cork that day. We'll never know because Cork weren't good enough to get to the final. That was a much better Offaly team than they got credit for. They won seven Leinster titles between 1980 and 1990, yet they always had to battle for recognition.

They lost status in the eyes of traditionalists when they flopped badly to Cork in the 1984 All-Ireland final, going down by 3-16 to 1-12. Diehards shook their heads knowingly and claimed that Offaly couldn't cope with the 'real' powers. Odd that, since nobody questioned Cork's resolve when they lost to Kilkenny by 3-18 to 1-13 in 1982. They were simply beaten by a better team! Cork lost to Kilkenny a year later as well.

Inevitably, there was a great sense of loss in Galway after the 1985 final. We felt luck hadn't done us any favours, but deep down I was satisfied that things were coming right. We might have lost the final but we had made a breakthrough of sorts. My biggest fear heading into that championship was that we might lose fairly heavily to Cork in the semi-final. It was a new-look team and, irrespective of how well-prepared you are, there is no way of knowing how players will react to their first big test. In the quiet, reflective weeks after the All-Ireland final, I knew that we had found a few gems. Finnerty, Keady and Cooney had all come through the test. They would be the better for it. Meantime, a lot of fresh talent was pushing its way to the surface. By the time we won the All-Ireland final two years later, we had six new players on board.

The 1983 minor team was maturing rapidly and it was only a matter of time before we were able to slot more of them into the senior squad. Ultimately, they were to be the final pieces in the jigsaw.

CHAPTER 6
ONE STEP FORWARD, TWO STEPS BACK

If the Lotto had been in existence back in 1985, the big jackpot prizes would have been under no threat from most of those involved in Galway hurling. It was a crazy year, one in which seven Galway teams, including College sides, lost All-Ireland finals.

The only winners were the county Vocational team which beat Offaly in the All-Ireland final. Elsewhere, it was misery all the way, with most of it experienced by the Galway senior squad. The footballers were not doing any better, failing to bring any Connacht title to Galway that year.

We started the year by losing the Railway Cup final to Munster in March. A month later Galway lost the Open Draw final (the competition had been introduced a year earlier to mark the GAA's Centenary) to Tipperary by three points. Later on we lost the All-Ireland final to Offaly by two points and finished the season with a four-point defeat by Cork in the Oireachtas final.

Galway club champions, Castlegar, who had made an important breakthrough by winning the All-Ireland club final in 1980, were back in the final in 1985 but lost to St Martin's, Kilkenny, in a replay.

The whispering campaign was thriving by the end of the year. Galway hurling was synonymous with losing. It couldn't cope with the big day pressures! It suffered from an inferiority complex! Several of the defeats were by tiny margins, but that wasn't taken into account. The fact that the senior team was still in the formative stage didn't get much consideration either. But then that's the reality of sport. The winner takes it all.

When you lose by a point, the critics will outline ten reasons why it happened. They will rewind the video twenty times and zoom in on allegedly critical incidents, which contributed to the defeat. If you win by a point the same 'experts' will give you plenty of reasons why the victory was deserved. It's from the kindergarten school of analysis, but is becoming increasingly common.

The video is both a blessing and a curse. It can be helpful in terms of detail, but a lot of commentators live by it and are unable to form an opinion without having viewed a game over and over again. We would all love to be able to play the match on our video, stopping play and rewinding when we are in trouble or fast-forwarding when we are on attack. But that's not the real world.

I sat down with Phelim Murphy and Bernie O'Connor at the end of 1985 and assessed exactly where the squad stood. We had lost four finals but had gained a lot of experience. The team was developing nicely. It's significant that eleven of the Galway team which lost to Tipperary in the Open Draw final in April 1985, played in the 1987 All-Ireland semi-final. Only four of the Tipperary team, Bobby Ryan, Conor O'Donovan, Nicholas English and Donie O'Connell, survived from 1985 (Open Draw final) to 1987. Clearly, you can never form a solid opinion on the basis of a single game.

Still, we were becoming increasingly conscious of the need to actually win something. Winning or losing can become a way of life and if a team acquires a reputation for losing finals, insecurity can creep in like a rust. So much depends on a team's mental attitude on the big day, so if players become infected by nagging self-doubt, it can be hard to eradicate.

Wexford hurlers are a classic example. They lost several Leinster finals to Kilkenny because deep down they didn't believe they could win. John Henderson often made the point that he could see the doubts in Wexford players' eyes when they came under pressure in an important game.

Whether he could or not doesn't matter. He was convinced that he could spot a weakness which, of course, made him feel better. That has always been part of the Kilkenny psyche against Wexford.

We were determined to do well in the 1985/86 League, on the basis that this side had won nothing and that it was important to make a fairly quick breakthrough. We had to experiment too, of course, but we cruised along pretty well in the League, beating Dublin in Croke Park and Cork in Pearse Stadium on an amazing scoreline: 0-25 to 0-10. It was one of Galway's biggest ever winning margins against Cork. Quite simply, we couldn't go wrong. I suspect that if one of our forwards took a shot from the Leisureland Complex in Salthill it would have gone over the bar. Cork were all over the place. Long before the finish we could sense that they were just willing the game away. It was one of those days as far as they were concerned.

Next stop was Nowlan Park, where we lost a niggly game by 2-9 to 0-9. Not surprisingly, given the nasty undercurrent, most of the scores came from frees. We finished the season with a comfortable win over Laois in Portlaoise to leave us joint top of the First Division. Seamus Coen, Sylvie Linnane, Peter Finnerty, Brendan Lynskey and Joe Cooney all won All-Star awards. That was important at the time because it made all concerned with Galway feel good about themselves. Over the coming seasons, Galway players were to capture several All-Star awards. I'm not so sure if it was always a good thing.

One of the problems with the All-Stars' scheme is the question mark against the knowledge of some of the selectors. A big name will always stand a better chance of winning an award than a newcomer, irrespective of how well he has played. It's a sort of safety option for a selector who doesn't know his sport. But it can do damage. There are times when the last thing a manager wants to see is a player winning an award when it's quite clear that it has been given on the basis of reputation, rather than a solid season's work. Believe me, it happens virtually every year. It can damage a player if he misreads the signals. Most players are smart enough to know if they deserved the award, but others are not and they may feel that they had a good year when, in fact, they had not. The implications of that are obvious.

Similarly, a player who did well all season may start getting doubts if he is not included on the All-Stars' team. He shouldn't. Team selection is an inexact science at the best of times, but when you have a twenty-strong selection committee, as in the All-Stars, the margin for error is great. Don't get me wrong. I am not saying that all journalists are bad judges. Far from it. But if you have twenty of them choosing a team, the chances are that there will be some who aren't quite up to it, or else vote with their map in one hand and their judgment in the other. A smaller selection panel would lead to greater accountability and, in my view, more consistent selections.

All things considered, Galway had made reasonable progress in 1985. We didn't have any silverware to show, but we had learned a lot about ourselves and the opposition. Precious experience had been gained and we had played a big number of matches. We would be the better for them all.

We started 1986 with an embarrassing thrashing. Limerick beat us by 5-6 to 2-10 in a League game in Loughrea. We played Sylvie Linnane at right half-forward that day and, while he scored seven points from frees, it was pretty clear that he was more suited to defence. Not only that, but we needed him in defence, judging by the room the Limerick attack enjoyed. Sylvie was restored to corner-back for our next game against Leinster in the Railway Cup semi-final in Pearse Stadium and we regained some equilibrium with a one point win.

The Railway Cup has been a good competition for Galway. It gives us extra games and a win can lift morale if things are not going well. Unlike teams in other provinces we don't have a Provincial championship to aim for, so it's nice to have the Railway Cup as a sort of compensation. Why the GAA don't settle on a permanent date for it is beyond me. It has been pushed all over the calendar and has lost considerable status as a result. It has been squeezed out by the club championships in the public's affections but I still think it has a role. The players like it, but to have any chance of regaining popularity, it must be given a regular place on the fixture list and marketed properly. Galway would really miss it, if it were to be abolished, an option which many seem to favour. Personally, I think that would be a big mistake, one which would only become apparent when it was gone.

Apart from being of value to Galway, it is also very popular in Ulster, among both footballers and hurlers. Some players from the leading counties in Munster and Leinster may have shown it scant respect in recent times but they should not be allowed to dictate to the rest. Besides, players from the so-called 'weaker counties' in both provinces see it as a vehicle to advance their careers. Meath's Pat Potterton has been a recent example. He has fitted in nicely to the Leinster team and I am sure he regards it as a big honour to play for his Province.

The 1986 Railway Cup final brought us great relief. We beat Munster by 3-11 to 0-11 in the final in Ballinasloe. The rest of the hurling world might not have taken much notice of it but it was a big breakthrough for us. We had finally shed the losers' tag. The players had become very conscious of having lost so many finals in 1985 and you couldn't read any preview of a match involving Galway, without seeing a reference to our poor record in finals.

Noel Lane scored two goals in that final, but the most-talked about incident was the magnificent point from a free, scored by Cork goalie, Ger Cunningham. He had the wind behind him and made full use of it to hoist the ball over the bar from 120 yards. It was not the last time that Ger's massive puck-outs would make an impact against Galway!

The week before the Railway Cup final, we made an important psychological point to Offaly in a League game in Birr. Each of us needed to win to be sure of a place in the knock-out stages and there was a lot of tension going into the game. Galway-Offaly rivalry has always been intense and, after the previous year's All-Ireland final, this was regarded as a crunch clash. A crowd of over 6,000, which is big for a game like that in March, turned out and they weren't disappointed. It was action all the way.

Brendan Lynskey was sent off a minute into the second-half. The scores were level at the time and it looked bad for Galway; but with Offaly playing their extra man in defence, they were unable to put us under any concerted pressure. A Michael Connolly goal proved the tiebreaker. We won by 1-10 to 0-9 and finished joint top of Division One with Cork.

That brought us directly into the League semi-final, where we met Wexford, who had beaten Limerick in the quarter-final after coming up from Division Two. Our clashes with Wexford in Thurles were to prove memorable in more ways than one.

Galway squandered a six-point second-half lead in the first game and with Tom Dempsey knocking in two goals for Wexford, they led by two points with ninety seconds to go. We were saved through late points by PJ Molloy and Anthony Cunningham.

It was the first time that Galway were to take any notice of Dublin referee, John F Bailey. We were most unhappy with his performance in the drawn game and even more so in the replay. We felt we got nothing from him, but it didn't matter this time because we won the replay 3-11 to 2-5 after a late burst. Little did we know then that the same referee would be in charge of the All-Ireland final against Cork in September.

The scoreline flattered Galway. We were just a point ahead with seven minutes remaining but sub, Michael Connolly, scored a goal and Wexford, somewhat surprisingly, folded. We were back in Thurles for the League final against Kilkenny a week later. Kilkenny had hammered Cork in the semi-final and hadn't the slightest doubt in their minds that they would beat Galway. They saw us in much the same light as Wexford – good for a time but always likely to melt when the heat was switched on in the closing quarter.

Their attitude was easy to understand. With the notable exception of the 1975 League semi-final, which Galway won by 1-9 to 1-6, Kilkenny had Galway under control. They had beaten us in six championship games going back to 1972, by margins ranging from seven to twenty-seven points.

We saw the 1986 League final as a crucial game. It was time to make a forceful statement to ourselves and the rest of the hurling world. The

Railway Cup had been a start. Now we wanted to press on and build an impressive momentum for the championship. Once again, we failed.

In a bad-tempered game on a wretched day in Thurles (only 18,000 spectators turned out), we were always chasing Kilkenny. Liam Fennelly and Christy Heffernan scored first-half goals and, for a time, it looked as if we would be completely demolished. They led by nine points at one stage and after twenty-seven minutes Galway had scored just a single point after shooting a string of wides. We were playing terribly badly. Thankfully, Noel Lane lifted the siege, scoring 1-1 before the break to revive our hopes slightly.

But we were playing so poorly that it really would have taken a miracle to rescue us. We seemed unable to lift the pace and were playing very much to Kilkenny's confident agenda. They dominated the third quarter and while a Conor Hayes goal from a penalty took the bleak look off the scoreline, we could have no complaints about the 2-10 to 2-6 defeat.

Overall, it was a nightmare. Ger Fennelly destroyed us at midfield and our attack made little or no impression on a tough, rugged Kilkenny defence. Martin Naughton, Anthony Cunningham, Joe Cooney, Bernie Forde, Noel Lane and PJ Molloy were our forwards that day and they allowed themselves to be knocked off the ball far too easily. Clearly, we needed an anchor man up front for the championship, somebody who wouldn't take 'no' for an answer. Brendan Lynskey, who was at midfield that day, was the obvious solution.

There was much comment afterwards about the amount of timber dished out in that game. We blamed Kilkenny and they blamed us. There was a fair amount of personal animosity between various players at that stage. I don't know where it came from but it was very definitely there.

We had played Kilkenny in a League game in Nowlan Park in the previous November and things got a bit out of hand once or twice. The following day's report in the *Irish Press* commented that 'teak hurleys would have been more appropriate as the ash sticks were far too soft to withstand the pressures exerted on them as Kilkenny and Galway clattered into each other'. Noel Lane got himself sent off in the last minute and we lost by two goals.

We felt around then that Kilkenny were dishing out the timber far more liberally than in previous years and we decided that, whatever else happened, we would not be intimidated physically. One of the things about tradition in hurling is that counties like Kilkenny, Cork and Tipperary can get away with things that others cannot.

It's part of the élitist factor, I suppose. The theory is that the 'Big Three' are all great hurling artists, who wouldn't dream of using anything other than pure, undiluted skill to win games. That is complete nonsense, of course.

Kilkenny could hand it out with the best of them, as they showed in the 1985/'86/'87 period. Tipperary and Cork could never be described as weaklings either. They had their own hard men, when the occasion demanded. Kilkenny claimed that Galway over-stepped the mark in the 1986 League final, singling out the treatment Liam Fennelly got. We had our casualties too, notably Ollie Kilkenny, who got a terrible time. In the end, though, all that mattered was that Kilkenny had won and we had lost.

The harsh reality was that as we trooped out of Semple Stadium on the evening of 12 May 1986, after losing another League final, it was becoming increasingly obvious that unless we did something different, we would never reach the top. We were on a plateau, just short of the finishing peak and every time we tried to clamber up, somebody stood on our fingers.

It was hard to accept that, but it was necessary if we were to make the sort of progress required to form a genuine championship side. Frankly, we had not improved anywhere near as much as we had hoped during the League. A Kilkenny player really endeared himself to Phelim Murphy in Hayes' Hotel afterwards by telling him that he doubted very much if that Galway team would ever beat Kilkenny. His arrogance appeared well-founded at the time, but it was something we bore in mind for a future meeting. Wild statements like that are best left unsaid. Today's throwaway remark can become tomorrow's motivation. Phelim would remind us all over and over again of what had been said to him when serious championship training got underway five weeks later. Believe me, Phelim has a long memory in matters like that.

That League final defeat was to prove very significant for us. In the end, we lost by just four points and it would have been easy enough to put a comfortable gloss on the defeat, which we did for public consumption. But once we dissected it, we knew the truth. Kilkenny had controlled all the important play. We had played a support role all day.

There were two routes open to us. Battle on in the same mode and hope that everything would be OK next time we met Kilkenny or plan a fundamental overhaul of our set-up. For our own sanity, that seemed the more logical step. It was time for a new approach. The old ways had let us down.

CHAPTER 7

NEW HIGHS AND OLD LOWS

The summer of 1986 was one of the wettest in history. Grounds were soft virtually right through; but we had a lot more to worry us as we began championship training in Athenry. We were waist-high in an identity crisis.

I have always been an optimist and, where Galway hurling is concerned, would feel that on a given day we could beat anybody. But after the League final defeat by Kilkenny, I began to wonder. Granted, it was only a fleeting feeling, but I hated it. Deep down, I knew the players felt the same, but I could never betray any sense of insecurity to them. My job was not only to have them physically right for the big day, but also to have them mentally tuned.

Nerves were getting frayed. We had been together as a panel for nearly two years and, while we had undoubtedly made progress, we seemed unable to push on and complete the job. We were being constantly reminded of all the finals we had lost and, although nobody said it publicly, the view was abroad that we were a bunch of 'chokers' who would never place the maroon and white flag on any meaningful summit. Outsiders were beginning to feel sorry for us in a patronising sort of way, while Galway fans were getting increasingly impatient.

There was a near-arrogance about the manner in which Kilkenny had blown us apart in the League final. Kilkenny believed we would never beat them. They reckoned that when the real heat came Galway would melt into a subservient mess in the corner. God, that infuriated me. You couldn't blame Kilkenny for thinking that way. History had deposited enough evidence at their door. They would never change, but what was to stop us? The League final was lost but there were still three months to the All-Ireland semi-final. We were due to meet the Leinster champions and the odds were that it would be either Kilkenny or Offaly who had, of course, beaten us in the previous year's All-Ireland final. Either way, it was a tall order for Galway.

The first task was to analyse what exactly had gone wrong in the League final. I spent hours discussing it with Phelim and Bernie and we reached the conclusion that the midfield area was one of our biggest problems, not in terms of individuals but in terms of pattern. Brendan Lynskey and Steve Mahon had played there against Kilkenny and Ger Fennelly had done terrible damage. Mahon was a fine hurler but was better on the ball than marking an opponent, while Lynskey was always more useful in attack.

We looked at all the options during the summer, while also keeping one eye on Leinster. First, of course, we had to get over the quarter-final, which we duly did, beating Kerry comfortably. When Kilkenny beat Offaly by eight points in the Leinster final, we knew we had to produce something special. We had been warned. Not that we needed to be after the League final.

Ever since I first started coaching, I always felt that not enough attention was given to devising tactics in hurling. That's probably due to the fact that, unlike soccer, rugby or even Gaelic football, it's very difficult to play a possession game in hurling.

Too often though, I think, coaches looked at it and said, 'It can't be done,' without going into it in any detail. That is not necessarily the case. It may not be as easy to devise tactics in hurling as in other sports but that does not automatically make it a non-starter. Given our predicament, it was time to be bold, maybe even crazy. Faint heart never won an All-Ireland title, so we came up with a plan.

Instead of playing two midfielders, three half-forwards and three full-forwards in the traditional 2-3-3 formation, we decided we would play a 3-3-2. Pearse Piggott and Tony Kilkenny were to be central to that ploy.

Both were very versatile sorts. Piggott had started at centre-back in the League final with Tony Kilkenny on his left and brother, Ollie on the right. We had Peter Finnerty, Tony Keady and Gerry McInerney back for the championship, so we could afford to drop Ollie Kilkenny back to the full-back line and push Tony up to midfield. The idea was that Tony and Piggott would play alongside Steve Mahon, with Anthony Cunningham, Lynskey and Martin Naughton in the half-forward line, leaving Joe Cooney and Noel Lane as a two-man full-forward line. It was mainly designed to capitalise on the great pace and acceleration of Cooney, Cunningham, and Naughton, plus Lane's cuteness around goal. Lynksey would be the target man with responsibility to set up 'second phase' ball, to use a rugby term.

There were risks involved. It meant that the opposition would have a spare man in defence – initially at least – so it was vital that the deliveries into our attack were quick and accurate. There was no point in firing the ball into an unmarked defender (something which unfortunately happened in the All-Ireland final). It was also important for the three midfielders to keep out of each other's way. The last thing we needed was bunching.

When we tried that in training some of the players thought it was plain daft. I had visions of them driving home at night muttering darkly: 'Farrell has flipped. He's gone completely this time. This is crazy.' I kept saying that there was no harm in trying a new approach. And besides, we had to do something to shake the Kilkenny monkey off our backs.

We could analyse it any way we liked but the record showed that it was 15-4 in favour of Kilkenny in All-Ireland semi-final clashes with Galway over the years. They had also beaten us in the 1975 and 1979 All-Ireland finals, plus the League final a few months earlier. We had to try something different.

We knew that they would have studied our set-up and seen nothing to worry them. Why should they? On the Tuesday before the semi-final, several reporters, both from the local and national papers, were in Athenry to watch us training and to get the team selection. It was an unbelievable evening. A deluge poured down unrelentlessly from an angry, leaden sky, leaving huge pools of water on Kenny Park. We hung around for a while, but decided that there was nothing to be gained from training. In fact, it would have been dangerous. I had planned a fairly lively work-out (without showing our hand in a tactical sense), but it just wasn't possible. The only consolation was that Kilkenny were in the same flooded boat down in Nowlan Park.

We had a team talk instead that evening and went through the fine details of our revolutionary game plan. It was a strange sort of feeling. We were sitting in the Kenny Park dressing-rooms with the rain lashing against the windows. It was more like a March night than an August evening. We should have been out on a golden, sunny, evening practising our skills – instead we were cooped up in a dressing-room plotting a game plan which, if it failed, would have left us the laughing stock of the hurling world. Any wonder team management gradually drives you mad!

Had it been a fine evening, our training schedule would have looked very normal. There were only five days to go to the game and there was no way we were going to show our hand to the assembled media who would have splashed it all over the papers the following day. No, we wanted to keep this little surprise until Sunday.

I'm not sure what the players thought on their way home that night, but the look of disbelief on the faces of the reporters and supporters when they heard the team said it all. Phelim called it out to the journalists and it was OK until he reached midfield: 'Mahon, Kilkenny, Naughton, Lynskey, Cooney, Cunningham, Piggott, Lane'. There was a short pause. 'Did you say Piggott at full-forward?' 'I did, sure he's a horse of a man,' replied Phelim Murphy with a dead straight face. The local reporters, in particular, knew that something didn't add up. Piggott at full-forward indeed! The team, as named, was completely unbalanced. The suspicion was that we would inter-change Lynksey and Piggott. Either that or we had gone stone mad! That could be the only other explanation.

The interest in team selection is incredible. All supporters have their own view of what a team should be and, in fairness, some of them are good judges. I am not talking about the once-a-year brigade, but rather the fanatical fans who see a club game every Sunday and who never miss an inter-county game, whether it's championship or challenge. Not only that, but the really sharp ones will study training sessions in detail and know exactly what is going on.

That's why hurling and football are the envy of so many other sports. What other sport do you get hundreds of people turning out just to see a training session? Crowds watching Galway training for an All-Ireland final are a damn sight bigger than the attendances at many League of Ireland soccer games or club rugby matches. It's the same in several other counties.

It gives fans a sense of closeness to the players. They see them arriving, wait for them to come onto the pitch, go through their drill and leave afterwards. We did most of our training in Athenry, which has a very cosy sort of atmosphere in terms of player-fan relationship. The dressing-rooms are situated behind one set of goals, a good distance from the pitch. The players have to walk down a little hill where the fans congregate, so there is a very close bond between all sides. That is important.

Apart from naming Mahon and Kilkenny at midfield with Piggott at full-forward, we also decided to inter-change Sylvie Linnane and Conor Hayes. Kilkenny were playing Liam Fennelly at full-forward and we felt that Linnane's close marking style would work better. Hayes switched to the right and John Commins had replaced Peter Murphy in goal and Bernie Forde was gone from the attack. The new line-up meant that only Steve Mahon lined out in the same position as in the League final. Kilkenny, meanwhile, had made minimal changes. Harry Ryan had come into the attack for Joe O'Hara – otherwise the team was the same as that which had beaten us in the League final, apart from a few positional switches.

I knew full well that my entire coaching reputation depended on the gamble. Had it failed I would have been skewered by Galway fans and, quite probably, the Galway team as well. Having gone for broke, I had to go all the way. In interviews prior to the semi-final, I kept referring to how Kilkenny had bordered on the 'dirty' in the League final. Frankly, I believed it. Their tactics had been questioned in other games also, so they were under a certain cloud. Kilkenny like to trade on a reputation as the goody-goodies of hurling, who are all wrist and class, but they can be as tough and steely as the next. You don't win as many All-Irelands as they have without being as tough as the occasion demands.

I did an interview on RTE television on the day before the game and made the rather pointed comment that I hoped we would get more protection from the referee than we did in the League final. At that stage, I was prepared to take whatever advantage was going and if there was a doubt about Kilkenny's tactics, why should I hang back? They certainly wouldn't have. They would later claim that they were unfairly depicted as hit-men, not just by me but also by media commentators, and that it inhibited them in the semi-final. I don't believe that for a second. It was stretching imagination a bit to believe that the Kilkenny backs were standing off our forwards, simply because they were afraid that referee, Terence Murray, would be hard on them. A county of Kilkenny's hurling pedigree would never make a silly mistake like that. As for the claim that there was a media conspiracy against them, it simply doesn't wash. I can hardly envisage a group of commentators getting together and deciding to 'get' Kilkenny. No, the truth was that Kilkenny were flying very close to the wind in the physical stakes around that period.

The day before a big game is always tough. It was more uncomfortable than usual for us that year because the semi-final was in Thurles. Normally, we would be heading to Dublin on the Saturday. That became a routine, so any time the semi-final was in Thurles, I always found Saturday a long, fidgety sort of day. That was very definitely the case that year. I dared not think ahead to Monday if our tactics backfired and Kilkenny won well. The longest of long knives would be pointing ominously in my direction.

We were hoping for a dry day, on the basis that our running, hand-passing type of game would be better suited by good conditions but, typical of 1986, it was wet. Ah well, too late to change now, although I was worried that the conditions would slow play down, which would definitely have been to Kilkenny's advantage. It had been wet on League final day and they positively thrived in it.

The day started badly when our minors lost the semi-final to Offaly by 3-13 to 2-10. That was disappointing, as hopes were high for the minors that year. Ray Duane played a blinder but it wasn't enough against an Offaly team which went on to win the county's first All-Ireland minor title, beating Cork.

Our fears about the wet day were unfounded. Our plan worked a dream from the start. Better, in fact, than we could have ever hoped for. Piggott, Mahon and Kilkenny won lots of ball around midfield and the forwards clicked immediately. We had worked for hours in training on hand-passing movements and inter-changing positions, but there is a world of difference between doing it in Kenny Park among ourselves and in an All-Ireland semi-final against Kilkenny in Semple Stadium. If anything, though, the forwards did it better that day than they had in training.

Noel Lane hand-passed the first goal and then Joe Cooney set up Anthony Cunningham who hand-passed the second goal. That score represented the perfect execution of what we had planned. Cooney, whose sense of vision suggested he had eyes on all sides of his head, won possession. Cunningham was already making his run so that he was running at full pace by the time Cooney fed him. The gallop through and the hand-passed goal. Sweet and virtually unstoppable. We could do no wrong. Kilkenny were completely mesmerised. It was one of those lovely moments when you look across a pitch and see everything working beautifully.

With things running so smoothly for us, I decided to wander up along the sideline to see what the Kilkenny mentors were up to. Coach, Pat Henderson, a man for whom I always had the utmost respect, was prowling up and down, chewing on his pipe and trying to work out what the hell was going on. He consulted a few times with his co-selectors, Eddie Keher, Pat Delaney and John Walsh and eventually they took off right corner-back, Paddy Prendergast. It was tough on Prendergast. It wasn't all his fault. Far from it, he was no more bamboozled than the rest of the defence, but I suppose the selectors had to try something. They were criticised afterwards for not reacting quicker to our tactics but, in fairness, it was very hard to do anything about them. Everything was going right for us.

Galway wrapped up the game just after half-time when Cooney scored the third goal after Lane's hand-passed effort had been blocked. Minutes later, Cooney scored a brilliant goal, chip-lifting the ball into his hand and beating a defender at the same time. Significantly, two of Galway's goals had come off the hand while a third resulted from a blocked hand-pass. A few years later the GAA authorities outlawed the hand-passed goal, which was a severe blow to Galway.

We eventually won by 4-12 to 0-13. Several Kilkenny players had thrown in the towel long before the end. I never thought I would see the day when Kilkenny players would be wishing a game away, but such was the case that day. Ger Henderson was a notable exception. He had incredible heart and his fierce pride in himself and the Black and Amber kept him battling away right to the end. He was beavering just as hard in the last minute as he was in the first, even though the game was long since over in a competitive sense. He was an example to all when it came to keep going even when the odds were stacked against him.

Kilkenny were disgusted. Bad enough to lose to Galway, but to be out-manoeuvred tactically was more than they could cope with. And by Galway too! I have no doubt that they under-estimated us. It's very hard to avoid complacency when you have a team caught in the sort of psychological grip which Kilkenny had on Galway up to then.

With Kilkenny beaten, our thoughts turned to the final where Cork were waiting for us. It was a dilemma. Would the same tactics work against Cork? Should we revert to an orthodox formation?

That would have meant sacrificing some of the team which performed so heroically against Kilkenny, which would have been very hard to do. Besides, I didn't think that we had players who were capable of beating Cork if we played with a standard line-up. That might seem odd, but I believe it to be the case. We needed something extra to give us a spark and the tactical shake-up had done that against Kilkenny. If executed with the same precision, it could work against Cork too. Had we gone back to an orthodox line-up, I don't think we were good enough to beat them. I have argued this with several people over the years and have been repeatedly told that we won the 1987 final with twelve of the team which lost in 1986. So where was the big difference? Simply in the fact that in 1987 we had added players of the calibre of Pat Malone, Eanna Ryan and 'Hopper' McGrath to the team. And with Noel Lane not starting in '87, we had a much stronger subs' bench than a year earlier.

Our first six subs in 1986 were Peter Murphy, Pakie Dervan, Seamus Coen, Michael Coleman, Gerry Burke and Michael Connolly. In 1987, we had Murphy, Michael Earls, Tony Kilkenny, Pearse Piggott, Noel Lane and PJ Molloy on the bench. All in all a much stronger back-up, certainly in an attacking sense.

The hype after the 1986 semi-final was unbelievable. The Mayor of Galway, in an outbreak of runaway optimism, suggested rather unhelpfully that it was only a matter of turning up on All-Ireland final day and collecting the McCarthy Cup. That was all we needed!

We knew that it was going to be very difficult to beat Cork. Our surprise tactics against Kilkenny were a surprise no more, so they had to be carried out to perfection to work again. They weren't. For whatever reason, we got it all wrong in the early stages.

The plan was to leave the right corner-forward position largely unoccupied. If Cork left corner-back, John Crowley, stayed there, more or less marking space, then our outfield men, who would have numerical advantage, were either to carry the ball in or take their long range scores or drive the ball down the centre or the left to Cooney and Lane. If Crowley came outfield, the instruction was to deliver the ball into the right channel for Cunningham and/or Cooney to run onto.

Unfortunately, amid the pressures of the day, some of our lads lost their focus and instead of adhering to the well-rehearsed game plan, they started driving the ball indiscriminately in on the full-forward line.

That meant that on several occasions the unmarked Crowley was left to simply pick up and clear all alone. It looked bloody awful. And when the ball was driven down the left, Noel Lane, who had been so brilliant against Kilkenny, was being beaten by Denis Mulcahy.

Lane was captain that year and I think it got to him. He seemed to tie up completely and didn't do himself justice. The strange thing about Lane was that All-Ireland finals didn't get to him at all around 1979-80-81 but later on, he became very nervous. Perhaps he was expecting too much of himself as he was now one of the senior figures on the team, whereas in the first 'coming' he was one of the younger set. Certainly being captain didn't help his game, but then it was our decision to appoint him captain so we must take responsibility in the matter.

With our game plan not working, we reverted to an orthodox formation, something I regret to this day. Cork had got two early goals, one off a free by John Fenton, the other from Kevin Hennessy, but we fought back well and were only a point adrift at half-time.

Had we stuck by our original formation for the second-half, who knows what might have happened? Instead, we went back to the old-fashioned game plan, which gave Cork a decided psychological advantage when the game was evenly balance midway through the second-half. As far as they were concerned, they had forced us to play their game, whereas against Kilkenny, we had them trying in vain to play our game. Luck wasn't going our way either. Nor indeed were the referee's decisions. The big break came when Tomas Mulcahy soloed virtually from the half-way line to score Cork's third goal. How many steps did he take without playing the ball? Who's counting? It was that sort of day for Galway. Hennessy added a fourth goal and it was all over. John Commins, from a penalty, and PJ Molloy pulled two goals back, but Cork deservedly won by 4-13 to 2-15.

I had no complaints about that. They had hurled well and had taken their chances. However, I certainly had complaints about the manner in which Dublin's John F Bailey refereed the game. Maybe there was something he didn't like about our style but, whatever the reason, we felt we got nothing from him. The awful thing was that ever since the League semi-final against Wexford earlier in the year, we didn't want him to referee any more big matches which we were involved in and I could not help feeling that if Cork had been as opposed to a referee as we were, he would not have been appointed for the final.

We were particularly angry about the manner in which Brendan Lynskey was treated. Clearly, he had been singled out for special attention by the Cork defence and got more wallops in the first-half than a player might reasonably expect in a lifetime. Cork had studied the semi-final closely and had identified Lynskey as the main target man in attack. Fair enough, but their efforts to curb him were not pretty. One first-half 'tackle', right in front of the Hogan Stand, was appalling.

It amuses me when I hear people saying that the super-powers like Cork, Tipperary and Kilkenny never resort to questionable tactics. Not half! They can be as physical as the next team when the occasion demands.

The GAA doesn't allow public criticism of referees, but as the disappointment of that defeat set in on the night of the All-Ireland final, I decided to speak out the following day. Naturally, the referee's performance was discussed at the post All-Ireland lunch in the Burlington Hotel and I let fly.

All the newspapers carried reports of my criticisms on the Tuesday. I was delighted with that. It wouldn't do anything to ease the pain of losing to Cork but it would put down a marker for the future. The days of staying quiet and accepting whatever Croke Park threw at us were over. I had been tipped off on the Monday that the GAA would not take kindly to any criticisms of the referee. But I didn't care. I reckoned that that they had two choices. Ignore what I had said, which by extension could be interpreted as agreeing with it or summon me to Croke Park to explain myself, which I would do with a degree of relish.

A couple of weeks later the letter dropped through my letter box. 'Cyril, A Chara, would you mind coming up to Croke Park to tell the Games Administration Committee exactly what you meant when you criticised the referee?' No, it wasn't worded that casually but the gist of it was the same. I was being charged with bringing the GAA into disrepute, or some such offence.

Ironically, the GAC chairman at the time was a Galwayman, Tom Cunningham from Mountbellew. Tom is a real gentleman and I have no doubt that the last thing he wanted was to have to hear a disciplinary case against me.

The meeting was held in Croke Park on a Friday night in late September and I remember taking a look at the pitch before going into the Ceannarus building. It was all quiet and almost eerie and as I stood looking across towards the Cusack Stand, I thought: 'What the hell is going on, why am I here?' There were a hundred more useful things I could have been doing right then.

I had devoted every spare minute to hurling all year and now I was being hauled before a Committee to explain why I had criticised the referee. Why should referees be above criticism? I had got lots of stick for the tactics used on the All-Ireland final day but I couldn't summon the critics to a meeting and give them a dressing-down or suspend them.

I made up my mind that, come what may, I was not going to back down before the GAC. I was eventually called and I gave them my version of events.

The GAC didn't want to suspend me – I knew that from the start. They repeatedly asked me if I was happy that I had been quoted correctly by the journalists who wrote the story on the day after the final. That irritated me even more.

Had I said, 'Lads, you know yourselves how journalists put a spin on things – I never really said all that and if I offended anybody, I'm sorry,' I would probably have got away with a mild rebuke. But I wasn't interested in impugning journalists' integrity simply to save my own neck. Besides, I had been quoted accurately. If anything, the journalists had watered down what I had said.

Eventually, I was called back in and told that I was being suspended for two months. It didn't bother me. I had made my point, but I thought it downright unfair that I could not speak my mind without being treated like some sort of anarchist. I was not the first to feel the GAA's hand across the wrists for criticising a referee. Dublin's Tony Hanahoe had got into trouble some years earlier for a similar 'offence'. For some strange reason, the GAA will not allow referees to make any comments on their handling of a game. I believe that an awful lot of the problems could be sorted out if referees were allowed to explain why they took certain decisions. I am not proposing that they explain every decision, but they certainly should have the option of making a comment if they wish. Most of the referees I know would favour that. The current situation is frustrating both for them and the general public.

The fall-out from the 1986 final lasted for weeks. Galway supporters blamed me for getting the tactics all wrong. A hero one month, a villain the next! Such is life for a team manager. Apart from the forward formation, the decision to play Conor Hayes at right corner-back and Sylvie Linnane at full-back was singled out for special attention, especially when Cork scored two goals in the opening minutes.

I still hold that the placings were right. Sylvie was a more tenacious defender than Conor, who had a poor record against Jimmy Barry-Murphy anyway. Besides, Conor had been at right corner-back on the Galway teams which won the 1978 All-Ireland U-21 final and the 1980 senior final. It wasn't as if he was a stranger to the position. Nor had there been any complaints about the fact that he was at corner-back in the semi-final against Kilkenny. But then, we won that day. Also Conor was at full-back in the 1985 semi-final and Cork had scored five goals.

Far too much is made of positional play in hurling. Within limits, a good player can perform in several positions and both Hayes and Linnane had the skills to do that. My 'crime', such as it was, hinged on the fact that Galway lost. I was the obvious scapegoat. I could handle that by then.

A huge crowd turned out to greet the team when we returned home on the Monday night. For the second year in a row, we told a thronged Eyre Square that we would be back next year. It was no more than words at the time, something to say to the fans, who were just as disappointed as we were. Deep down the doubts were beginning to grow into ugly monsters.

In the space of a few short weeks, my own stock had dived dramatically. Galway fans felt I had botched up the final and the GAA authorities thought I was an impertinent boyo for speaking out of turn. Just as well I had grown immune to criticism by that stage.

Still, one silver lining had peeped through the dark clouds. In fact, it turned out to be a real boost. On the Sunday after the senior defeat by Cork our U-21 team faced Wexford in the All-Ireland U-21 final in Thurles. I was also coaching the Galway U-21s.

Being involved with them helped me to get over the disappointment of the senior setback, as we were back training on the Tuesday night. That was a very good U-21 team. It had most of the lads who won the minor title in 1983. John Commins, Pat Malone, Gerry McInerney, Joe Cooney and Anthony Cunningham were all fully-fledged seniors, out for some compensation for the previous Sunday's defeat.

Wexford had a handy team too with lads like Larry O'Gorman, Tom Dempsey, Paul Bridges and Eamonn Synnott on board. We really needed to win that game, to inject some hope back into Galway's bloodstream. Wexford needed to win too as they had been out of the All-Ireland frame in all grades for a long time.

On the morning of the game, I discovered that two of our sub backs had gone down injured, leaving us with little defensive cover. Sean Treacy, who had starred for us in the 1983 minor final, had been in America that summer but I had heard that he had returned home a few days earlier. He had been playing in the US, so I knew he would be fairly fit.

I drove out to his house in Portumna and found him sitting in the car, reading the papers after Mass. 'Get your boots, Treacy. I need you on the bench today.' He protested that he could not possibly join the panel at such a late stage and besides, he had left his boots in America. I told him to let me worry about bringing him back on the panel, so he borrowed his brother's boots and we sped off to rejoin the team coach on its way to Thurles. A few hours later, he was the proud holder of an All-Ireland U-21 medal, although he had not come on as a sub.

It was a fine game. Wexford stretched us all the way but, as he had done the previous Sunday, John Commins came up from goal and scored a penalty. We won by 1-14 to 2-5. The relief was unbelievable. Galway hurling badly needed that win to prove that we were not allergic to winning All-Ireland titles. In fact, it rescued the season for us. It also provided another plank in the development of the senior team. Lads like Cooney, Commins, McInerney, Malone and Cunningham had now won minor and U-21 All-Ireland medals in the space of three seasons. The maturing process was continuing nicely.

Chapter 8

THIS IS THE START –
THERE'S A LOT MORE TO COME

'Get yourself, ready, Earls, we're going to need you. Have you the slip ready, Phelim?'

We were well into the second-half of the 1987 League final against Clare in Thurles and our world was crumbling again. We had played Clare off the pitch for long periods of the first-half, yet we were trailing. Clare full-forward, Tommy Guilfoyle, was hurling rings around Conor Hayes. He had scored one goal and set up another when Hayes fouled him. Gerry McInerney (Clare's Gerry that is – our Gerry was in America at the time) rocketed the resultant free to the net.

Michael Earls was our sub full-back and a good one at that. Still, the last thing we wanted to do was to take Hayes off. He was more than just our full-back and captain. He was a sort of reference point for all Galway's aspirations. Hayes was very popular inside and outside Galway. A big, inspirational man in every sense. But on this particular day, he was a big man having a stinking bad game.

There were risks involved in taking him off. The rest of the Galway players would see it as a bad sign. There was a danger that heads might drop. Nerves were raw after losing so many finals in 1985-86, so it would not have taken much to pull the confidence plug. Also, Clare would interpret Hayes' substitution as another important bridge blown up. It would have galvanised them even further at a time when they were going well. So what the hell were we to do? Guilfoyle was on a roll.

That represented the greater risk. We had to do something to quell the panic every time the ball came in towards our goal. It wasn't all Hayes' fault. Our outfield men were giving Clare too much room. The momentum was very much towards our goal and Hayes was at the sharpest end of the mauling and seemed unable to play his way out of it. Earls was warming up and I moved round the back of the goal behind Hayes. He was about to be replaced. I think he sensed what was going to happen. It was typical of Hayes to produce his best when his back wasn't so much to the wall but through it. He caught the next ball which came in… and the next. A couple of long clearances followed.

The defence steadied and the crisis passed. Stability had been restored. Michael Earls returned to the dug-out.

We edged back in front and, as the game ticked to a conclusion, Galway were two points clear. Then came an incident which I believe fashioned the course of hurling history over the next few years. Michael Guilfoyle hoisted a high ball into the Galway square. It broke loose in front of Gerry McInerney. He was no more than a few yards from goal, faced with the match-winning shot. It seemed he couldn't miss but, somehow, he topped his shot and it bobbled slowly towards the goal line where Peter Murphy saved. He cleared it out to Joe Cooney, who had drifted back to defence and as he prepared to drive the ball downfield, referee, Gerry Kirwan blew the final whistle. The sense of relief was incredible.

We had been granted a last-second reprieve when all seemed lost. Gerry McInerney was devastated. Had it been any other day, I would have felt genuinely sorry for both him and Clare. Like ourselves, they had been dealt more than a fair share of misery over the years and while a League title might not compare with an All-Ireland crown, it would have been some consolation to that Clare team. But frankly, we needed to win more, purely to retain our sanity.

Going into the final, we had done our best to play down its importance. But how could we have explained away another big-day defeat? It was all very well telling a packed Eyre Square the previous September that we would be back the following year but it was futile unless we delivered.

That League was crucial to us. It had started out in Pairc Ui Chaoimh in the previous October with a match against Cork in an All-Ireland final repeat. I was suspended at the time, but seeing that nobody has ever explained what exactly it means to suspend an official, I ignored it and managed the team as usual.

I patrolled the sideline as if nothing was amiss. It was only afterwards that I heard that Games Administration Chairman, Tom Cunningham, was at the game. I was half-expecting another 'Cyril, A Chara' letter from Croke Park but it never came. To be honest, I think the GAC were not interested in another controversy. Anyway, I never did believe that they felt happy about suspending me in the first place. Either that or Tom, being a Galwayman, decided to turn a blind eye in Pairc Ui Chaoimh.

We beat Cork by 2-21 to 5-8, with Joe Cooney in splendid form, scoring 1-8. We followed up with a win over Kilkenny but were shocked by Westmeath in Loughrea, losing by a goal. With respect to Westmeath, I think we were a bit over-confident that day. It was the only match we lost in the League. In fact, we weren't to lose another competitive game for sixteen months.

We beat Limerick easily and then hit a goal strike to beat previously unbeaten Clare by 5-7 to 2-8 in Ennis in the final game of the year. We beat Offaly and drew with Wexford in our first two games of 1987, to easily qualify for the League semi-finals.

Eanna Ryan was a significant discovery during that League. In hindsight, we probably should have had him in the panel for the 1986 championship. He was a marvellously gifted player with great skill and a sharp instinct when it came to anticipating the break of a ball. A natural goal poacher, if ever there was one. He really went to town in the December game against Clare, scoring 3-1. Apart from being a great opportunist, he was very versatile and could play anywhere from midfield up.

So why was he not on the panel in 1986? Simply because we didn't think he was quite up to it then. A mistake, probably, but then team management is not an exact science.

Michael Coleman was another who came through during that League, but he played poorly in the final against Clare. He couldn't do anything right. He was very raw at the time and we left him off the championship panel. That was a mistake. We should have kept him on the scene, even if he wasn't ready for the 1987 championship. Sixteen months later, he was to emerge as a trump card in the All-Ireland final against Tipperary.

Sometimes it's difficult to pinpoint a match which turns things round for a team but, in Galway's case, there is no doubt that the 1987 League final was crucial. There was a strange atmosphere in the county going into that game. We trained mostly in Garbally College, Ballinasloe. The present Bishop of Clonfert, Most Rev John Kirby, was President of Garbally at the time and he kindly let us use the pitches. Hardly anybody knew where we were training. I'm not so sure they even cared.

Not that we over-exerted ourselves. We cruised into the final with a massive win over Waterford in Portlaoise and it was only then that we really got to work. We had been expecting a semi-final date with Cork but they were surprisingly beaten by a point by Waterford, who flopped badly against us, losing by 5-16 to 1-12. Joe Cooney and Anthony Cunningham had a field day, scoring 4-10 between them. On the other side, Tipperary were showing hopeful signs. It was 'Babs' Keating's first season as manager and, although they were in Division Two, they were attracting quite a bit of notice.

They won promotion and then beat Limerick by a point in extra-time in the quarter-final. Nicholas English and Pat Fox, names which were to be to the forefront of so much important action after that, got the points which initially sent the game into extra-time and then earned Tipp a clash with Clare in the semi-final.

Clare, who like ourselves went directly for the semi-finals, generally had the upperhand on Tipperary around then. Tipperary were without English for the semi-final and lost by 2-11 to 1-11 in Pairc Ui Chaoimh. Nobody could possibly have envisaged that evening that Tipperary would win five of the next seven Munster titles and that they would also capture two All-Ireland and two League titles.

Coming up to the 1987 League decider, we kept saying that our training schedule was geared for the championship — and it was — but once you are in a final, you have to cram in as much as you can in a short time. It's like facing an exam without having covered the course. Not a nice feeling. You curse the fact that you didn't do more work earlier while, at the same time, telling yourself that an early season training campaign would not have fitted in with the overall plan.

There didn't seem to be a whole lot of interest among the Galway supporters in that League final. We never could figure out whether they thought we would win easily or that we would flop in another final. One could hardly blame them if they were pessimistic. We had hammered Clare in a Division One game five months earlier, but that was not going to count for much in the final.

I suppose we were lucky to beat Clare. We hurled well enough in patches, but we still had problems putting teams away. All the important breaks went our way that day but after the previous two years we felt entitled to them. It's a strange phenomenon but a team can go through a phase where they don't get one lucky break and then hit a patch where everything goes their way. That League final was the start of a lucky phase for Galway.

I'm not saying that luck was solely responsible for our great run. Far from it. But at least in 1987-88 we were getting a decent share of the breaks, unlike other seasons when we could not be sure that we would back the winner in a one-horse race.

As we left the pitch in Thurles after the presentation, Phelim Murphy remarked to me, 'This is the start, there's a lot more to come'. We had no idea how much.

The bulb was blown in the tunnel leading into our dressing-room and it was a most strange sensation walking in from the bright sunlight to almost total darkness. Victory's bright glow was all around, however, and I doubt very much if any team ever felt greater satisfaction, not to mention relief, from winning a League title. The Clare lads stayed on the pitch for the presentation and waited to congratulate us as we came across with the trophy. As always, they took their defeat very sportingly but they were very, very disappointed. Understandably so.

There may have been more celebrations when Galway won the 1975 League title after a twenty-four year gap but that team could have afforded to lose the final to Tipperary. They would still have been regarded as heroes after beating Cork and Kilkenny to reach the final. In 1987, all had changed. Reaching finals was no longer enough.

Ironically, that League final was to prove a watershed both for Galway and Clare. We went from strength to strength while Clare went into decline. I fancied them to do very well in the Munster championship that summer. They had come very close to Cork in the 1986 Munster final and had a very experienced team.

What we didn't realise was that a new power was emerging in Munster. Clare drew with Tipperary in the Munster semi-final, thanks to a late goal by Gerry McInerney (he made no mistake this time) but, were surprisingly blitzed 4-17 to 0-8 in the replay. It was an amazing turnaround in the space of two weeks.

I always thought that Clare reacted too hastily after that. They saw it as the end of that particular team and too many of them were let go. You have got to be very careful about making decisions like that. You must ask yourself if you have better replacements because there is no point making changes simply for change sake. It might look good initially but, once the novelty wears off, you can be worse off than before.

I always had a soft spot for Clare hurlers. Apart from being near neighbours, they have a lot in common with Galway. Tipperary and Cork don't really rate them (even if they have beaten both in the last two championships) and always feel that there must be something wrong if Clare get the better of them. They play the patronising game with Clare, telling them how good they are if they win while silently thinking: 'What the hell went wrong. Clare shouldn't be beating us.'

Ger Loughnane, Sean Stack, John Callinan, all of whom were magnificent hurlers, were gone by 1988. They had given a lifetime of dedicated service to Clare but were destined to finish up without either a Munster or All-Ireland medal. It was so unfair.

Clare's loss in 1987 was very much Galway's gain. Colm Flynn had been a key sideline figure with Clare for years and I made up my mind when Tipperary beat them that I would approach him to join us. He took that defeat very badly so I left him to get over his disappointment for a few weeks. He took a holiday and I approached him when he came back and asked him to join us. He was reluctant at first. His heart was in Clare but, gradually, he came round and, after a bit of persuasion, he agreed to join us as a physio.

I had got to know him over the previous years and had the utmost respect for him. Sylvie (Linnane) and Steve (Mahon) and some of the other lads in South Galway knew him very well too and thought the world of him. Colm was another piece of the Galway jigsaw. By now, Michael McGloin had joined us as team doctor. He looked after the more serious injuries while Colm worked on the niggling ones. They were both fantastic and played a huge part in the Galway success story.

Michael was incredibly generous with his time and rarely missed a training session. He was more than a team doctor, he was an enthusiast. He still is.

Colm had vast experience both with both Clare and Eire Óg, Ennis and he was also involved in boxing, so apart from being brilliant with injuries, he also knew how sportspeople thought. Some players imagine they have injuries when, in fact, they haven't. Others will try to ignore warning signs in the hope that they can train or play their way out of an injury. Colm was a great man to cut through the exterior and get right down to the heart of the matter.

So if we had somebody injured and I asked Colm when he was likely to be fit, he invariably got it right. If he pointed to his head, I knew it was all imagination on the part of the injured party and we worked accordingly. But if Colm said it was serious, I accepted that. Believe me, he was very good at spotting the difference between a genuinely injured played and a player who thought he was injured. It was to prove helpful more than once.

We all had great confidence in the medical back-up, which was important. It's a vital part of the set-up. It helps too if the medics are genuine enthusiasts. Michael and Colm certainly were, just as Dr Mary McInerney was before them.

As we headed into the summer 'recess' in 1987, things were looking good. The players' confidence had soared after the League final success and, overall, there was a more professional shape about the entire set-up. Everybody had a job to do. There was no over-lapping, nor were there any gaps. We travelled everywhere on Miko Donoghue's coaches and Miko and his team became part of ours too.

Nevertheless, Phelim, Bernie and myself had certain doubts. The championship would be altogether different. We had won a fairly handy League. Even then we had struggled against Clare. A big, big improvement would be required if we hoped to win the championship. It would demand a lot of careful planning, several late nights and, quite probably, some very tough decisions.

A win covers a multitude and it was only in later years that we realised the significance of the League final success over Clare. Those who say the League doesn't count know nothing of the relief we felt after beating Clare. We knew that deep down the likes of Cork and Kilkenny looked on that League final as no more than an irrelevant sideshow between two moderate teams and would still feel that Galway had not made the breakthrough. As events transpired, Cork had a lot more to worry them in Munster than they might have thought, while Kilkenny would feel the cutting edge of our growing maturity.

The Galway squad felt good about themselves as they returned to the club championship scene awaiting the summer call and, while the management were not convinced that everything was right, at least we had a solid base to work on.

Chapter 9
HOT AUGUST AFTERNOON

It was Phelim Murphy's idea. We had spent many long hours assessing the options, examining the problems, identifying the risks. We knew that we weren't far away from the championship breakthrough, but the margin for error was getting smaller.

Even after winning the 1987 League final, we still felt the team needed an extra lift for the championship. Unlike 1986, when we possibly showed undue loyalty to the team which had beaten Kilkenny in the All-Ireland semi-final, we were prepared to do anything required to give us that vital edge in 1987.

That included persuading Peter Finnerty and Gerry McInerney to return from the US. They had been there since the previous autumn but the understanding was that they would be back in good time for championship training. Their return would spark off change. It meant no place for Pearse Piggott in defence. We left Michael Coleman off the panel altogether. Tony Kilkenny would be omitted for the All-Ireland final. We had a further trick up our sleeves, planted there by Phelim in one of the many late-night sessions the selectors indulged in through that summer.

We had noticed that over the previous two years our game had tended to run out of impetus at crucial stages. Fitness-wise we were fine, but for some strange reason, our game would die for a time, very often in the second-half. There was no obvious reason for it but there was no escaping the damage it was doing. It had happened against Clare in the League final and, while we lived to tell the tale, the danger signs were there. Phelim suggested that maybe we should try holding one of our big names in the subs and introduce him as a 'springer' in the second-half. It just might be the catalyst the team needed.

Noel Lane immediately sprang to mind for that lonely, but vital role. Lane had been captain in 1986 and had frozen completely in the final against Cork. He hadn't done much better against Offaly a year earlier. We had talked it over several times but we never sorted it out. He was getting far too tense going into finals and wasn't doing himself justice.

That doesn't in any way detract from his fantastic talents. He gave Galway hurling twelve magnificent years and more than paid his dues, but we had to do what we thought was in the team's best interests. He was ideal for the super-sub role. His first touch was always good which meant he could play himself into a game immediately. He never had any problems adapting to the pace of a game when he came on. Others can take time to adjust when they come on as a sub. Not Lane. He would get on his game straightaway, in fact, often much quicker than if he had started the game. Don't ask me why, it was just the way he was.

He was also a big name with a great record. He made a very definite impact when he raced out as a replacement. Here was a man who had won an All-Ireland medal, a League medal, several Railway Cup medals and two All-Star awards. He lifted his colleagues' spirits while sending panic waves through the opposition. It was a hard role for him, one which understandably he never accepted, but I'm convinced that it was very much in Galway's best interests in 1987-88.

Early summer is a sort of limbo time in Galway hurling. The club championships are in full swing but because the inter-county team doesn't have a game until late July (every second year) or August, all we can do is sit back and watch the drama unfolding in the other provinces. Boy, was there some drama in 1987, especially in Munster.

Cork, who were the reigning All-Ireland champions, were the favourites to retain the Munster title. They duly made it to the final, beating Limerick in a semi-final replay. Tipperary had beaten Clare in another semi-final replay but were still underdogs going into the final in Thurles. Obviously, nobody told them that because they led for most of the way before a typical Cork rally put them a point ahead in the closing minute. Once again, it looked as if Cork's survival instincts had squeezed them through, but Pat Fox equalised from a free to send the match to a replay in Killarney the following Sunday.

Most people thought that Cork would win the replay, claiming that Tipperary had blown their chance in Thurles. I didn't agree. I fancied Tipp to win the replay. I felt that they were maturing rapidly and that they stood to gain more from the drawn game than Cork who were badly missing Jimmy Barry-Murphy, who had retired the previous spring.

Tipperary did win eventually but not before the game went into extra-time. We were watching the drama from afar, not quite sure what to make of it at first. The whole of Tipperary went into ecstasy when they beat Cork. It was understandable. After all, they hadn't won a Munster final since 1971.

Their return home was unbelievable. The team stayed in Killarney on the Sunday night and made a triumphant trip back home on the Monday evening. Had Cork won they would scarcely have been noticed as they slipped back home on Sunday evening, but this was something special.

Tipperary's win presented us with a whole new ball-game. The entire country seemed to be sucked in by the blue-and-gold euphoria and, with Kilkenny coming out of Leinster, the old cliches were back in business. The traditionalists wanted a 'real' final, Kilkenny v Tipperary. Galway and Antrim were seen as no more than irritants to be blown aside to make way for the 'Big Two'.

I made up my mind to be bold and brash in the team talks. Galway had spent far too long paying tribute to the super-powers. It was time to fight back. I felt the players were disappointed that they wouldn't be meeting Cork and I turned that into an advantage.

I tried to brainwash them into believing that they were far superior to Tipperary. Why didn't we know more about Tipperary, I kept asking? Simply because they hadn't been in an All-Ireland semi-final for sixteen years and, even in the League, they had been up and down between Divisions One and Two like a yo-yo. Croke Park would be new to them on All-Ireland semi-final day, while we were old hands there. Also, they had beaten a Cork team which was over the top while we were still improving.

It was a somewhat risky approach but I wanted our team to feel superior to Tipperary on All-Ireland semi-final day. Besides, I had a trump card up my sleeve. I kept harping back to 1983 when Galway beat Tipperary at both minor and U-21 level. If they were good enough to win then, why not do it now as seniors four years later?

The whole focus was on Tipperary coming up to the game. It was as if the year's entire momentum had gathered behind them and wasn't going to be stopped. We had Finnerty, McInerney and Commins back for the game. We moved Tony Kilkenny to midfield alongside Steve Mahon and played the same forward line as in the League final. Peter Murphy, Pearse Piggott and Michael Coleman lost out.

We all knew it was make-or-break year. It was our third season together and if we didn't deliver an All-Ireland title, the team management would have to resign. The turnover among the team would have been high too.

There was incredible tension coming up to that game. It was only afterwards that we heard of the humourous side. It seems some mischievous Kilkenny fans had erected signposts around Urlingford and Johnstown proclaiming 'Croke Park this way', by way of send-up for the Tipperary followers passing through on the Sunday morning of the game. Travelling to Croke Park for big games was a new experience for many Tipperary fans. I suspect that most Kilkenny people thought Tipperary would beat us and they wanted to plant the seeds of doubt for the final.

As it happened, 1987 was one of the years when we didn't have an All-Ireland quarter-final game. That meant that we were without a competitive fixture between 3 May and 9 August. Tipperary had played five championship games in the same period.

I know people will say that a quarter-final means nothing to Galway. I never accepted that. OK, so maybe the All-Ireland 'B' champions are a notch below the big powers, but the quarter-final is still a fence which has to be cleared. It gives Galway an earlier focus than when they go straight into the semi-final.

I never was one to dwell on the past but it was impossible to avoid the historical baggage which was being unloaded in the media prior to the semi-final. One reporter phoned to ask if I knew that this would be the 10th semi-final meeting between Galway and Tipperary and that the score stood 8-1 to Tipp? I replied that 'no', I wasn't aware of that and what's more I couldn't care less. What John and Jimmy Doyle, Donie Nealon, 'Babs' Keating and all the previous greats had done to Galway didn't count as far as I was concerned. I was sick and tired listening to grim tales of past Galway failures. What had they to do with anything?

Match-day dawned bright and sunny. Good! It would suit our running game. It would suit Tipperary too, but I wasn't worried about that. Better to get your own game right than worry about the opposition. Let them worry about us for a change.

The scenes as Miko Donoghue edged the team coach to Croke Park were unbelievable. Two years earlier, only 8,200 turned up for our semi-final against Cork. We would hear later that almost 50,000 were in Croke Park for our clash with Tipperary. There really was an All-Ireland atmosphere around.

The match programme had a blue and gold (Tipperary colours) front, with a picture of a very determined-looking Bobby Ryan. It was a small point but it made a statement. The focus, even at official level, was on Tipperary. Understandably so. They were the new kids on the semi-final block and everybody wanted to know about them. Galway fans were reminded of the disappointing past with an article on 'Babs' Keating which hailed his great achievement in scoring 2-12 for Tipperary against Galway in the 1971 All-Ireland semi-final in Birr. Were Galway forever to be reminded of the past?

The excitement among the Tipperary fans was incredible. There was a more subdued atmosphere among the Galway crowd. They were almost afraid to hope, after the disappointments of 1985-86. Tipp minors beat Galway 4-12 to 1-9 in the curtain-raiser. A sign of things to come?

Tipperary had named Nicholas English at left full-forward with Bobby Ryan at full-forward but we never believed for a second that they would line out like that. English would be at full-forward. He would try and run Conor Hayes into submission. Quite what Bobby Ryan was doing in attack would always remain a mystery. Bobby was a fine defender, tough, durable, brave and honest. But in 1987, 'Babs' and his co-selectors, Donie Nealon and Theo English obviously felt that they needed his leadership qualities up front. Trouble was that Bobby was a defender at heart and never liked playing in attack. We figured that he would not cause us many problems. He was restored to the defence by 1988.

One of our main concerns was to prevent Tipperary from making a good start. We felt that if we gave them an early jolt they might show their lack of big-time experience, so our plan was to sprint from the off. As it happened, they struck first, with a Nicholas English point. Galway's response a few minutes later was to prove crucial. It came a few minutes later. Brendan Lynskey gathered possession, sucked in a few defenders and slipped the ball out to Martin Naughton. He let fly from twenty-five yards and the ball flew past Ken Hogan into the Tipperary net.

That goal convinced me that we were on our way. Tipperary's naïvety in congregating on Lynskey had left Naughton clear and he had the confidence to go for goal from twenty-five yards. Galway might only have beaten Tipp in one previous semi-final, but that score left nobody in any doubt that times had changed. A few minutes later we were six points clear. Joe Cooney was doing all sorts of damage, but English was equally menacing at the other end. Pat Fox goaled a penalty just before the break to revive Tipp hopes. Galway 1-13 Tipperary 1-9 at half-time.

Tipperary dominated the third quarter and one could sense the Galway fans preparing for the worst. Fox's second goal fourteen minutes from the end gave Tipp the lead. The atmosphere was unbelievable. Tipperary fans were convinced that they would be in the All-Ireland final. It was time to put the super-sub theory to the test. We sent on Lane.

The next few minutes characterised the changed attitude in Galway. There was a time when we might have folded after allowing a team back into a game, but not anymore. That inner resolve was strong by now. Besides, luck was beginning to go our way. A miss by Tipperary wing-forward, Martin McGrath, after a fine run was a perfect example. In previous years, the net would have shaken.

The sides were level with nine minutes left when an incident occurred which many believe decided the game. Few in Croke Park spotted the late tackle on our goalie, John Commins, just before English knocked over a point. Thankfully, referee, Gerry Kirwan did and awarded a free out. Tipperary momentarily lost concentration and Conor Hayes hoisted the free deep into Tipp territory. Lynskey caught it, broke a tackle or two, flicked it to Eanna Ryan, who was enjoying a brilliant championship debut. He galloped forward and hand-passed it to the net. Thank God for the good old trusted hand-pass. Instead of being a point behind, we were a goal in front in the space of ten seconds. Anthony Cunningham made it a four-point lead before English and Donie O'Connell scored two points for Tipperary. But, in a tense finish, Lane did his suber-sup trick, scoring our third goal. Joe Cooney added a point: Galway 3-20 Tipperary 2-17! Phew! We had made it.

'Babs' Keating claimed afterwards that the Tipperary team were stone dead from all the effort they had put in during the Munster championship. He could have fooled me. They played well enough to win most semi-finals (let's face it, 2-17 would win most games), but Galway were approaching a peak at that stage.

There was a hunger, born of fear and frustration, buried deep in the players' souls. They knew that had they lost, it would have been the end for them as a team. The management set-up would have changed and obviously those coming in after us would have brought in new ideas and, in many cases, new players. I think the fear of failure motivated

Galway that day, almost as much as the unbelievable hype which had surrounded Tipperary.

The arrogance which exuded from Tipp after beating Cork was hard to take. In many ways, it's part of their armoury. They love to propagate the 'Premier County – Home of Hurling' theory. There was a time it would have intimidated Galway. We would have played well for a long time but ended up losing. By 1987, that had changed. Hurling was becoming a classless society as far as were concerned.

The 1987 semi-final was one of the classic games of the 1980s. I would have loved to have been a neutral on the stands, taking it all in and enjoying it. You don't really enjoy games when you are closely involved. You are switched in to every shot and move and it's as if part of you is out there on the pitch. It can be very frustrating for a coach. He can have all the influence he likes outside the white line but the real action is inside. You worry for every player and worry too in case you have made the wrong decisions. There is no second chance in a big game. When you win, it's much later that the satisfaction of success sinks in.

Unquestionably, there was a great deal of inner delight at having beaten Tipperary in 1987. Over the next few years, we would have many more famous battles with them. Oddly enough though, that first meeting was probably the best of all in terms of quality hurling.

Chapter 10

BURNING THE MIDNIGHT OIL

In an age when there is a tendency to overplay the importance of a team manager in most sports, I am the first to admit that any manager is only as good as his squad. There is absolutely nothing you can do unless you have the raw material. I would define a good manager as a person who is able to extract the maximum level of efficiency and performance from the available talent.

Sometimes that will be enough to win an All-Ireland title. Maybe even two or three All-Irelands if you have an extra-special panel. Alternatively, you might not get past the first round of the championship, but that does not make you a bad manager if you don't have the resources to work with in the first place. All that might seem very obvious, but I'm afraid that a great many commentators are unable to differentiate between good and bad managers. Thus, the manager who presides over an All-Ireland triumph is automatically deemed a success, while his counterpart who fails to make the breakthrough is dubbed a failure. The fact that the managers had different squads to work on tends to be overlooked.

I was extremely fortunate with the calibre of players I dealt with in Galway. Apart from their obvious talents, they were, for the most part, focused on winning and were prepared to make whatever sacrifices were necessary to achieve success. Ultimately, that is just as important as being talented.

I was lucky too with the selectors. Back in 1980, the late 'Inky' Flaherty and Bernie O'Connor were my co-selectors while Bernie and Phelim Murphy were with me from 1984 on. 'Inky' was a legend in Galway hurling, having been a star player back in the 1940s and 1950s. Even more importantly, in the context of modern Galway hurling, he was coach to the team which made a significant breakthrough by winning the 1975 National League title. That really was the rebirth of Galway hurling at senior level and was due in no small way to Inky's ability to get players believing that they could win.

'Inky' was a lovely man. I always referred to him as 'The Boss' as he had that fatherly sort of personality. I got on famously with him when I took over as coach in the autumn of 1979. He was a joy to work with. He knew that I was a stickler for physical fitness and, although I am sure there were times when he felt I might be driving some of the older players too much, he trusted me enough and let me get on with it. Believe me, there wasn't a happier man in Croke Park than Inky when the fifty-seven year All-Ireland famine ended the following September.

On our way to Croke Park that day 'Inky' had a broad smile on his face. Every time, we passed a knot of cheering Galway supporters, he would say, 'This is our day. I'm telling you, this is our day. I can sense it.' But then he was very much an optimist, a man with a vision for success. Tradition didn't count as far as he was concerned. Galway hurling was an entity in its own right and should fear nobody. Amen to that.

Bernie O'Connor had given many long, faithful years to the Galway cause as a player. Unfortunately for him, he played in an era when Galway was wasting its time in the Munster Championship. The closest he came to a major success was in 1969 when Connacht reached the Railway Cup final for the first time since 1959.

The Railway Cup was a major competition then and was invariably shared between Leinster and Munster. It was a big surprise when Connacht beat Leinster in the 1969 semi-final as Leinster had won their previous meeting with Connacht by 10-10 to 3-2 in the 1967 semi-final. Connacht drew with Munster in the 1969 final in Croke Park but lost the replay by six points in Galway. It was a big disappointment at the time.

When I was given the option of choosing my own selectors for my second managerial stint in 1984, I had no hesitation in choosing Bernie and Phelim Murphy. Phelim, who was also Hurling Board Secretary, had been a selector with me when Galway won the U-21 title in 1978 and we hit if off straightaway. In hurling terms, we were on the same wavelength.

Bernie and Phelim shared one vital characteristic. They were both above club considerations. Never once did either of them push a player from his own club. Martin Naughton was the only man from Turloughmore (Phelim's club) to hold down a regular place, while Pat Malone was the sole Oranmore-Maree (Bernie's club) up to 1991, when Richie Burke took over in goal. Turlo's Gerry Burke was on the team in 1989 but, overall, nobody could ever say that club loyalties played a part in our deliberations.

That was a prime consideration for me. I wanted people around me who put Galway first, clubs second. Don't get me wrong. Club activity is very important, but once you are involved in the county scene, that has to be the priority.

Both Phelim and Bernie had something else in common. They both got great support from their families. Phelim's wife, Nellie, and Bernie's wife, Joan, were immersed in hurling just as much as we were. Nellie has washed every Galway jersey since Phelim took over as Hurling Board Secretary in 1982. More than that, she lives hurling almost as much as Phelim does, and probably knows just as much about it! The same goes for Joan O'Connor.

There were dozens of nights over the years when we sat until all hours in either Murphy's or O'Connor's, discussing, debating, teasing out things in an effort to get the right blend. Phelim's mother was alive then and I'm sure there were nights when she felt like saying 'Have ye no homes to go to?' as we sat until dawn, drinking tea and talking hurling. But deep down she was a great hurling woman too and was fiercely proud of Phelim's involvement with Turloughmore and Galway.

Phelim had a fine pedigree as a club manager, having been at the heart of the Turloughmore set-up which won six Galway county championship titles in a row between 1961 and 1966. Galway were going through their Munster nightmare at that stage and made no impression on the county scene, but the club structure was strong.

One of the reasons I got on so well with Phelim and Bernie was that, although generally we thought along the same lines, we came at it from different directions. Overall, we agreed on the type of player we wanted but saw it from different angles. We worked out a plan early on which worked very well. We would meet on a Monday night after the fixtures for the following Sunday had been made. We would pick a game each to watch certain players and report back on the following Monday night.

If somebody had spotted something interesting in a certain player, another of us would take a look at him the following week. We always had a fair idea of what we were looking for, based on the requirements for the team. For instance, Steve Mahon was a naturally left-sided midfielder, so we set about finding a right-sided player to complement him. It took quite some time to sift through the candidates and we eventually discovered Pat Malone, who turned out to be a real gem.

We rarely attended club games together. We didn't need to. I knew when Bernie or Phelim suggested that I take a look at a player, he was compatible with the general philosophies under which we operated. Quite simply, we each knew how the other thought and we respected each other's views.

Phelim played a vital role, not just as a selector, but also in terms of liaising with the clubs. As Hurling Board Secretary, he was in constant touch with the clubs and was able to manoeuvre the fixtures' schedule to dovetail with the county team.

There are people who claim that the clubs must always come first, but that's an over-simplification. Yes, of course, they must be looked after and treated properly, but the truth is that nothing boosts the club scene like a healthy inter-county set-up. It's all very fine having your club fixture list running like clockwork, but it won't do a whole lot to make sure that you are in Croke Park on the first Sunday of September.

A rising tide lifts all boats and if your inter-county team is going well, clubs will prosper as there is an inevitable surge in public interest. That theory is borne out by the fact that in 1981 the total gate receipts at Galway hurling championship games were £51,000 while in 1993, they brought in £157,000. It's fair to say that club hurling has never been stronger in Galway, as borne out by the fact that Kiltormer and Sarsfields have won the last three All-Ireland club titles.

The key to it all is common sense and a bit of give and take here and there. Phelim was a master at achieving that. He is, what you might call, a democratic dictator! But then people like that are vital in the GAA because of its multi-layered fixtures' structure.

Phelim is a very clear thinker on players and tactics. He operated one simple theory which, the more I studied it, the more accurate it appeared. Basically, he believed that a player who flopped once on the big day was likely to do it again. The old country saying about never trusting a horse which ran away was central to his approach.

Bernie had a theory about certain clubs. He knew every club's background inside out and felt that, for whatever reason, some clubs were far more likely than others to produce inter-county players. It wasn't simply a matter of numbers, it was more a question of attitude. More than once, Bernie was proved right. I'm not saying that we would ignore a player, simply because he was from a certain club; but we knew that some clubs had their players better prepared both mentally and physically for the step up to county hurling.

Bernie was also the coolest of the three of us. He would stand back where Phelim or I would be inclined to shoot from the hip. But God help anybody who criticised the players when Bernie was around. It was about the only thing which ever made him angry.

Never once in our seven years in charge did we have a vote about team selection. It wasn't that we always agreed. Far from it. But we reckoned that taking a vote would be a cowardly way of reaching a decision. Our job was to tease out all the possibilities and we owed it to the squad and to Galway to do that systematically and professionally. If it took all night, so be it. If it took half the following day, we would give it that too. Once we had reached a decision, there were no recriminations,· even if it backfired badly. We had enough critics without turning on ourselves.

Phelim always regarded the lads on the Galway panel as ultra-special. He would give each one of them a gold hurl if they asked for it, but would go through the roof if somebody went to the boot of his car and took a hurl without asking. It was a mortal sin in his book.

If Phelim was an expert at manoeuvring the clubs to fit in with the county scene, he was a positive genius at getting around me. I always wanted to play our League games at venues which I reckoned suited us against certain teams. I couldn't care less if that meant playing every game at the same venue in any one season. Phelim wanted to give all the venues a fair share of games to keep everybody happy and he had a great way of going about it.

Pearse Stadium could be a pretty dismal place on a miserable winter's day. If the wind and rain was whipping in from the Atlantic, Pearse Stadium was about the best advertisement you could get for sitting at home by the fire. I remember walking across the pitch on one particularly dark, wet, November evening after winning an awful League game when Phelim piped up, 'Do you know what, but this is the best ground in the county for winning games?' I looked at him and was about to launch into a tirade when he walked away with a mischievous look on his face. I knew damn well that he had already promised some other game to Pearse Stadium and he was simply trying to make a case for it.

I left all that sort of thing to Phelim and the Hurling Board. Phelim and Board Chairman, Tom Callinan got on well and I knew that ultimately the team's best interests would come first. There was one thing which used to drive me daft about Phelim. As Hurling Board Secretary, he took charge of the distribution of tickets for the All-Ireland final.

Believe me, it's a horrible job. The amount of traffic up to his house in Waterview was unreal every time Galway got to a final. It would start as early as eight o'clock in the morning and continue all day and well into the night. As for the crowds at training, they were massive.

If word went out that Phelim might be allocating tickets on a particular evening, hordes of fans would converge on Kenny Park in Athenry, hoping to get lucky. Phelim would look like the Pied Piper as hopeful fans walked around after him. It was a comical sight. They operated on the basis that it was best to be within striking distance if, and when, the share-out began. That was the thing about Phelim. You never quite knew when or where he would begin dispensing the goodies.

Trouble was that there were hundreds who were left disappointed and they would try their case with the rest of us. The last thing I wanted was players being hassled on the week of an All-Ireland final, but a fan without a ticket is a troubled soul who will try anything or anybody to get his hands on the priceless piece of cardboard.

I kept telling Phelim that he should form a small committee to preside over the distribution of tickets, thereby saving himself and us a lot of hassle. He would promise to do it the next time Galway got into an All-Ireland final but he never did. Deep down I think he enjoyed it. How, I don't know, because it would drive me mad.

Only once did I see him losing his temper with the players. It was back in early 1986 after we had played rubbish in a challenge game against Offaly in Tullamore. Back in the dressing-room, one of the squad, in what had to be the essence of bad timing, asked, 'Phelim, where are we going for the feed?' Phelim exploded in a fit of rage. 'Feed! What feed? Ye think ye deserve to be fed after that? Poisoning some of ye need.' There were no further questions!

Yes, he really was a man to call it as he saw it, a policy which scarcely endeared him to the GAA authorities. He had regular rows with them but never once flinched from speaking his mind. In an odd sort of way, I think the authorities respected him for his convictions, even if they did (and still do) suffer at the end of his sharp tongue from time to time.

Irish Times sportswriter, Sean Kilfeather, tells a lovely story of one night when Phelim was appearing before the Games Administration Committee in Croke Park. It was probably around 1989, as we spent half our time in the Croke Park offices that year, explaining ourselves.

Journalists were waiting outside the meeting room and as Phelim opened the door to go into the meeting, Kilfeather called out to him, 'Be careful, Phelim, they're sharpening the guillotine in there.' Phelim paused and within earshot of the GAC members shouted back, 'Guillotine, I'll give them f——— guillotine.' It wasn't an approach which a public relations school would advocate but then Phelim wasn't one for mincing his words.

After the 1990 All-Ireland final defeat we decided to bring in a fourth selector to spice things up a bit. Fresh thinking – especially when a selection panel is heading into its seventh season – is always valuable, so we invited Jimmy Cooney to join us. He fitted in well but it was a bad time to have come in. The edge was going, both from the squad and the management and there wasn't a whole lot he could have done to revive it. He did bring one thing to the committee. He too showed utter integrity when it came to picking the team and in no way tried to push his own Sarsfields' clubmen beyond what their talents were doing anyway.

The fact that we were losing the edge was not apparent at the time but, in hindsight, it was very much the case. I suppose it's the story of life. Irrespective of how dedicated or committed you are to something, there is a tendency for automatic pilot to take over after a certain length of time. We all need to recharge our batteries from time to time.

As the team manager, it was inevitable, I suppose, that I had a high profile during the 1980s but I can honestly say that Phelim and Bernie made just as big a contribution as I did. None of us contributed as much as the players, of course, but from my viewpoint, working with Phelim and Bernie was a delight. I had been through it with Bernie in 1980 but winning a senior All-Ireland was new to Phelim in 1987 and I'll never forget the journey home on the Monday evening.

Phelim sat at the front of the coach, proudly clasping the McCarthy Cup. He had a permanent beam on his face as he peered ahead, wishing the miles away back to his beloved Galway. Nobody deserved to enjoy that winning feeling more than he did.

Chapter 11
'THERE'S GOT TO BE A BETTER WAY'

I sat and watched, feeling angry and confused. It was the sort of occasion that had I been a drinker, I would have got twisted. The whole thing seemed so bloody pointless.

It was the night of the 1979 All-Ireland hurling final and the Galway 'wake' was in full swing in the Green Isle, Hotel. We had lost another All-Ireland final, this time to Kilkenny by 2-12 to 1-8.

Only it wasn't a 'wake'. I looked around and couldn't believe what I was seeing. It was more like a celebration. The mood was far too jolly for my liking. Had strangers walked in who didn't know the result, they might easily have thought that the McCarthy Cup was lurking in a corner, playing some silly hide-and-seek game.

But no. It was at the Kilkenny team hotel. Again! Here we were, the gallant losers, who knew how to celebrate, even when we lost. Years of practice, I suppose. Good old Galway, great for hurling, terrible at winning finals. Two more pints, please!

Tomorrow the newspapers would be full of it. We could relive in graphic detail how we came to Croke Park, flying high on optimism and had our silly little wings clipped by the masters. But we didn't mind. This was our role in hurling life. Weren't we lucky to be even near Croke Park on All-Ireland final day? Such honour was usually reserved for Kilkenny, Cork and Tipperary. Real hurling counties!

I hated what was going on around me. I was team trainer that year. I had no real power and no real responsibility, other than to have the team physically tuned. The defeat shouldn't have bothered me any more than anybody else. In fact, it should have mattered a lot less. I could easily have off-loaded the responsibility onto the team, the selectors, coach 'Babs' Keating, or I could have done what everybody else seemed to be doing – take it in great spirits.

The fact was that I couldn't. I kept asking myself if there was anything I could have done to make the team better. Where did it all go wrong and why? It kept going round and round in my head and it gradually dawned on me that part of the problem was there, right in front of me, in that crowded, noisy, boisterous function room.

The defeat was hurting me a lot more than many of the players. I was feeling sick, remote, isolated. Everybody else involved in the set-up should have been feeling the same but they weren't. Not all of them, anyway.

It was as if Galway had invested in a padded cushion which was always waiting there to soften the thud when we lost. The problem was that with a cushion underneath, losing didn't seem so painful after all. We could blame it on tradition or the fact that we didn't have a provincial championship of our own to tune us up through the summer months. Excuses were plenty. But as I sat there that night, the harsh reality seemed very clear. We weren't thinking like winners. We had too much respect for the outside hurling world.

Yes, we had beaten Cork in the semi-final and were always capable of a one-off explosion, but deep down we lacked conviction. We were great at guerrilla warfare, ambushing major opposition forces and beating them. But ask us to stay on the battlefield and fight on and we lost our nerve.

We kept peering over the fence, seeking help. 'Babs' Keating in 1977, Joe McGrath in 1978, 'Babs' again in 1979, who in 1980? What we needed wasn't going to come from the outside. No, we had to look to ourselves. Be self-reliant and positive. Looking over the fence, understandable as it might have been, had brought us nowhere.

I made up my mind there and then that if I was given the coaching job for 1980, there would never be a similar atmosphere after a big game. If we lost, it would hurt the players a lot more than it seemed to be hurting them that night. By God, it would!

I know that players have different ways of showing hurt and disappointment and I'm probably doing them a disservice by claiming it didn't upset them as much as it should have. But that was how it seemed to me after the '79 final. After all, this was the second big disappointment of the season, as Galway had also lost the League final to Tipperary by a whopping sixteen points.

Sean Conroy, Bernie O'Connor, Michael Howley, PJ Qualter and Paddy Egan were the selectors that year. I was trainer and 'Babs' Keating was brought in as coach. In many ways, it was impossible to argue with his appointment. He was a proven winner as a player with Tipperary and was popular with the players. They looked up to him. He could tell them about winning All-Irelands, something nobody in Galway could have done at the time.

Whether or not that eventually became a cop-out, we will never know. But in those situations, there is always the danger that a successful outsider will be regarded as a Messiah and that whatever expertise he brings is off-set by a proportionate off-loading of responsibility elsewhere.

'Babs' concentrated an awful lot on the hurling end of things. In fairness, he was very good at it. I got to know him well that year as we travelled up and down to Dublin together for training sessions.

Everything seemed to be going well when we beat Offaly in the League quarter-final and Limerick in the semi-final to qualify for the final against Tipperary in Limerick. With 'Babs' in Galway's camp, there was a great hype going into the game. Boy, was it a let down. They walloped us off the pitch, winning by 3-15 to 0-8. At least we learned one thing that day, Joe McDonagh was not a full-back. Not that he was the sole culprit. There were difficulties in virtually every line.

There wasn't much consolation to be taken from a defeat like that. Poor old 'Babs' was getting it from both sides. As we were walking down the Ennis Road afterwards, Tipperary fans were jeering him for being a 'traitor' while Galway fans were accusing him of having 'thrown' the match. Quite how he could have gone about that is a mystery, but then there is no accounting for the vicious bile which emanates from losing fans. 'Babs' took it all in his stride. He never was one to let other people's opinions worry him.

By the time we next appeared in a competitive game, there were even more curious selections. Niall McInerney was at full-forward for the All-Ireland quarter-final against Laois in Birr. Laois were in the 'B' championship then but had a very useful side and came very close to causing an upset. They were four points up on us well into the second-half but a PJ Molloy goal from a free launched the revival and Galway eventually won by 1-23 to 3-10. It was a long way from the sort of performance which would have sent punters around to their local bookie's shop the following morning with a wad of money on Galway for the All-Ireland title.

Cork were bidding for their fourth All-Ireland in a row that year and, quite rightly, were the hottest of favourites to beat us in the semi-final. The experiment of playing McInerney at full-forward was dispensed with for the semi-final. He returned to corner-back with Noel Lane taking over at full-forward. Andy Fenton and Joe McDonagh were also back.

The All-Ireland hurling semi-finals were not nearly as popular back then. Only 12,000 spectators turned up in Croke Park for the game against Cork, with probably eighty per cent of them supporting Galway. Cork fans didn't make the trip, convinced that Galway had no chance where the likes of Kilkenny had failed the year before. Cork were rated very, very highly at the time.

But, as in 1975, Galway tore into Cork and were six points clear after twenty-five minutes. Cork rallied but Galway were far more tuned in and won by 2-14 to 1-13. It was a splendid effort. There was a power and a conviction about it, which was a delight to watch. Cork had no excuses, they were beaten by a better team on the day.

Cork were bitterly disappointed. They were chasing the four-in-a-row, something they had last achieved in the 1940s and regarded Kilkenny as the only real problem. The last thing they expected was to be caught by a Galway side which had been hammered in the League final.

Kilkenny were waiting in an All-Ireland final which turned out to be one of the most disappointing in Galway's history. We lost by 2-12 to 1-8, after failing to score from the forty-eighth minute on. Noel Lane's goal put Galway 1-8 to 1-6 ahead but it all fell apart after that.

Mick Brennan scored a long-range goal (Kilkenny's first goal had been directly from a '70') in a game which Galway goalie, Seamus Shinnors, will not have enjoyed, while John Connolly missed a penalty at a stage when a goal would have put Galway a point up. He never got hold of it at all and it was easily saved by Kilkenny goalie, Noel Skehan, who was always magnificent in those sort of head-to-head situations. Add in the fact that Galway shot eleven wides in the first-half and you have a litany of blunders which ruined the day.

Shinnors became the obvious scapegoat afterwards. While accepting that it wasn't one of his better days, it was too easy to blame him. The fact that he was a former Tipperary goalkeeper made it all the more convenient for Galway people who wanted a quick answer to what went wrong. On the one hand, we were looking outside for help, but, when we got it, we blamed the 'outsider' if things went wrong. Realistically, the blame for the 1979 defeat has to rest with the attack. If you score 1-8 in an All-Ireland final, it's most unlikely that you will have the Cup on the team coach afterwards.

All in all, it was a fiercely frustrating season for me. For while I was in charge of training, I couldn't decide when, and how often, the side would train. Frankly, there were times when I felt they could have done with more sessions. No, I am not trying to shed responsibility, but I was playing to somebody else's agenda that year and consequently could only implement some of the things I wanted.

As I sat in the Green Isle Hotel on the night of the final, I made up my mind that I would never again be part of a similar set-up. I would either have full control or I would not be involved at all. I'm not saying that we would have won the '79 final had I been in total charge. But it was very frustrating being involved without having the power to make any real decisions.

What worried me most about that defeat was that yet another withdrawal had been made from the team's dwindling confidence reserves. I felt that defeat was now almost acceptable and that unless something happened quickly that particular team would never win an All-Ireland title. Time was running out… and fast.

Chapter 12

DOING IT MY WAY

John Connolly was quoted in Jack Mahon's book, *The Game Of My Life*, as saying that towards the end of the 1980s, I had improved an awful lot as a team manager.

Take what you will from that but, I suppose, the obvious inference is that early on, I left a fair bit to be desired. I probably did but I'm honest enough to admit it. Nobody walks into a dressing-room on their first day in charge and says, 'Here I am lads, I know it all... and a bit more besides'. It doesn't work that way. You have to find your feet, get to know the players, decide exactly what you want and work from there.

The Galway dressing-room I walked into in the autumn of 1979 was not exactly full of winners. Big reputations, maybe, winners definitely not. In fact, the slide towards self-pity had begun. 'Why won't that big bad world let us win an All-Ireland title? Everybody seems to think we are entitled to one.' Everybody, that is, except the teams Galway met towards the business end of each championship season.

I can understand how John Connolly and some of the more experienced players felt uncomfortable when I was appointed team manager. For a start, I was younger than John (I was thirty at the time) and was only a year or two older than Niall McInerney, Sean Silke, Frank Burke and PJ Molloy. Iggy Clarke and Joe McDonagh were a few years younger but were household names after several seasons in the fast lane. They were instantly recognisable everywhere. Cyril Farrell was not.

They had each won at least one All-Star award. John Connolly had, in fact, been honoured in the All-Stars' inaugural year, 1971, after an outstanding performance in the All-Ireland semi-final against Tipperary. He had captured another award in 1979 and, in between, had been very much a central figure in everything that moved in Galway hurling.

A deep sense of frustration hung over Galway hurling after losing the 1979 All-Ireland final to Kilkenny. It was the original 'near and yet so far' syndrome. The more experienced players wanted something dynamic to happen. 'Babs' Keating had coached them that season and a year earlier, Joe McGrath had been brought in for the summer campaign. Now they were told that I was to be coach and team manager, with 'Inky' Flaherty and Bernie O'Connor as selectors. I knew damn well that they were not impressed. How on earth could a moderate club hurler from Woodford coach them to win an All-Ireland title? If I was any real use, I would have made it as a hurler and done it on the pitch, not on the sidelines.

I would love to have been a great hurler. But it wasn't to be. But I knew what I wanted in a hurler. Most of all, I knew that Galway's failure to win an All-Ireland was not simply down to a lack of skill or strength. No, it had more to do with attitude and, on a few occasions, fitness. It was a time of change in hurling and football. Kevin Heffernan and Mick O'Dwyer had pushed the fitness frontiers onto new horizons in football. Hurling was slow to react, operating on the basis that it had different requirements and that hi-tech fitness was not all that important. I disagreed. A good, ultra-fit hurler is far more valuable than a good hurler.

Being involved with UCG had been a huge help to me. It was a great character builder. I came across people from several other counties and quickly realised that they were no different to us in Galway. They all had their doubts, their insecurities, their secret fears and that applied in hurling matters too. It was just that they managed to disguise them better than Galway. We wore an inferiority complex as if it was something to be proud of, rather than a handicap which had to be blown sky-high if we were ever to make the breakthrough.

We tended to look at Kilkenny, Cork and Tipperary as if they were superior beings. Weren't we honoured to be on the same pitch as them? Great if we caught them on an off-day but really, all things being equal, they were better than us. And when it came to looking for advice, we had no shortage of people prepared to rush off and ask the superpowers what they thought. Yes, and that applied to some of our top players too!

The theory that if we were ever going to make the breakthrough, we would have to get outside help infuriated me. That attitude simply nourished the insecurities which were thriving already. There was talk of hoodoos and curses as puzzled fans tried to fathom out why the All-Ireland success was proving so elusive. We were told that we wouldn't win the All-Ireland while there was a Castlegar man on the team. Apparently, God had taken a personal distaste for Galway hurling after being called on to do so by a priest who spotted some Castlegar lads leaving Mass early to go to a hurling game years ago. I kid you not, there were people who actually believed that nonsense.

I still remember the night I was told that I had been appointed team manager. I was living in Dublin at the time and I got a call from from Noel Treacy, the present-day Energy Minister, who was on the Galway Hurling Board at the time. Initially, I felt honoured at being chosen but then apprehension set in. What made me think I could succeed where people like 'Babs' Keating, Joe McGrath and 'Inky' Flaherty had failed in previous years?

The McCarthy Cup was still behaving as if it was allergic to crossing the Shannon, although it was being edged closer all the time. As far as I was concerned, one big push could heave it across in 1980. My job was to get that through to the players.

One of the lessons I learned as trainer in 1979 was that if you are going to carry the can, you should make sure that nobody else puts holes in it. I would do things my way. I knew that I would have the younger squad members with me and I didn't give tuppence what the older crowd thought. Yes, they were good hurlers, but they would conform to my strategy or not at all. There would be no prima donnas on board, irrespective of how many All-Star awards they had on their mantle-pieces.

They might look at me and think, 'What the hell does he know about coaching, or indeed top class hurling?' But equally, I could look at them and respond, 'What do you lot know about winning All-Irelands? Not one bit more than I do?' In fact, less in many cases. At least I had been in charge of the U-21 team which had won the 1978 All-Ireland final. Not only that but we had beaten Tipperary, one of the so-called élite. And in a replay too!

I was lucky to have 'Inky' and Bernie as co-selectors. 'Inky' was very popular, inside and outside Galway, and older Galway fans felt happy that he was was still involved. He was seen as a safe pair of hands. But deep down, 'Inky' knew the score well and was quite happy to let me be as ruthless as I liked. He felt the whole scene needed that. Bernie felt exactly the same so we got on very well from the start.

Once the initial doubts subsided, I felt I could do the job as well, if not better, than anybody. I wasn't being arrogant or cocky. It was simply a question of looking at it logically and clinically and asking: 'Why shouldn't we win the 1980 All-Ireland final? We are just as good as any of the other contenders.'

It irked me to think that some of the more senior players might be more interested in looking for excuses than in actually getting down to it and proving that they were the best in the country. There is less pressure and responsibility when you are losing on a regular basis, especially if you are playing for a county which has not achieved a whole lot.

You get a lot of sympathy and encouraging words but not much else. The All-Star selectors might throw you a token award or two at the end of the year but if any player is relying on them for his kicks, then he has not set his standards very high.

John Connolly had been a Galway hero for years. He was one of the most gifted hurlers the county (and indeed hurling) ever produced but unfortunately the best days of his career came at a time when he lacked quality support around him. By 1980, John's powers had waned a little but he was still a very fine player. Generally though, he had been used to calling the shots. He was used to people heeding what he said but I wasn't inclined to listen too much. Everybody was equal as far as I was concerned.

The first task was to appoint a captain and we settled on Joe Connolly, John's younger brother. It was a carefully considered choice. I knew Joe from UCG and liked his approach. Also, he was neither one of the old or the new set. He was in-between and we reckoned he would be a unifying force. He had plenty of leadership qualities and, equally importantly, would not let the captaincy effect him. Some players buckle under the responsibility but Joe thrived on it. In fact, it made him play better.

I made up my mind straightaway that I would not be influenced by what anybody on the team told me. If Galway were going to lose in 1980, then I would at least be able to satisfy myself that I had failed through my own initiatives, rather than by taking on board a hotch-potch of theories which players had learned from other sources over the years. 'Babs' and others had had their chance – now it was my turn. The only people I listened to were 'Inky' and Bernie.

I knew, for instance, that John Connolly wanted to play at centre-back. He was such a fine player that, at one stage, he could have played virtually anywhere, but I reckoned that at that stage of his career, centre-back was not his best position. Not by a long way. Besides, he was needed in attack. Still, John was very keen to play at centre-back so we positioned him there for our first League game against Kilkenny in

Pearse Stadium in early November. Long term, we had no intention of leaving him there. The game was a repeat of the All-Ireland final but the extent to which Galway supporters had become disillusioned was underlined by the fact that fewer than 2,000 spectators turned out.

In fairness, it was a horrible day and the game was almost abandoned at one stage. We won by 0-9 to 0-7, a result which looks better on the history books than it did on the pitch. Kilkenny had only nine of their All-Ireland winning side in action and were completely out of touch after returning from an All-Stars trip to America a few days earlier.

Still, a win is a win, and we headed for the Gaelic Grounds in Limerick two weeks later in good spirits. Dear oh dear, what a disaster. They ripped us apart. They led by 4-6 to 0-1 at half-time and eventually won by 6-8 to 0-5. It was a most awful humiliation but I learned something that day which, I'm convinced, was crucial to our All-Ireland win over Limerick ten months later.

Joe McKenna was very much the in-form full-forward around that time. Big and strong with a great eye for the dropping ball, he was very hard to stop. He scored three goals off Conor Hayes that day. Hayes was only learning the full-back trade and McKenna exploited it ruthlessly. When it came to choosing the team for the 1980 All-Ireland final, that League game was very much on our minds.

The League went into the Christmas recess after that but the planning didn't stop. I decided to start the new season as early as possible in January. One of the frustrations I had experienced in 1979 was that while I was team trainer, I couldn't call the shots on how often we trained. I could offer an opinion but it was up to others whether or not we trained two, three or four times a week.

That was not the case in 1980. The Christmas dinner had barely been digested when I had the panel back in training. Frankly, I always had doubts about whether or not they had ever been fully fit, so I was leaving nothing to chance that year. They would be driven like never before.

We were hurling as early as 6 January in frosty conditions on slushy surfaces. I knew that some of the squad thought I was quite mad. Any resemblance between that and summer hurling is purely co-incidental, but I reckoned that it would give us an edge early in the season.

Besides, it would bring home to the players the sort of sacrifices and commitment I was expecting. Anybody who didn't want to do it – and that included the high-profile stars – could sign off the panel there and then. They weren't being forced to stay. But under no circumstances would I tolerate an early season opt-out while all the tough, nasty work was being done on horrible nights.

The training routine that spring was, to put it mildly, savage. I had them on the go all the time. It was risky in one sense as older players can blow up if you push them too hard. But I reckoned that this squad could take one more hard push and that the possibility of making the breakthrough would keep them going.

The older lads hated it but I kept telling them to think of the rewards. Mind you, All-Ireland success seemed a long, long way off on those miserable January and February days when I ran the legs off them in Fahy's Field. I always believe that you train as you play and in some of the practice games, we managed to get up quite a pace and tempo. I would have a few lads around to make sure that if the ball went out over the sideline, for instance, another one would be thrown in straightaway. The idea was to keep the squad going as hard as possible all the time.

I had a plan in mind, although I didn't tell them at the time. It seemed to me that what the team needed more than anything else was to win a title of some sort to boost their confidence. The Railway Cup was the first available option and I reckoned that with a fair bit of work, we would win it.

The year before Connacht (Galway) had beaten Munster by 4-9 to 2-7 in the semi-final but lost the final to Leinster by 1-13 to 1-9. The Railway Cup was treated more seriously then than it is now, certainly by Leinster and Munster. Connacht was usually represented by thirteen or fourteen Galway players and one or two from Mayo, Roscommon or Sligo.

Connacht's previous success had been as far back as 1947 when they beat Munster in the final. 'Inky' Flaherty had been on that team so he was delighted with the idea of making a push for it in 1980. We didn't over-emphasise it to the players because it was a high-risk situation and the last thing we wanted was to target it publicly and then lose out. No, the plan was to creep up on it and pounce.

We started the 1980 season with a three-point win over Offaly in the League and a week later, we beat Leinster by 1-13 to 1-10 after extra-time in the Railway Cup semi-final at Ballinasloe. Sylvie Linnane and Joe Hennessy were sent off in a really competitive game. We were delighted by the win. Not only had we beaten Leinster, but we had won in extra-time. It was an important breakthrough. We had held our nerve. In other years that would not happened.

Reality revisited us with a mischievous leer the following week in Pairc Ui Chaoimh where we lost by ten points to Cork in a League game, but we ensured a quarter-final place with a six point win over Clare in Ballinasloe two weeks later.

As we headed for Croke Park for the Railway Cup final against Munster on St Patrick's Day, few could have envisaged just how important it was for us. In 1979, Galway had lost the All-Ireland senior and U-21 finals and the Railway Cup final. We needed to win something… and quickly.

It would be downright dishonest to claim that the 1980 Railway Cup final was a great game. Icy rain and a small crowd (7,351) conspired to make Croke Park a rather miserable place to be that particular afternoon, but the result brought a warm glow down on Galway hurling.

Sean Silke scored a goal direct from a '70' and with Munster shooting a lot of wides, we hung on in there. Iggy Clarke, who had also been outstanding in the semi-final, had another blinder and we eventually won by 1-5 to 0-7. I doubt very much if a score of 1-5 would have won any previous Railway Cup but we were not complaining. Joe Connolly made a bold prediction after the presentation that Galway would be back to collect the McCarthy Cup in September. It was typical Joe, always thinking ahead and in no way afraid to talk confidently. I liked that. He was a good ambassador for Galway hurling and represented the positive attitude I wanted the county to be portraying.

It was an important win. Finally, Galway had a Cup to bring home from Croke Park. I was teaching in Dublin at the time and didn't travel home with the team, but there was a right party in Hayden's Hotel, Ballinasloe, and in points west that night.

The team which won the final was: Seamus Shinnors; Niall McInerney, Conor Hayes, Jimmy Cooney; Sylvie Linnane, Sean Silke, Iggy Clarke; Steve Mahon, John Connolly; Michael Kilkenny, Joe Connolly, PJ Molloy; Noel Lane, Gerry Curtin, Finbarr Gantley. It was a sweet victory; but the picture was still far from complete and, by September, there were quite a lot of changes on the team.

Expectations soared after the Railway Cup win but three League games in April gave us plenty to chew over. We drew with Waterford (1-12 each) in the League quarter-final in Thurles before beating them

3-15 to 2-7 in the replay to set up a semi-final clash with Cork in Limerick. In a tough, physical game, a Ray Cummins' goal proved the difference and we lost by 1-12 to 0-12.

We were upset by that. It was the sort of game we should have been winning but, despite the Railway Cup success, the whiff of insecurity still hung around us. Nonetheless, we had made progress.

We had an awful lot of hard, physical work done, which would stand to us later on. We had one trophy on the sideboard, had reached a League semi-final and, most importantly of all, had discovered a lot of things about the side. It would be an interesting summer.

Chapter 13

WINNERS, BUT NOT ALL RIGHT

Big Mike Conneely had lost his place as Galway goalie after conceding three goals in the last five minutes of a League game against Clare in Tulla in February 1979. It was one of those nightmare occasions. Galway were cruising to victory, leading by 2-9 to 0-7 when suddenly the roof fell in as Clare scored three goals to win the game.

Clare played most of their League games in Tulla around then and it was about as popular among visiting teams as the Parc De Princes is for the Irish rugby team. Poor Mike took most of the blame for the defeat and was replaced by Frank Larkin for the next game. He later lost out to Seamus Shinnors, a former Tipperary goalie, who was then playing for Ballinasloe.

Seamus mixed the good with the bad in a sort of disappointing mix which left selectors wondering what the hell they should do. By the summer of 1980, I had no doubts what must be done. Big Mike would have to be brought back as No 1 goalie. Deep down, my instincts said that he would be a safer option on the big day and I have always believed that you should never ignore your instincts.

There was a problem with Big Mike. His puck-outs were, to put it mildly, dire. He was thirty years old then but somehow he had never managed to get a consistent swing into his puck-outs. It was just one of those things which seemed to be generally accepted without asking why. Some people told me I was mad when I said that I was going to work on his puck-outs. They quite simply thought that an old dog like Mike could not be taught new tricks.

Still, there was no harm in trying. And so the process began. I had watched him closely and reckoned that he had a number of problems. He rarely took the same number of steps before hitting the ball and his follow-through was erratic, to say the least.

We worked out how many steps he needed, the point at which he hit the ball and adjusted the follow-through. That was the easy part. The hard work was down to Mike. His instructions were to devote most of the training sessions to puck-outs. There were evenings when he spent two hours pucking the ball out. It was downright monotonous for him counting steps… hitting the ball… following through… counting steps… hitting the ball.

We had a series of flags for him to aim at. He had his targets for each evening and it was easy to check how he was getting on. Often, after going through two full hours of pucking-out on a Tuesday evening, his shoulder would be dead on the Wednesday evening. He wouldn't be able to lift his arm. We would give him a rest but would have him back at it again on Thursday. His attitude to the gruelling toil greatly encouraged me. I don't know what he said behind my back but he never complained to me, except when his arm was killing him.

Mike was delighted with the progress even if he was bored to tears belting the ball out all the time. By All-Ireland final day, he was driving the ball as long and as accurately as Limerick's Tommy Quaid, who always had a fine puck-out. Those long, lonely hours had yielded a rich harvest.

I always regarded the visible improvement in Mike's puck-outs as one of the most satisfactory aspects of my early coaching campaign. It proved, as if proof was needed, that a player is never too old to learn if he is willing. Mike was prepared to work as hard as was necessary and it paid off. He was also prepared to listen and try new things. That's why he has turned into such a fine coach with Sarsfields. Mike was (and is) one of my favourite people in hurling. A perfect gentleman in every way.

With his puck-outs much improved, Mike was pencilled in as our No 1 goalkeeper in the Summer of 1980. We worked on some other little tricks too, notably the use of the hand-pass out of defence. It seemed to me a most constructive way of using it and I felt that Galway had not exploited it nearly enough in previous seasons. It involves one back 'showing' for the ball when a colleague gets it. It happens all the time in football but there is a tendency in hurling for a defender to be left to make his own clearance, irrespective of the pressure.

Further up, we had knocked the idea of playing at centre-back out of John Connolly's head. Failing that, he would have liked to play at centre-forward, but we felt he would be more value to the team at full-forward. I knew he didn't like it but I didn't care. In fact, he hated it. Again though, I had to back my instincts.

The Connollys got a great boost that summer when no fewer than five of them, John, Padraig, Joe, Michael and Gerry powered Castlegar to an All-Ireland club title against Antrim champions, Ballycastle, in

Navan. Two more, Murt and Tom, were on the subs. Ballycastle were backboned by the Donnellys and the final was seen as a Connolly v Donnelly clash. The Connollys won the day, as Castlegar got through by 1-11 to 1-8. John had played at centre-back, which accounted for his eagerness to play there for Galway, but we weren't having it. We wanted him up front and besides, Sean Silke was doing fine at centre-back.

Castlegar's success was a significant breakthrough as they became the first Galway club to win the All-Ireland title. Nowadays that's almost taken for granted, but back then it represented another plank in the divide between success and also-rans. It was also a nice little boost for Galway as it meant that we had now won a Railway Cup and an All-Ireland club title within three months of each other. Every little bit helps when you are trying to make the breakthrough.

Things were taking shape all round. Michael Connolly was back to full fitness and Frank Burke, who hadn't played since the 1979 final, was also back. Our options were increasing.

Kildare awaited us in the All-Ireland quarter-final and they didn't put up much of a fight. We won by 5-15 to 1-11. A more interesting development had taken place in Leinster that year. Offaly finally tore up the traditional script, beating Kilkenny in the Leinster final.

As we were due to face the Leinster champions in the All-Ireland semi-final, I went to Croke Park for the Leinster final and before long I was an avid Offaly fan. Kilkenny, who were defending All-Ireland champions, had beaten Wexford in the semi-final in a game which was seen by many as the real Leinster final. Offaly weren't regarded by the traditionalists as being in the same class.

Only 9,500 turned up for the game, emphasising exactly what the hurling public thought of it. It was the lowest Leinster final attendance since the 1940s. I was sitting among a group of Kilkenny supporters and they were sickeningly smug, even when it became apparent that their side were in trouble. They were convinced that ultimately teams like Offaly and Galway always pressed the self-destruct button. They just sat there waiting for Offaly to blow up.

Offaly didn't and won a splendid game by a point, 3-17 to 5-10. I could hardly stop myself jumping up and down on the stand because apart from being delighted at Offaly's first Leinster final success, I figured that we would find them easier to handle in the semi-final. Besides, it was one-up for the underdogs, a family to which we firmly belonged at that stage. The Kilkenny crowd around me could hardly believe what had happened. Straightaway, they accused the team of being over-confident! This from a group who had earlier been predicting a gloomy end to the day for Offaly! If they wanted to see over-confidence, all they had to do was check in a mirror.

I stopped in Birr on my way home that night and met a few Galway lads who brought me down to the golf club. It seemed to me that there were more Offaly people there than in Croke Park earlier. Not even Offaly fans had expected a win and hadn't bothered to travel.

It would have been easy for Offaly to consider the year's work finished after that historic triumph. They didn't. They were coached by Kilkennyman, Dermot Healy, and he did a great job in keeping the lid on things. Deep down, he would have figured that having beaten Kilkenny, the All-Ireland title was within their grasp, especially as Limerick had beaten Cork in the Munster final.

We had to play the semi-final without Conor Hayes, who had gone to work in Holland for the summer after injuring his thumb. We switched Niall McInerney to full-back and brought Seamus Coen in at corner-back. Steve Mahon wasn't going well so we slotted Paschal Ryan in at midfield.

Once again, a small crowd (well relatively small) of 21,280 turned up. Galway fans had clearly lost faith in the team's capacity to make the breakthrough. Offaly had a much bigger support than for the Leinster final, but die-hard neutrals couldn't be bothered travelling for a semi-final between Galway and Offaly. In hindsight, they were probably good judges because it was one sloppy game.

Just about everything that could go wrong for us did go wrong! The forwards could not have been any more inaccurate had the goalposts been moving from side to side in a mocking dance. They shot seventeen wides, several from easy positions. Iggy Clarke had to go off with a bad shoulder injury, Sylvie Linnane was sent off midway through the second-half and Big Mike had a nightmare game in goal. So too had Frank Burke in attack.

Iggy's injury and Sylvie's dismissal were severe blows. Iggy was in his prime and playing brilliantly as usual. Joe McDonagh was first wing-back sub, but as it was a a drizzly day and Joe was wearing contact lenses, we decided to bring on Gerry Glynn instead. Gerry and his brother, Micheál, were wing-backs on the Castlegar team which had won the club final that year. Gerry had been on the fringes for a long time, having won an All-Ireland U-21 medal in 1972.

Two goals by John Connolly and one each from Noel Lane and Bernie Forde had us nine points clear with thirteen minutes left. Then came the Offaly revival through a Brendan Bermingham goal and another by Mark Corrigan, whose shot from fifty yards spun past Big Mike. The gap was down to two points (4-9 to 3-10) when Waterford referee, JJ Landers sounded the final whistle.

Offaly protested that he blew at least fifty seconds too soon but, as far as we were concerned, the game was well over! Just as well. We really were hanging on at that stage. Padraig Horan came into our dressing-room afterwards and told us that Limerick were very confident about beating whichever of us had won. He was living in Limerick at the time so he knew the mood well. 'But if you go in hard and keep at it, I think you'll beat them,' he told us. Encouraging words, but we had a lot to think about as we headed home that night.

Limerick had won the Munster championship in fine style, beating Clare (by six points) and Cork (by four points). Their win over Cork was especially significant as, earlier on in the year, they had lost the League final replay to Cork by nine points. Clearly they had improved a great deal through the summer and would go into the final with the memory of that crushing League win over us the previous November very much on their minds. The bookies released their odds the day after the semi-final and had no doubts about where the McCarthy Cup was heading. They installed Limerick at 4/6 favourites with Galway on 5/4. We were underdogs again, only this time we were planning a very big bite.

Chapter 14
MIND OVER MATTER

The Moscow Olympics closed on the day we beat Offaly. The world's greatest sporting festival had all but passed me by over the previous two weeks and when I woke up on the following morning, I wondered what life was all about.

Were we taking sport too seriously? Did it really matter who won the All-Ireland final? Why get so excited about it all? Those philosophical dilemmas lasted all of two minutes. Damn sure it mattered who won the final. An entire year's work hinged on it. More than that, the credibility of Galway hurling and of a loyal squad of players depended on it. Come to think of it, my reputation as a coach rested on it.

Another All-Ireland final defeat would have wrecked that squad. Players like John Connolly, Sean Silke, Niall McInerney, Frank Burke and Michael Conneely would have had their careers slammed shut without ever standing on the Hogan Stand and waving the McCarthy Cup to the Galway fans.

I just couldn't accept that. Galway were as good as the rest, but years of persistent rejection, fuelled mainly by that dreadful decision to play in the Munster championship through the 1960s, had left the county hypnotised by flashy images of Cork, Tipperary and Kilkenny.

Were we afraid of winning? Why did we always play down our own achievements? We kept hearing and reading about how we were as good as any side in the country but we weren't delivering. It was as if we fed on being patronised and lacked the resolve to finish what we had started.

A book called *Sportsmen Under Stress*, written by Angela Patmore, dealt in considerable detail with this phenomenon, which is quite common in sport. One particular extract was very relevant to the Galway team of 1980, even if it was written with professional sportspeople in mind.

'Professional sportsmen, unlike their gladiatorial predecessors, enter the arena of their own free will because the rewards are high. They think they will simply be competing against their opponents' skills but, once the sport experiment begins, the opponent they face is the Monster. Sportsmen refer to it, when they speak of it at all, as 'pressure'. Pressure makes them exhilarated, confused, frightened. It makes them extend themselves, break records, forget pain, lash out at fellow competitors. Often, it paralyses their skills and they experience strange terrors and even shellshock. The purpose of sport is to see whether the Monster makes them or breaks them.'

All of those sentiments apply just as much to amateurs as to professionals and certainly apply to a squad of players who have given everything in pursuit of an All-Ireland medal. Up to then, I'm afraid the 'Monster' had crushed, rather than lifted, Galway. That was certainly the case in 1979.

In the 1980 semi-final against Offaly, we were uncertain and unconvincing. We had gone into a big lead and should have killed the game off, yet we ended up hanging on by our fingertips. The 'Monster' was still travelling far too comfortably with us. It was time to accelerate and lose him. It was also a time to be bold, to take chances, to let others worry about us.

First, though, we had plenty of worrying to do on practical matters. Iggy's shoulder injury would keep him out of the final; Sylvie was awaiting a disciplinary hearing and might be suspended for the final; Big Mike's confidence was nowhere to be seen and Frank Burke's form was also a source of considerable worry.

First things, first. It seemed quite idiotic to have a talent like Conor Hayes picking tulips in Amsterdam (or whatever he was doing) while we were facing up to such a crucial game. We didn't want him to leave in the first place but he had paid his air fare and, with his thumb injured, he didn't see any point in staying for the semi-final.

I rang him from Bernie O'Connor's house after the Offaly game and asked him to come back. He hesitated at first. The thumb was OK by now but he felt that he would be seen as a glory hunter if he returned home for the final, having missed the semi-final.

I told him to forget about that and to let the selectors worry about it. A few days later, he was back home and training with the squad. We considered our options and whatever way we looked at them, Hayes's name came up. He was far too good to leave off.

But where would we play him? Most people thought that he would come back in at full-back with McInerney switching to the right. Hayes had played full-back in 1979 but had been at corner-back (something a lot of people forget) the year earlier when Galway won the All-Ireland U-21 title. Besides, McInerney had done well enough at full-back against Offaly.

We were conscious of Limerick's full-forward line-up, which had Ollie O'Connor on the right, Joe McKenna in the centre and Eamonn Cregan on the left. McKenna had scored three goals off Hayes in their previous meeting in the League and we felt he would like playing on Hayes again.

Cregan, on the other hand, might not. Hayes was younger and more mobile than McInerney. We would put him on Cregan who, at thirty-four years of age, may have been past his best but who was still very dangerous. Cregan had played all over the pitch in a long and distinguished career with Limerick (he was centre-back when they won the All-Ireland in 1973) but had now settled at corner-forward where his prowling instincts made him lethal.

If Cregan was the split-second opportunist, McKenna was the inspirational figure. A giant of a man, his speciality was the high catch and the flicked goal. He really was difficult to stop if he got the right sort of possession and if he was in the right mood.

That's where Niall McInerney came in. 'Mac' was as cute as a fox and was expert at putting his opponent off his game. He was the ultimate percentage player, more at home with the short flick away from goal than the flashy clearance. He had one great trait. He was brilliant at staying goal side of his opponent. McKenna had a reputation for goal-scoring and we reckoned that if we could curtail that, it would be a huge psychological boost. Much the same happened with Nicholas English in the 1988 All-Ireland final.

It's amazing the way some players with reputations for scoring goals tend to get upset if they don't hit the jackpot. The fans expect goals from them and even if they score several points, it never has the same impact.

The plan was for McInerney to 'sit' on McKenna, who liked to catch the ball, turn and hit on his left side. Mac would watch his left all the time. Of course, the only goal McKenna got was off his right-side and 'Mac' gave me some stick over it afterwards, claiming I had overdone the coaching in this particular aspect.

'Mac' was also a master at the psyching game. 'How many goals have you got today, Joe? The crowd are expecting goals from you, Joe, where are they? Time is running out Joe.'

Deciding where to play Hayes and McInerney wasn't the only tough decision. What were we to do with Big Mike, who felt totally deflated after the semi-final? If we were prepared to listen to the fans, we not only would have left him off the team but would have banished him from the subs' bench as well.

As far as we were concerned, dropping him was not an option. We had decided he was the No 1 goalie earlier in the Summer and it would have been very disruptive to omit him for the final. Besides, we still had a hunch that he would produce it on the big day.

There was nothing for it but try to rebuild his confidence, brick by brick from the foundation up. His form wasn't great in training after the semi-final and we always made sure that he was down in the far goal in Kenny Park, away from the crowd, to take the pressure off him.

I talked a lot to him, trying to convince him that he was an outstanding goalie, who had gone through a bad game. It was behind him now and he would be judged solely on the All-Ireland final. Play well in the final and he would be a Galway hero forever.

He worked very hard to get his game right. PJ Molloy, who lived in Athenry, used to go down to Kenny Park with Mike most lunch-times, practising shots. It was typical Molloy, always willing to help out. It also gave PJ a chance to work on his shooting. It went well and gradually Mike regained his confidence and composure. On All-Ireland final day – when it really mattered – he didn't put a hand or foot wrong.

Next item on the agenda was to decide who would replace Iggy Clarke at wing-back. Gerry Glynn had done very well when he came in as a sub in the semi-final, while Joe McDonagh had lots of big-day experience. It was tough on both, but we decided to switch Seamus Coen out from the corner, now that we had Hayes back.

Glynn was a lovely first-touch hurler and would probably have got the nod on another day, but we felt that Coen's dogged determination would be a bigger asset against the Limerick half-forward line. Coen had been with me as an U-21 in 1978 and had done very well at left half-back. As with Hayes at right-corner, I trusted he would repeat that form in a senior final.

We eventually settled on the following team for the final: Michael Conneely; Conor Hayes, Niall McInerney, Jimmy Cooney; Sylvie Linnane, Sean Silke, Seamus Coen; Michael Connolly, Steve Mahon; Frank Burke, Joe Connolly, PJ Molloy; Bernie Forde, John Connolly, Noel Lane.

The media were intrigued by the selection. Frankly, I don't think they believed the team would line out as selected. Paddy Downey wrote in *The Irish Times* that Limerick people were amazed by the selection, in particular, the positioning of Hayes and McInerney and Burke and Joe Connolly. Donal Carroll noted in his *Irish Independent* preview that one of the reasons he was tipping Limerick was because he didn't believe the Galway gambles would work out.

Once again, we had a strategy in mind. I had noticed that much of Joe McKenna's possession came from captain, Sean Foley, who was very much an attacking left half-back. When he got the ball, he nearly always tried to get round his man, before firing a long drive down into the opposition square. Right half-back, Liam O'Donoghue, tended to whip the ball cross-field.

Frank Burke was given the specific task of ensuring that Foley wasn't allowed to burst forward and deliver those high lobs, which McKenna loved so much. Burke was very strong and was under instruction not only to put the pressure on Foley but to actually drive him back at every opportunity. Under no circumstances was Foley to be allowed to surge forward and hoist those dangerous lobs down on McKenna. The problem was that Burke had played poorly in the semi-final. But he picked up in training afterwards and did exactly what was required against Foley in the final.

Iggy Clarke played an important role in the build-up to the final. He became very much the media front-man. His heart-break story captivated all the journalists and kept the focus away from the players. Not that I put too much emphasis on so-called media pressures before a game. Most journalists are fair and I reckon that a player who cannot handle a straightforward interview is unlikely to be of much use to you in the tense, demanding atmosphere of an All-Ireland final. Nonetheless, Iggy's skills with the media were much appreciated. It was no fun for him, for while he kept a brave face on it, a deep personal disappointment was lurking beneath. Missing an All-Ireland final after putting in so much effort for so long was hard to take. From our perspective, losing a player of Iggy's stature was a huge loss.

Despite Iggy's absence, I felt a lot happier going into the 1980 final than I had a year earlier. Galway's form in the semi-final had been patchy, to say the least, but sometimes that can be a good thing. A brilliant semi-final performance can create a false impression, as had happened with Galway in previous years and, indeed, subsequently. Also, the training for the final had gone well. We had put in an incredible amount of training sessions, stretching back to the first week in January and, all in all, I felt we had the squad and the tactics to beat Limerick.

The team talks had been positive too. We went into things in great detail and identified specific targets for every player. We did it in a positive way, at all times emphasising our own strengths. The more we weighed them up, the more we seemed to have, even if the rest of the hurling world was muttering darkly about Galway's tendency to flop in finals. As far as we were concerned, that was all in the past.

We had made quite a few adjustments from the team which had lost to Kilkenny a year earlier. Big Mike had replaced Seamus Shinnors in goal; Jimmy Cooney was in for Andy Fenton at corner-back; Sylvie Linnane and Seamus Coen replaced Joe McDonagh and Iggy Clarke as wing-backs (the Coen for Clarke move was forced on us); Michael Connolly was in at midfield with brother, John moving to full-forward; Noel Lane switched to the corner in place of Finbarr Gantley. In fact, centre-back, Sean Silke and midfielder, Steve Mahon were the only two players who lined out in the same positions as in 1979.

It was difficult to judge how Galway supporters felt going into the 1980 final. Certainly, there was no great confidence, due largely to the shaky semi-final form and also because Galway fans had come to fear the worst. They coped with 1975 but the 1979 All-Ireland final defeat was hard to take. It was seen as another example of Galway yielding, not so much to a great Kilkenny team as to the assumption that when things get tight the traditional powers were better than the likes of Galway.

Limerick were not regarded as a traditional power in the Cork-Kilkenny-Tipperary mould but, nonetheless, they had a solid enough record and were lying third in the All-Ireland winners' table. They had been bubbling just below the top layer for some seasons and, having finally shaken off Cork in Munster, were favourites to beat us. Although they would never admit it now, I think the majority of Galway fans headed for Croke Park on All-Ireland final day fearing the worst. The atmosphere was altogether more positive inside the Galway camp.

Chapter 15
'PEOPLE OF GALWAY, WE LOVE YOU'

On the Thursday before the 1980 All-Ireland final an old man came up to me in Eyre Square in Galway and, with Padraig O'Conaire's statue staring at us, he said: 'I'll die happy if Galway win on Sunday'.

It was both a beautiful and a frightening experience. It was lovely to think that, even allowing for exaggeration, winning an All-Ireland could mean so much. But equally, it was intimidating to have so many hopes, so much expectation loaded onto a group of players. The old-timer was echoing the thoughts and sentiments of every Galway person, not just at home but all over the world.

My well-wisher was certainly old enough to remember Galway's previous All-Ireland senior success in 1923. Since then, Galway had played in nine hurling finals and had lost them all. Not only that but Galway footballers, market leaders in talent, flair and invention in the 1960s, had also come under a losing spell, having been beaten in the 1971-73-74 finals. Galway badly needed a lift.

Some weeks after the final I came across the same old man. There were no handshakes, no congratulations, simply a command, 'Ye'll have to win the two-in-a-row now'. More than anything, it summed up the remarkable change Galway hurling underwent on the afternoon of 7 September, 1980.

The atmosphere was electric in the weeks prior to the final. It can be a draining experience for players, unless they learn to relax and separate what's important from what's not. Above all, they must always keep the focus right. It's all about the match, not about the trappings that surround it.

We stayed in the Clarence Hotel on Dublin's quays on the Saturday night before the final and it really was chaotic. It seemed to me that just about every Galway and Limerick fan was either staying there or was in for the disco. When the disco was over a sing-song started and finally, in desperation, Bernie O'Connor and myself went downstairs to ask the revellers to tone things down a little. After all, an All-Ireland squad was trying to get some sleep upstairs and it was five o'clock in the morning!

A year later we stayed in the Ashling Hotel, further up the quays, which was also pretty packed and noisy. Some senior administrators in

Galway GAA affairs later claimed that this was part of the reason we lost to Offaly. The fact that things were every bit as noisy in the Clarence a year earlier was conveniently ignored. That's the difference between winning and losing. Little things become important when you lose, but are ignored if you win.

Personally, I was never too fussy where we stayed on the Saturday night. If players are depending on a sound sleep on the night before a big game, then they are not properly focused in the first place. Many of them wouldn't sleep even if they were in a sound-proofed room anyway. No, the energy and the really important rest must have come long before the Saturday night.

In fact, I think it's good for players to be involved in the hustle and bustle of the big occasion, provided it's controlled. Before the 1986 final, we stayed out in Malahide, where there was very little match atmosphere. It wasn't until we got within a few miles of Croke Park on the Sunday that we sensed the All-Ireland mood. I felt we lost out, somewhat. Perhaps it was pure coincidence, but it took us fifteen minutes to tune into the match. We were back in the Ashling amid the fans and the noise and the chaos in 1987 and 1988 and we won both finals.

There was a genuine sense of optimism among the squad on the morning of the 1980 final. All the players had been through it before and, even if their experiences were bad, they knew how to cope with the pre-match build-up.

Nonetheless, a tingle goes down the spine when you turn down Jones' Road and come within a '65' of Croke Park on All-Ireland final day. Irrespective of how often you have been through it, there is a special feeling attached to it. It's as if there is a fusion of passion and expectation, awaiting to be released. Heart beats increase and it's then that players realise that this is it. We are playing in an All-Ireland final, the cherished ambition of every young lad who ever played hurling or football.

The dressing-rooms were under the Cusack Stand then and we went into the first one we came across. Mike Conneely darted for what he regarded as his favourite corner, but a steward came in and told us that we should be in the other dressing-room. Big Mike didn't like it. He regarded that one as 'our' dressing-room (we had been there for the semi-final) and felt we were being messed about. 'Don't worry, Mike, we haven't won an All-Ireland out of either dressing-room so it hardly makes a whole lot of difference,' I said. Mike wasn't impressed and gathered up his gear, still grumbling.

Those who were looking for bad omens certainly got one even before the game started. Team doctor, Mary McInerney, had to give Noel Lane a few stitches after he got a cut over the eye as the team came onto the pitch. He was accidentally caught by a colleague's hurley and had blood pouring down his face. Mary did a great job on him while the rest of the team had their usual puckaround. Thankfully, it wasn't too serious and Lane was able to play.

It would have been an awful setback if he had to withdraw as, together with our other corner-forward, Bernie Forde, he was central to our attacking strategy. We had analysed the Limerick full-back line closely and figured that their corner-backs, Dom Punch and Donal Murray were vulnerable. They tended to lay in parallel to full-back, Leonard Enright and were susceptible to runs on the outside. At least we hoped they were!

We knew they would definitely lay in against us, as sort of safeguards against John Connolly, who was greatly feared by Limerick. They reckoned that we would pump every ball down on Connolly and Enright so, quite naturally, the Limerick corner-backs were inclined to stay inside their men, ready to pounce on the breaking ball. Our plan was to spray the ball wide and take them on the outside. It worked very well. But before we got a chance to test that tactic, there was an early examination for Big Mike at the other end.

Galway hearts were popping up in their mouths as the ball sailed in towards him. A first touch is always important for a goalie, but in Mike's case it was absolutely vital, after his jittery semi-final. He gathered safely and despatched the ball downfield. Relief all round! His confidence was back and it intensified as the game wore on. Galway got a great start. Bernie Forde skipped in and kicked a goal, Joe Connolly pointed a free and PJ Molloy, showing just how important it is to play the whistle, kept going when others stopped after he had been up-ended and his persistence paid off with a great goal. 2-1 to 0-0 up after ten minutes! Not bad!

It couldn't last, of course, and Limerick bounced right back with a palmed goal by Cregan, who was causing Hayes problems. Hayes would come into his own later on. Still, McInerney was doing well on McKenna and Jimmy Cooney was giving Ollie O'Connor no room.

Elsewhere, things were going well for us too. Frank Burke was doing exactly what was required on Sean Foley, denying him space to make his clearances. Joe Connolly was drawing Limerick centre-back, Mossie Carroll, all over the place (Carroll would later be replaced in a move which baffled many people) and our full-forward line was dangerous on every half-chance. Limerick were chasing the game all the time and we were very happy at the interval, leading by 2-7 to 1-5.

We lost the second-half by 2-4 to 0-8 but we had enough on deposit to cope with that. Not by much, mind you, but enough nonetheless. It took a marvellous save from Big Mike to keep McKenna out at a crucial stage but a little later Joe did find the net. We led by five points with ten minutes to go, but Cregan's penalty goal relaunched Limerick's effort.

A few minutes from the end Hayes made a wonderful interception from a Cregan pass to an unmarked McKenna. It was one of those awful moments we dreaded. You would have banked on Cregan every time to get the ball into McKenna and after that it was odds-on a goal. But Hayes calmly stepped in and timed his interception to perfection. The width of a hurley saved us but, after so much heartbreak and misery, the gods had finally smiled on us. John Ryan, who had come in as a sub, scored the insurance point. Cregan had one late chance from a penalty, but his drive was deflected over the bar. Galway 2-15 Limerick 3-9. Success at last!

Those who watched the post-match scenes either 'live' or on TV say they were the most emotional ever witnessed at Croke Park. Out on the pitch, it was difficult to take it all in. It was as if a giant gusher had opened in front of the Hogan Stand and we were being hoisted higher and higher by its magical force. Adults wept openly as they tried to come to terms with the fact that Galway had finally won an All-Ireland final.

It's at times like this that you realise the value of the GAA and of Gaelic Games. Winning an All-Ireland title brings a unique sense of bonding to a county, a feeling that, yes, we're better than the rest (for now anyway). It works wonders for a county's self-esteem.

I don't know if any study has ever been done on it, but I'm quite sure that productivity increases in counties which win All-Ireland titles. It might take time for that to show but, once the celebrations are over, I'm certain that people work better because they feel good about themselves and their county.

If ever there was an ideal captain for such a momentous occasion, Joe Connolly was the man. His victory speech was never going to be of the 'Is Mór An Onoir Dom' variety. The Connollys are native Irish speakers and there is a passion and sincerity in their love of the Irish language. Joe gave a splendid oration. And when he switched to English, his 'People of Galway, we love you' theme brought tears to Galway people at home and abroad, especially when it was followed by Joe McDonagh's beautiful rendering of the 'The West's Awake'. It was a truly emotional occasion.

My own immediate reaction was one of relief and pride. For me, this was a victory for self-belief. Galway's days as a subservient force were over. John Connolly announced his retirement in the dressing-room immediately afterwards. It was understandable amid the euphoria of the occasion for a man who had given thirteen years of service to Galway, but at thirty-two years of age, he still had plenty to offer. It was always going to be a difficult decision to stand by and John was coaxed out of retirement for the 1981 All-Ireland semi-final replay.

Iggy Clarke was beaming in the middle of the celebrations but, deep down, it was very hard on him. His injured arm had ruled him out and while he had been a central part of our preparations and team talks, he was not playing. He had handled the media brilliantly in the run-up to the final and played his part as best he could, but it was a great pity for him that he missed Galway hurling's greatest win since 1923. Sadly, when he did get his chance to play in the following year's final, Galway lost, so his great career passed him by without actually figuring on an All-Ireland winning side.

That win changed the entire complexion of Galway hurling. It put us very much on the map, not just as decent triers, who were a notch below the top level, but as a force in our own right.

Personally, I felt very fulfilled by the whole experience as my coaching career was on the line in 1980. I knew deep down that many people doubted my ability to coach a team to win a senior All-Ireland. I couldn't blame them.

Nobody can ever be sure how many people turned out to greet the team on its journey home on the Monday night, but it's estimated that there were at least 30,000 jammed into Eyre Square alone. It was nearly 2 am when we finally reached Galway and as the sea of faces looked up like a joyous ocean, 'Inky' Flaherty nudged me and said, 'I told you we'd do it'.

That homecoming was especially emotional. Galway had returned empty-handed in 1975 and 1979 and, deep down, there was a fear that our turn would never come. But as the whole of Galway turned out to line the route home that night, the feeling that the West was very much awake had seeped right into all our hearts. It would be lonely round the fields of Athenry no longer!

Chapter 16
TALL STORIES FROM A NON-CHAMPAGNE PERFORMANCE

If you were to believe even a fraction of the stories which circulated after the 1981 All-Ireland hurling final, the only obvious conclusion to be reached was that at half-time the Galway dressing-room resembled a cross between an after-hours drinking club and a bare-knuckle fight venue.

Grim details about unspeakable deeds deep in the bowels of Croke Park became a thriving growth industry as Galway fans attempted to adjust to the shock of losing to Offaly. The rumour machine was as inventive as the young scientists' exhibition, as supporters vied with each other in the frantic search for the most far-fetched explanation. Stories of rows and unrest spread way beyond Galway and, in time, there were dozens of different versions doing the circuit.

War is not the only enemy of truth. So too, it seems, is defeat in an All-Ireland final. There were so many rumours about what happened in our dressing-room that if even half of them were true, the action in there was a lot more interesting than anything that happened on the pitch.

The most popular explanation for Galway's second-half fade out was that instead of getting things organised for the second-half, I was trying to take off John Connolly, who steadfastly refused to go. While that was going on, the rest of the team, waist-high in over-confidence after going into a six-point lead, were already swigging champagne in anticipation of a great victory.

Both are so far off the mark that I'm almost reluctant to deal with them but, as the rumours persist to this day, I had better not ignore them or people will say, 'We were right all along, there was a row in the dressing-room'.

Firstly, there was no row with John Connolly, any other Connolly or any member of the team. Why in heaven's name would we want to take off John Connolly? We had gone to him after the drawn All-Ireland semi-final against Limerick and asked him to rejoin the panel. He hadn't played for us since the 1980 final, having announced his retirement in the dressing-room afterwards.

We felt that he still had a lot to offer and that his mere presence alone would be a boost. That was proven in the replay against Limerick. John had been suffering from tonsillitis coming up to the final but there was no way we were going to play without him, unless we really had to. As far as I was concerned, he should never have retired in the first place. A player of that skill could survive well into his mid-thirties.

I had no problems with John Connolly. I know that full-forward was not his favourite position but, when I took over as team manager, I was not in the business of accommodating players' individual tastes. In fact, that may have gone on for too long. No individual, irrespective of how good he was, was bigger than the team. That included John Connolly.

I knew where I stood with John and vice versa. He was one of the most gifted players hurling has ever produced and was a household name at a time when not many households could name another Galway player. The pity was that when he was in his prime, Galway hurling was not. By the time Galway eventually won an All-Ireland crown, John had gone back a little. He was still a great hurler, but not as dominating as five or six years earlier.

As a senior and respected figure on the Galway scene, other players looked up to him. He was very much in favour of bringing in 'Babs' Keating in 1979. When the All-Ireland title still didn't come Galway's way and a very average club hurler from Tommy Larkins was appointed team manager and coach for 1980, I could well understand if John – and indeed other senior squad members – thought Galway were going nowhere.

Equally, I'm sure they could understand that I wasn't going to be intimidated by reputations. I might have been an average hurler, but I had no doubt about my ability to coach others. Nor indeed about my confidence in Galway people and Galway hurling. I wasn't being arrogant, but it always drove me mad the way the West of Ireland was looked on (it still is in some quarters) as some sort of pathetic outpost, buried in bogs behind the Shannon.

An image is like a reputation. Once acquired, it's very difficult to discard. Connacht people tend to be too submissive, too meek, too fearful of standing up and shouting, 'We're here in the West and proud of it'.

So when I took over as Galway coach in the autumn of 1979, my one and only ambition was to win an All-Ireland title. I felt we had the players. What we needed mainly was a change of outlook.

'We've done it! We've won the two-in-a-row.' Miko Donoghue, who has been ferrying Galway teams on his coaches for years is first on to Croke Park to offer his congratulations after beating Tipperary in the 1988 All-Ireland final.

Happiness is… scoring a goal against Kilkenny late on in the 1987 All-Ireland final. Ray Duane leads the dance on the sideline with Michael Connolly, Michael Earls and Martin Naughton joining in the celebrations.

Concentration is written all over Joe Connolly's and Mike Conneely's faces as they lead the parade prior to the 1980 All-Ireland final.
Both were to play splendidly.

'People of Galway, we love you.' The McCarthy Cup is on its way to Galway at last and proud captain, Joe Connolly, shows it to the fans from the steps of the Hogan Stand after beating Limerick.

Sometimes they listen and sometimes they don't! Sylvie Linnane and Steve Mahon laugh when my back is turned in training, but there is much more concentration as I give the final rundown prior to the 1990 All-Ireland final. I always liked to get the players together just before the throw-in to refocus them.

Hardly the recommended way of handling the McCarthy Cup, but Conor Hayes and Noel Lane always did have safe hands.

Pete Finnerty and Michael Coleman are called to the bar at the Burlington Hotel prior to an All-Star dinner.

'Selectors how are you? They should never have left me off the team.' A euphoric Noel Lane prepares for take-off after scoring yet another super-sub goal in the 1988 All-Ireland final. Tipperary's Ken Hogan ponders the hazards of being a goalie.

PJ Molloy is going very much the one way in both the 1980 and 1985 All-Ireland finals. He had Frank Burke and Bernie Forde in support in 1980 while Offaly's Pat Delaney and Aidan Fogarty were in hot pursuit in 1985.

Tony Keady and Brendan Lynskey were both based in Dublin during Galway's glory run in the 1980s. They seem to have O'Connell Bridge virtually to themselves on this occasion.

You can't beat winter hurling! Ask Steve Mahon and Brendan Lynskey as they get some resin from Phelim Murphy in a Thurles downpour in November 1987.

Galway's National League success in 1975 was a huge lift to hurling in the county. This classic shot of Niall McInerney keeping half the Tipperary forward line at bay in the final typified the growing spirit of Galway hurling at the time.

That winning feeling for John and Joe Connolly as Galway fans celebrate the All-Ireland breakthrough in 1980.

The two faces of 1989. Galway captain, Conor Hayes, is all smiles after beating Tipperary in the League final in April, while three months later Tony Keady is a picture of misery as he sits out a challenge match against Antrim in Kells after being suspended for playing in the US.

Galway's three-in-a-row hopes are shattered and it shows on the faces of Hurling Board chairman, Tom Callanan, physio, Colm Flynn, Tony Keady, Martin Naughton, Pearse Piggott and selector, Bernie O'Connor, as the 1989 All-Ireland semi-final draws to a close.

Joe Cooney, my choice as the best Galway player of our generation, threads his way between Bobby Ryan and Paul Delaney in the 1988 All-Ireland final.

'You score them, I'll save them.' That seems to be Mike Conneely's advice to John Connolly prior to a big game in Croke Park.

John Commins, who came through from the great minor team of 1983, was one of the few hurling goalies in history to keep a clean sheet in two consecutive All-Ireland finals. But what's he doing in a Dublin jersey?

'Know what I mean, Harry?' Sylvie Linnane has some mischievous comment for Kilkenny's Harry Ryan in the 1987 All-Ireland final.

Big Joe McKenna can only look and watch as Niall McInerney and Jimmy Cooney stay goal side of him in the 1980 All-Ireland final. Closing Joe down was central to our tactics against Limerick that day.

Sean Treacy and Conor Hayes, sporting his GOAL shirt, seem less enthusiastic for training than I am at a session in Ballinasloe prior to the All-Ireland final. The decision to leave Hayes out of the team later drew criticism on the selectors.

'You're as well off doing it yourself.' Babs' Keating gets into the swing of things! He was one of my great rivals but I always had great affection for him.

A Galwayman in Croke Park for the 1992 Leinster final! I enjoyed my stint with Wexford but would have needed a lot longer than three months to change things.

The Kiltormer sandwich! Ollie Kilkenny and Conor Hayes have all the angles blocked off for Tipperary's Pat Fox in the 1988 All-Ireland final.

The haunting presence of Johnny Flaherty is in the background as Niall McInerney prepares to clear in the 1981 All-Ireland final. Johnny's goal would destroy us later on.

History makers – the Galway team which ended a 57-year famine by winning the 1980 All-Ireland title. *Back:* Conor Hayes, Steve Mahon, John Connolly, Michael Connolly, Mike Conneely, Frank Burke, Noel Lane, Sean Silke. *Front:* Niall McInerney, Seamus Coen, Jimmy Cooney, Joe Connolly (captain), Sylvie Linnane, PJ Molloy, Bernie Forde.

Another breakthrough in 1987 as Galway beat Tipperary and Kilkenny to win the All-Ireland final. *Back:* Brendan Lynskey, Pete Finnerty, Steve Mahon, John Commins, Tony Keady, Martin Naughton, Ollie Kilkenny. *Front:* Joe Cooney, Pat Malone, 'Hopper' McGrath, Sylvie Linnane, Conor Hayes (captain), Anthony Cunningham, Gerry McInerney, Eanna Ryan. (The mascot is Nigel Murray).

I couldn't teach John Connolly anything about hurling. But then who could? A talent like his didn't need coaching. Others were different and I felt I could make a contribution in terms of little adjustments in technique. After all, you don't have to be a cow to know the difference between cream and milk. It's pure nonsense to claim that because you weren't a star player, you cannot be a good coach.

That has been proven over and over again. Both Dermot Healy and Eugene McGee were very successful coaches after ordinary club careers while Sean Boylan has been an outstanding success with Meath footballers, although his main playing interest was in hurling.

I always felt that players like John Connolly, PJ Molloy, Niall McInerney, Sean Silke, Iggy Clarke and Frank Burke paid too much respect to the likes of Kilkenny, for instance. That was understandable, up to a point, since they had spent most of their careers losing to them.

When I took over, I saw a change of attitude as absolutely vital. I could scarcely assert my beliefs on the squad without taking a strong line. I'm not talking about discipline. There was never any problem with the squad in that regard. No, I wanted them to think bigger, like winners. I wanted John Connolly, who was a massive man with a massive reputation and who evoked great respect everywhere, to play to that image.

I wanted the other senior players to think big too. The younger lads had come from a different background, one where Galway hurling had some experience of winning, so it was easier to harness their positive energy.

What I didn't want – or wouldn't tolerate – was senior players telling me where they wanted to play or what sort of training programme they would like. Good and all as they were, their way had failed. I wanted to try mine.

Now I might have made mistakes in my time, but trying to take John Connolly off at half-time in the 1981 All-Ireland final was not one of them. Galway had gone beautifully well in the first-half and were in total control at half-time when we led by 0-13 to 1-4. Indeed, Connolly was very unlucky to have had a goal disallowed ten minutes before the break when referee, Frank Murphy, adjudged that John had fouled Offaly goalkeeper, Damien Martin, before hooking the ball over the goal line. We felt it was harsh but we were going so well at the time that it didn't appear to carry much relevance. How wrong we were.

So what did happen in the second-half? How did an Offaly team which was out of it for so long in the first-half win the second period by 1-8 to 0-2? First of all, let me explain what happened at half-time. The lads sat down as usual, some went to the toilet, some drank tea, while others had little knocks seen to. I singled out a few players and had a few words with them about little adjustments they should make. I talked to the whole team before they went back out, at all times emphasising the need to maintain concentration.

Some players said in interviews afterwards that over-confidence crept in. Perhaps it did but it shouldn't have. I think, in fact, that is a cop-out. Anybody who knew Offaly (and our lads knew them inside out) was aware of what they had achieved in the previous fifteen months.

Apart from winning their first Leinster title and running Galway to two points in the 1980 All-Ireland semi-final, they had reached the League final in May 1981. The remarkable feature of that was that they had to play all their games away from home. Clare had to do the same after a row during a League game against Offaly in Tulla in December 1979.

Despite that handicap, Offaly reached the final against Cork in Thurles. For some strange reason, Offaly played against a gale force wind in the first-half, despite winning the toss, and were 2-3 to 0-0 down after ten minutes. They out-scored Cork by 2-8 to 1-8 for the remainder of the game but that early blitz buried them. Later on that summer, they retained the Leinster title, beating Wexford.

Galway had seen Offaly at first-hand on League final day. We were, in fact, involved in the curtain raiser. Not a very auspicious one either. We had won just two of six League games and faced Wexford in a relegation play-off, which we won by three points.

Some teams prosper in the League after winning the All-Ireland title. That was certainly the case with Galway in 1987/88 but it was different in 1980. The celebrational trail had to be undertaken after Galway's long spell in the wilderness and League points were a long way from the players' agenda that autumn.

Given Offaly's background, Galway had absolutely no excuse for over-confidence in the second-half of the 1981 final. We went seven points clear through a Steve Mahon point just after half-time, but scored just a single point from there on in. Little things mean so much at this level. Damien Martin made a stunning save from Noel Lane seven minutes from the end at a time when we were still three points ahead. A goal then would have won it for us.

The decisive score was Johnny Flaherty's palmed goal near the end when he was left unmarked. A year earlier, Conor Hayes had made a vital interception in similar circumstances but this time, of course, Hayes was on the bench due to an injured back. He was a huge loss.

Losing in such circumstances was hard to swallow, but when the initial pain had subsided, the fact that we had lost to Offaly made it a bit easier to take. Like ourselves, they had been outside hurling's golden circle and had to put up with the usual patronising rubbish about being great triers, without actually achieving much. To this day, the validity of their 1980 and 1985 All-Ireland wins is questioned in some quarters because they beat Galway on both occasions.

The same sort of begrudgery was aimed at us when we beat Offaly and Limerick in 1980. That's why it was so satisfying to beat Tipperary and Kilkenny in 1987 and to repeat the dose over Tipp in 1988. My one regret was that we never beat Cork in an All-Ireland final. That would have buried the myth of the 'golden circle' once and for all.

The irony of the 1981 championship was that while we felt unlucky to lose to Offaly, we really were very fortunate to survive the semi-final against Limerick. They had re-grouped well after losing in 1980 and retained the Munster title with a six-point win over Clare in the final.

The All-Ireland semi-final turned out to be a torrid affair. Sean Foley was sent off after just nine minutes for a foul on PJ Molloy. It should have been the signal for us to click into gear but we never struck any rhythm all day. It was an amazing game with not one goal coming from four penalties. Possibly the most significant miss came ten minutes into the second-half when Eamonn Cregan had a penalty saved at a time when Limerick were leading by 0-9 to 1-3. We never once led in the match and it took a late point from a free by Finbarr Gantley to earn a draw, 1-8 to 0-11. A wretched game all round finished on another sour note when Joe Connolly and Jimmy Carroll were sent off. Each got off with a two week suspension and they were back for the replay but Foley was still suspended.

As the scoreline indicates, all our problems were in attack in the drawn game. We were without Frank Burke (injured) and John Connolly (retired) but after scoring just 1-8 we reckoned we had to coax John back into action. We talked to him in Croke Park that evening and he answered the call. He was actually on his way to the

South-East for a holiday but he changed his plans and resumed training with us the following week. He was restored to full-forward for the replay.

Limerick had all sorts of problems in the second game. Foley was suspended, Dom Punch and Pat Herbert were out injured, they lost Michael Grimes and Leonard Enright in the course of the game and still gave us one hell of a fright.

Once again, the penalty jinx struck (thank God!) with Leonard Enright missing in the first-half at a time when Limerick were 0-5 to 0-1 ahead. We eventually won by 4-16 to 2-17, with Joe Connolly scoring 2-7. Limerick felt they simply ran out of men and that with a full squad, they would have beaten us. They might well be right.

I still don't accept that there was a sort of poetic justice about Offaly's victory in the final. It was claimed that we exhausted every morsel of luck against Limerick and that we could expect no more help in the final. That might well be the case but a forward line of the calibre of Gantley – Joe Connolly – Molloy – Forde – John Connolly and Lane would be expected to score more than a single point (midfielder, Steve Mahon got the other one) from fifty yards on a dark night if they had thirty-five minutes to do it. Yet, they couldn't do it on a pleasant September afternoon in Croke Park. Amazing!

It remains one of those great mysteries. I suppose, in the circumstances, it was inevitable that all sorts of weird and wonderful stories would take root, but there really was nothing sinister behind Galway's second-half fade-out. Quite simply, Offaly's momentum peaked at the right time and our attack fizzled out for some strange reason.

A great deal had changed by the time Galway next appeared in Croke Park in a championship game. We had a mixed League in 1981/82. Our first game was against Offaly in Birr. After what happened in the All-Ireland final we were determined to gain some measure of revenge. The match turned out to be a pretty stormy affair. Let's put it this way, a lot of old animosities crept to the surface. We won the game by thirteen points but lost our way in the League after that and eventually had to play Offaly in a play-off in Limerick the following spring. We won that one too, by 1-11 to 1-7. That earned us a quarter-final game against a re-emerging Kilkenny. They beat us, 1-11 to 1-6.

Our first championship game in 1982 was against Antrim, whom we beat handily. We left Jimmy Cooney, whose form had suffered that year, off but recalled him for the semi-final against Kilkenny. Injuries and retirements left us with a new-look team that day. Frank Larkin was in goal, Conor Hayes at centre-back, Ollie Kilkenny at left-half back, Pearse Piggott at centre-forward and Brendan Lynskey at full-forward.

There were aspects of the preparation that I still regret to this day. I decided to let the players have more of an input than in previous years and it was a bad mistake. A manager should never be obstinately dictatorial but he must always, always make his own decisions. I let the team decide which way they would play if they won the toss and they opted to play against the wind. It was a mistake. Our team was breaking up and we needed a good start. Instead, Kilkenny hit us like a tornado and were 2-11 to 1-3 ahead at half-time. They eventually won by 2-20 to 2-10. The Galway team which played that day was: Frank Larkin; Seamus Coen, Niall McInerney, Jimmy Cooney; Iggy Clarke, Conor Hayes, Ollie Kilkenny; Michael Connolly, Steve Mahon; Joe Connolly, Pearse Piggott, Bernie Forde; PJ Molloy, Brendan Lynskey, Noel Lane.

By now, Galway fans had grown accustomed to being in Croke Park on All-Ireland final day and we took terrible stick for that defeat. The odd thing was that Cork, who went into the final as favourites, were beaten by eleven points. That Kilkenny team went on to win another All-Ireland crown a year later and were clearly a very special side, so maybe we were not as bad in the 1982 semi-final as everybody seemed to think.

Still, it was time for me to step down as manager. I was still teaching in Dublin and the travelling was becoming an awful chore. It involved leaving Dublin at 4 pm, driving to Athenry for training, sitting around discussing things afterwards and then driving back to Dublin, arriving at 2 am. Besides, I was quite aware that the critics were lying in wait. I wasn't going to be pushed – I resigned instead.

CHAPTER 17

SOWING THE SEEDS

I grew up thinking that All-Ireland hurling titles were for other counties. Galway, and their likes, were the warm-up acts, whose role was to tune up the major powers for the big days. Sadly, Galway were not even good at that during their disastrous decade in the Munster championship.

There had been some tantalising days for Galway hurling during the 1950s but I was too young to remember most of them. I had been told about Galway's epic battle with Cork in 1953, how Wexford had beaten Galway in the 1955 final and how Tipperary had no problems with a Galway team which got a bye into the 1958 final. Even before I saw him, I had formed the definite theory that the late Joe Salmon was the best hurler in the country. Galway played in three All-Ireland finals in the 1950s and lost them all. It was a habit which was to haunt us again in the 1970s and 1980s.

In 1959, the season after Galway got a bye into the All-Ireland final, they put one mistaken foot in front of another and marched into Munster to begin ten years of abject misery. Apparently the theory was that the existing system was serving Galway badly and that playing in Munster would give them more competitive games. History reveals otherwise.

My first recollection of watching Galway in the championship was in their first match in Munster in 1959. Like any ten year-old, I was excited and thrilled when my father promised he would take me to Limerick for the game against Waterford. Galway had been in the All-Ireland final a year earlier and, in my childish innocence, I took it for granted that Waterford would prove willing hosts for Munster's new visitors. They didn't. In fact, they beat Galway by 7-11 to 0-8 in one of the most one-sided games you could ever find. Waterford, of course, went on to win that year's All-Ireland final, but their worth was of little interest to a disappointed boy as he left Limerick.

Galway had not so much been beaten as humiliated. Men whom I believed to be ten-foot tall, with talent to match, had been left leaden-footed and dispirited as Waterford ran through them. It was an awful disappointment, not just to a ten year-old from Woodford but to a county which believed that a spell in Munster would be beneficial.

Nobody will ever know for sure how much damage the Southern campaign did to Galway hurling. The bare, cold statistics of Galway's 'exile' in Munster do not make pretty reading, but it's important to recall them to remind present-day Galway players and fans what life was like in Munster. Nowadays, Galway fans are disappointed unless they see the McCarthy Cup in Eyre Square every second year at least. Back then, getting over the first fence in Munster was the extent of Galway's ambition. It was achieved only once. Even then the 'prize' for beating Clare was a heavy defeat by Tipperary next time out.

1959	WATERFORD	7-11	GALWAY	0-8
1960	WATERFORD	9-8	GALWAY	4-8
1961	GALWAY	2-13	CLARE	0-7
	TIPPERARY	7-12	GALWAY	5-6
1962	LIMERICK	2-13	GALWAY	2-7
1963	LIMERICK	3-9	GALWAY	2-7
1964	CORK	4-14	GALWAY	2-7
1965	CLARE	4-8	GALWAY	3-10
1966	WATERFORD	2-16	GALWAY	1-9
1967	CLARE	4-12	GALWAY	1-11
1968	CORK	3-15	GALWAY	1-6
1969	CORK	3-15	GALWAY	1-10

Played twelve, lost eleven, won one! Any wonder that a Galway generation grew up wondering what on earth hurling was all about. As I was living close enough to the Tipperary border, tales of their great deeds wafted across and I really thought they were on a different planet hurling-wise. My father brought me to some Munster finals and they all looked so impressive, so high-powered, so important.

Looking back on it, the sense of occasion was frequently more dramatic than the actual games. Several of the Munster finals during the 1960s were drearily one-sided. In fact with the exception of the 1960, 1962 and 1963 finals, which were close, all the others were won by margins ranging from six to twenty points. But it scarcely seemed to matter. The Munster final was a sort of sporting institution. Hurling fans talked of it with reverence. Of course that added to Galway's burden every year.

There were some temporary rises in spirits when Galway reached two Munster U-21 finals and two minor finals (losing all four), but progress at senior level seemed a dim and distant prospect. Ironically, Galway football enjoyed its best ever decade in the 1960s, reaching four All-Ireland senior finals, winning three. Had anybody predicted at the end of 1966 that Galway hurling would win three All-Irelands before 1989 and that the footballers would still be waiting for their next one, he would have been accused of being out in the heat for too long. But that is precisely what has happened.

Behind the scenes, though, things were changing. Alf Murray, who was GAA President in the 1964-67 period launched a campaign to revitalise hurling when he came into office. Galway, which had a deep tradition in the game even if things were going badly, was an obvious target for such an initiative.

Canon O'Dea, Fr Jack Solan and Jack Whelan, who were then president, chairman and secretary respectively of the County Board, were enthusiastic supporters of the new thinking and Coiste Iomana na Gaillimhe came into being in 1965, under the chairmanship of Maitias McDonagh, Joe's father. PJ Callanan was its dedicated secretary. Its brief was to concentrate mainly on juvenile hurling.

One of the priorities was to make more hurleys and sliothars available. They were the basic tools of the trade but had not been available in the numbers required, mainly because of cost. I remember as a juvenile using hurls which were a few sizes too big for me. It was a common complaint at the time. It was very hard to improve with a hurl which didn't suit you, but you had to make do with what was available.

Ironically, the Football Board generated much of the finance for the hurling project. With the three-in-a-row team going so well, football was raising most of the cash. Club games were well supported and Galway also got a lot of money through their high profile in the National League.

It's different nowadays and I often think that many people in Galway hurling tend to forget the contribution the football side made to hurling back then. We cannot afford to have short memories since no sport is immune to change. Indeed, I am very sad at the manner in which Galway football has deteriorated over the years. There was a time when it was talked of in the same respected tones as Kerry and Dublin. Galway were, in fact, the third most successful force in the land but have lost that position now, even if they are still next in line behind Kerry and Dublin as All-Ireland winners. The truth is that such a lofty position was achieved a long time ago. As with hurling in the 1960s, it's time to go back to basics and work on the young lads. There is absolutely no reason why a county like Galway cannot regain its former greatness in football. It won't happen by accident though – it will take a huge amount of effort and sacrifice.

Putting a hurley in the hand of every young lad who wanted one was the principal aim of Coiste Iomána back in the 1960s. Some 4,500 hurleys were distributed throughout Galway in the first year. They were heavily subsidised (twenty hurleys and a sliothar could be bought for £3). Juvenile competitions were also revamped. Prior to then, the only juvenile grade was for U-16s. An U-14 competition at parish level was now added.

Another interesting innovation was the decision to ban U-14s from lifting the ball. There was a feeling around at the time that Galway's senior hurlers were obsessed with getting the ball into their hands when ground strokes would have served them better.

I cannot comment on whether or not that was the case but I doubt if it mattered all that much. Clearly, Galway senior hurling had a lot more problems than that but when a team is going badly, all sorts of theories will sprout wings. 'Keep the ball on the ground' has always been an easy catchphrase, even if it is woefully simplistic. The 'no-lift' rule only lasted a year as it was feared that, while it might have a certain validity, there were long-term risks in forcing U-14s to effectively play a different type of game than everybody else. However, the emphasis on ground hurling was to be stressed by coaches.

A little later more fresh thinking emerged which was to prove very beneficial to Galway hurling. A scheme was devised for summer courses which combined learning the Irish language and hurling at a month-long stint in Spiddal. Trials were held to choose fifty of the most promising juveniles. The scheme was to cater for all Connacht counties, but only Galway and Mayo took it up. The lads who qualified for the course spent two and a half hours each morning learning Irish, followed by two hours in the afternoons working on hurling skills. Guess which they preferred!

Several coaches gave a hand, including Donie Nealon, who was then a Tipperary star. Among the young lads who did especially well were Andy Fenton, Gerry Glynn and Michel Coen all of whom later went on to better things. Former Irish rugby captain, Ciaran Fitzgerald, was also on the course as was former Minister for Sport, Frank Fahey.

At the end of the course, the top twenty were selected to represent Galway in a juvenile match and were also brought to Croke Park to see the All-Ireland final. It was a watershed development in some ways. Apart from encouraging young talent, it proved that Galway had energetic and innovative administrators who were willing to work as hard as was necessary to ensure that hurling plotted a safe course back to the top.

While the Spiddal course was seen as the shop-window development an awful lot of quiet, unseen work was going on throughout the hurling part of the county. It would take time for that to manifest itself at senior level.

The wisdom of escaping from Munster's clutches was seen in Galway's first season of freedom. They gave Wexford a real fright in 1970, losing by just two points in the All-Ireland semi-final. Galway scored 5-9 that day while a year later, they managed 6-8 against Tipperary and still lost by nine points. In those days, the team had virtually no preparation. It was simply a question of being chosen to play in an All-Ireland semi-final and doing your best. Organised training, if it existed at all, only went on a week or two before a big game.

Unfortunately, that was having a very negative effect, other than just losing games. Personal insecurities set in and Galway were seen as gallant losers. Players began to respond accordingly. With the establishment of the Galway Hurling Board in the early 1970s, things got better. A great many energetic people became involved and the foundations were put in place. They would take time to set.

CHAPTER 18
SERVING MY APPRENTICESHIP

Nobody else must have wanted the job. But then there was never going to be a queue to coach a Galway minor hurling team back in the early 1970s. I was involved with UCG at the time, which probably explains how I came to be invited to coach Galway minors in 1973. I was only twenty-three years old and scarcely over-loaded with sideline experience.

The establishment of the Galway Hurling Board had provided a massive boost for the game and with structures improving all the time the base was getting more secure. But it was still asking a lot for Galway's U-18s to match the best from Munster and Leinster, where the roots were so much deeper. Particularly so, when Galway were going straight into an All-Ireland semi-final which was, in effect, their first competitive game together. It's the same today but the choice of players is much bigger. Nonetheless, it's still a disadvantage.

Galway have won three All-Ireland minor titles since 1983, but that doesn't alter the fact that the system is wrong. Once in a while an exceptional team comes along which is able to cope with being thrown directly into an All-Ireland semi-final but, in general, it is not a satisfactory situation. I have no doubt that some promising Galway minor teams would have done much better if they were in an open draw where they would enter the championship at the same stage as the rest.

A breakthrough of sorts was made in 1970 when Galway reached the minor final for the first time since 1958. They lost to Cork by sixteen points but it turned out to be a good Galway team, many of whom progressed to win All-Ireland U-21 medals two years later. Some made it as seniors later on. Iggy Clarke, Andy Fenton, Joe McDonagh, PJ Molloy and Gerry Holland were all on the 1970 minor team, while the full-forward was none other than Ciaran Fitzgerald, who of course went on to become an international rugby star.

It was back to the bad days in 1971 and 1972. Cork hammered Galway by 4-13 to 1-4 in the 1971 semi-final while a year later, it was Kilkenny's turn, winning by 7-9 to 2-8. So, as you can imagine, there was no great hope of a breakthrough at the start of 1973, although the county's spirit had been lifted by the success of the U-21s in 1972.

Coaching the 1973 minors was a great experience for me, in more ways than one. Team manager JP Cusack invited me in to work with himself and the other selectors, Brendan Murphy, Sean Fahy, John Furey, Gerry Corbett and Noel Treacy. We had a neat, tidy outfit and caused quite a stir when we beat Tipperary by 3-14 to 3-10 in the All-Ireland semi-final in Croke Park. Galway seniors had been surprisingly beaten by London that year, so a very close watch was being kept on emerging young talent. Nobody gave us much of a chance against Tipp as they had beaten Waterford, Cork and Limerick to win the Munster final. They were highly rated, but Galway rattled them from the start and were ten points ahead after twenty minutes. Tipperary fought back and looked to have timed their recovery to perfection when they cut the lead to a single goal with seven minutes left, but we held on and qualified for the final against Kilkenny.

It was all brand new to me although, even then, I had no hang-ups about tradition. We would beat Kilkenny if we were good enough. Prior to the final, we were all invited to Croke Park for a briefing as to what was expected of us on the day, in terms of presentation etc.

That was where I first came across the late Paddy Grace, who was Kilkenny's Mr Hurling at the time. Paddy was an institution in the game, a man who presided over Kilkenny hurling with a pride and devotion which was legendary. Dealing with Croke Park officials was old hat to him, something to be endured prior to an All-Ireland final.

All was going well until we were told that there was to be a clamp down on mentors running onto the pitch. Paddy was not impressed and made his views abundantly clear. 'If a Kilkenny player breaks a stick, God help anybody who tries to stop me getting a replacement into him,' he said. He turned to me and added: 'I advise you to do the same.'

I was very impressed by the manner in which he had cut through the red-tape and got down to the basics. The game was bigger than the occasion as far as he was concerned and nothing was going to prevent him from serving his county to the best of his great ability.

On the day of the match, he came over to me before the start. He knew that I had no experience in dealing with Croke Park officials, so he marked my card. 'They'll be telling you where you can and can't go.

I'm telling you to do what you have to do. Young man, coach your team and good luck.'

I thought it was a lovely touch. His whole life was dedicated to hurling and the idea of any Kilkenny team losing an All-Ireland final would sicken him. Nonetheless, his sheer love of the game was strong enough to prompt him to give a rookie coach like me a few words of advice, even if I was trying to plot Kilkenny's downfall. Paddy didn't know how good or bad the Galway team was at that stage, so it wasn't as if he could afford to be kind because we were certain to lose anyway. There was more to it than that. Quite simply, he disliked the idea of big day protocol getting in the way of the real business of hurling.

As it happened, Kilkenny did win… but only just, 4-5 to 3-7. We were a goal behind at half-time but we put on a great second-half spurt and were two points clear with three minutes left. Sadly, we gave away two late goals which destroyed us. We were devastated afterwards. We had a young red-head at midfield that day, whom I would get to know very well over the years. He was, of course, one Sylvie Linnane. Frank Larkin, who later played for the seniors too, was in goal.

Paddy Grace came to me afterwards and said, 'We'll never win the senior final, we used up all our luck there'. He was right. Limerick beat Kilkenny by seven points in the senior final. Not, mind you, that Kilkenny enjoyed much luck prior to the game. They were ravaged by injuries and eventually had to line out without Eddie Keher and Jim Treacy.

I formed quite a bond with Paddy after that. I loved his utter dedication to the Kilkenny cause. Some years later I was down in Nowlan Park for an All-Ireland club semi-final. Paddy saw me at the gate and brought me in on the pitch. It was a pleasant day and at half-time we were standing on the sideline chatting about hurling.

Nowlan Park wasn't looking very well that day but Paddy had his priorities in order. Chewing on a piece of grass, he winked at me knowingly and remarked, 'We mightn't have great grounds down here but we have great hurlers. Isn't that what counts?'

Indeed. That is the sort of vision which the GAA so badly needs. I'm all for improved facilities and better conditions for players and spectators but, ultimately, the promotion of the games has to be of paramount importance. The Paddy Grace vision of the GAA was not one which sees one-third of the counties not participating in the All-Ireland hurling championship. No, his was a practical vision. And if that involved allowing young lads to puck around Nowlan Park at half-time during inter-county games, so what? What harm were they doing? Weren't they learning the game? If it involved walking over to a young, inexperienced rival coach and telling him to do his own thing in Croke Park on All-Ireland final day, so what? Paddy wouldn't have seen it as big deal, simply a decent thing to do. No doubt about it, he made a lasting impression on me as a man of genuine substance.

Our defeat in the 1973 minor final alerted me to one thing. Being a coach virtually guarantees you criticism if your side loses. The *Connacht Tribune's* report noted: 'Unfortunately, the tactical aspect of their (Galway's) game was not on a par with the glorious play, and the far too long delayed positional switches in the forwards had a distinct bearing on the final outcome.' Sounds to me that they were saying I made of mess of it! Now when would I hear that again?

I had no further involvement in a coaching capacity with a Galway team until 1978 when I took over the U-21s. I suppose I still held out hope that I might make the Galway senior team. I won a Fitzgibbon Cup medal as a forward with UCG in 1977 and was also involved in coaching the team.

University life was a great help to me in terms of improving as a coach. You meet people from all over the country in university and it gives you a broader outlook. I came across dozens of hurlers from outside Galway and quickly realised that they weren't any different to what we had ourselves. Those from successful counties had more confidence, that was all.

I read a lot of books, dealing with psychology, especially as it related to sport and always kept an eye on trends in other sports. If there was a touring rugby team playing in Galway, I would go along to watch their training sessions. It's a different game, but you never know what you might pick up. I remember watching the All-Blacks on a few occasions and noticed that they used a ball in every drill. Even prop-forwards seemed keen to get their hands on the ball at a time when Irish props were there for one purpose only, to shove like hell in scrums and to protect the jumpers in the line-out. All very necessary work, but not exactly a model of inventive thought. Even then, the New Zealanders were expanding their horizons, something which they and the Australians, in particular, are still at.

Later on, I spent a few days with Shamrock Rovers. Johnny Giles was manager at the time and I was keen to see how he did things after a lifetime playing at the highest level in English soccer. Former Irish international, Paddy Mulligan, who was always a great fan of Galway hurling, was playing for Rovers at the time and he set it up for me. It was an interesting experience.

Although there may not appear to be many similarities between hurling and soccer, there are inter-changeable principles in all sports. I was always very impressed by the Liverpool way of playing soccer. At their peak, they operated three very simple basics: control, pass and move.

It sounds straightforward and it is. What is not simple is acquiring the skills to combine all three effectively. Liverpool did it magnificently. Kevin Heffernan introduced that type of strategy to Dublin when he took over. Mick O'Dwyer came along later and his Kerry team did it even better. Nowadays, all football teams are using it.

It's more difficult to operate in hurling but it's not impossible. Certainly it wasn't until the latest change of rule which restricts hand-passing. If you have a big target man who can win the ball in attack, you are half-way there. He feeds the ball to a colleague running at speed. You now have a distinct advantage as the forwards are all going in the same direction. The options are endless, provided the passing holds up. Why hasn't it been used more? Simply because there doesn't seem to be any great interest in devising new tactics in hurling. Too many people say it cannot be done and leave it at that.

Instead there is endless twaddle about ground hurling, as if it's somehow a superior way of doing things. It most patently is not. Yes, it has its uses if a player is in a tight corner, but it can never be as beneficial as getting the ball into your hand. A player with the ball in his hand is in control. The ground pull may look good but, at best, it gives your team a 50-50 chance of winning possession. A properly executed hand-pass has 100 per cent success rate.

I was always impressed by Kevin Heffernan's approach to coaching. I first came across him at a coaching course in Gormanston in spring 1974. Dublin were going nowhere at the time, or so it seemed. Heffo was giving a talk on football coaching and, although I was there for the hurling sessions, I decided I would drop in to hear what he was saying.

He was a very impressive speaker and one aspect of his thinking stuck in my mind. He was addressing the problem of what to do if you don't have an ideal player for a certain position. His basic line was that you pick out somebody whom you think you can work on and mould him into what you require.

He said that he was doing that with a big centre-back at the time and that it was working out well. As Dublin were going badly nobody took any great notice, but the centre-back turned out to be Alan Larkin. Five months later, Larkin didn't put a foot wrong as Dublin re-emerged after a spell in the doldrums to win the All-Ireland final.

While there are plenty of tips an aspiring young coach can pick up, he must also be self-reliant. Mick O'Dwyer once said that while he had four or five physical education teachers on his great squad, he always conducted the training sessions himself. Handing over any responsibility might be interpreted as a sign of weakness and could be damaging in other areas. It was a sound principle.

For while PE teachers are experts in their field, they are not necessarily the best at training teams. Different teams need different approaches and I would always prefer to run my own show rather than bring in a PE teacher. You quickly learn by your mistakes.

Anyway, there is more to managing players than simply training them. You have to be their psychologist, and sometimes even their psychiatrist. I'm always amused when I hear of team managers who are all hung up on discipline, for instance. Yes, it's important, but it must be handled very carefully.

It's absolutely pointless making rules if they cannot be kept. It's equally futile to issue an ultimatum. What if you do that and your bluff is called? What if you make a rule which says that no player can miss training under any circumstances and somebody doesn't turn up, citing a reason which you don't think is satisfactory?

The choice is clear. You either drop him off the panel or climb down. Either way you lose, simply by having a rule which cannot work. That's why a coach should never create a situation where he is left standing at the top of the cliff. The alternatives are to jump or back off. All in all, not a sound policy. I would always prefer to have discipline imposed from within. The trick is to make every panel member feel that if he misses a session, he is letting his colleagues down. It works well, if you have a dedicated, ambitious squad. In fact, it's one sure way of deciding what sort of squad you have.

CHAPTER 19

THE SHAPE OF THINGS TO COME

Sunday, 25 May 1975. Galway 4-9 Tipperary 4-6. National Hurling League final, Limerick Gaelic Grounds.

It's a date, a match, a venue and an occasion which will forever remain etched in the minds of Galway hurling folk. It was, in every sense, a watershed. Those who belittle the League as an irrelevant sideshow to the championship know nothing of the joy that the 1975 success brought to Galway.

Put it in context. It was only five years since Galway had slipped free of their ill-conceived 'affair' with the Munster hurling championship. They had returned to producing brave, but losing, performances in All-Ireland semi-finals, except of course in 1973 when there was nothing brave about their five-point defeat by London in the quarter-final. Spirit was marked absent that day. A year later Kilkenny beat Galway by twelve points in the All-Ireland semi-final and there was no great sign of any dramatic revival, although things were improving at underage level.

All that changed in the spring of 1975 when, after qualifying for the League quarter-final, Galway beat Cork, Kilkenny and Tipperary to win their first title since 1951. It was a remarkable triple against the three top hurling powers in the land. Coincidentally all three games were won by three point margins.

The attitude to Galway hurling changed overnight. Three years earlier an U-21 team, which featured Iggy Clarke, Frank Burke, PJ Molloy, Gerry Glynn, Andy Fenton, Marty Barrett, Tom Donoghue and Gerry Holland made a significant breakthrough by winning the All-Ireland final against Dublin. A year later I had my first taste of inter-county coaching with the Galway minor team which reached the All-Ireland final against Kilkenny.

They were important developments and a tribute to the improved hurling structures in the county, but it was the 1975 League success which did most to accelerate the development of Galway hurling. The good work was maintained in the All-Ireland semi-final when Galway beat Cork by 4-15 to 2-19 in a remarkable game. Galway had three goals on the board in ten minutes in an incredible start and, although Cork inevitably came back at them in the second-half, Galway held on to reach the final for the first time since 1958. Unlike 1958, of course, when they went directly into the final, they had done it the hard way this time.

It was difficult to believe that in the space of three months Galway had not only won the National League title but had also qualified for the All-Ireland final. Any wonder that coach, 'Inky' Flaherty was being treated as a hero? He deserved every accolade he got. He had injected great spirit into the players and his own natural sense of pride in Galway hurling was also very important.

Things had certainly changed. It was only three short years since the *Kilkenny People*, in a preview of the 1972 All-Ireland semi-final against Galway, had referred to it as 'a mere formality'. In fairness, you could hardly blame them since Kilkenny won by 5-28 to 3-7.

There was an incredible atmosphere in the county going into the 1975 All-Ireland final. In a sense, there was a beautiful naïvety about it all because we (the supporters) were inclined to think that nothing could go wrong. It was all going to lead to the McCarthy Cup at the end of the maroon and white rainbow. We never thought about the possibility of defeat.

By now, the rest of the hurling world had sat up and taken notice. The days of taking Galway hurling for granted were gone and Kilkenny set about counteracting Galway's strong points for the final. They did it brilliantly and although Galway started well enough, Kilkenny emerged easy winners, 2-22 to 2-10.

Nonetheless, it had been a smashing year. There was better to come, of course, in the 1980s but great credit must go to the team of 1975, who announced loud and confidently: 'Galway Hurling Is Back'.

The team which played in the 1975 All-Ireland final was: Michael Conneely; Niall McInerney, Joe Clarke, Paddy Lally; Joe McDonagh, Sean Silke, Iggy Clarke; John Connolly (captain), Sean Murphy; Gerry Coone, Frank Burke, PJ Molloy; Marty Barrett, PJ Qualter, Padraig Fahy.

Subs: Michael Connolly for Barrett, Ted Murphy for Lally, James Grealish for Murphy.

The 1975 breakthrough had an immediate impact. It heightened expectations in Galway and it also alerted the rest of the hurling world to Galway's potential. That was always going to be a problem. Many people cannot understand why it took five more years before Galway won the All-Ireland title, but the reality was that once the '75 side didn't go all the way, its limitations were exposed and there was no alternative but to wait for young, fresh back-up to arrive on the scene.

The following year was a huge disappointment. Galway drew with Wexford in a fantastic All-Ireland semi-final in Pairc Ui Chaoimh (Why in heaven's name were Galway and Wexford forced to play in Cork?) before losing a controversial replay by a goal the following Sunday.

The momentum seemed to ebb away a little after that. Galway had 'Babs' Keating in as coach in 1977 but lost the All-Ireland semi-final to Cork by five points on a day when PJ Molloy gave an exhibition of point-scoring. Joe McGrath was brought in as coach in 1978. Hopes were high that year, but Galway got a dreadful start in the semi-final against Kilkenny and were 3-11 to 2-6 behind at half-time. They recovered well in the second-half but had far too much leeway to make up and eventually lost by 4-20 to 4-13.

I had been appointed U-21 coach that year and we put together a handy team. Offaly came through to win their first-ever Leinster title but we beat them by four points in the All-Ireland semi-final to set up a final with Tipperary. We drew with them in Limerick (3-5 to 2-8) after letting a 3-5 to 1-6 lead slip. Given Tipp's record in replays nobody gave us a chance second-time round, but we played an awful lot better and won easily by 3-15 to 2-8.

It was only afterwards that we learned how seriously Tipperary had taken the U-21 championship that year. They had come together for their first training session on 31 December 1977 and between then and the replayed final on 23 October, 1978, they had trained forty times, which was very high-powered for an U-21 squad. Their season was given a further boost when, after drawing with Cork in the Munster final in Thurles, they won the replay by two points in Pairc Ui Chaoimh, a venue which traditionally frowned on Cork opposition in the championship.

That All-Ireland final win was important to us in a number of ways. With the senior scene having lost some impetus after the heady days of '75, Galway badly needed an injection of fresh blood. Winning the U-21 final in a replay was also important. It removed another brick from the old traditional wall.

Phelim Murphy, who was a selector that season, claims it was the best U-21 team ever to represent Galway. I'm not so sure myself, but certainly it had several players who went on to great things. Conor

Hayes, Seamus Coen, Steve Mahon, Bernie Forde, Michael Earls, Michael Kilkenny, Joe Greaney, John Goode and the Ryan twins, John and Paschal were all on that team. Strangely enough, not that many of the Tipperary team progressed to senior status. But then Tipp were going through a bad patch at the time and had a huge turnover in players.

That always happens in a big county where expectations are high. A player comes in, gets a short run on the team and, if he doesn't look a world beater, he is discarded. Cork football was famous for that in the days when they couldn't match Mick O'Dwyer's great Kerry team. Players were given one championship season to have a shot at Kerry and if they failed (as they usually did) they were thrown out and a new crew brought in.

Things don't work that way in the real world. Players have to be given a chance to settle in and even if they are beaten, it's important to analyse the reasons why. Were they up against a better team? Were the opposition better prepared? Is there room for improvement?

I have always believed that the basis that players have to be given a chance to develop at inter-county level. A player making his debut is under obvious pressure. Inevitably, he is nervous and uptight. All eyes are on him and if he makes the slightest mistake it's noticed, whereas the old-hand can get away with it.

A player needs three or four games before you can make a genuine assessment of him. Some people will tell you otherwise, claiming that they know straightaway whether or not a player will make the grade. I don't accept that.

About the only definite statement you can make after one game is whether or not a player is cowardly. That becomes obvious pretty quickly and I'm afraid there is not a whole lot you can do about it. Courage comes from within and cannot be coached into a player.

There are other pre-conceived notions which don't stand up either. Far too much emphasis is placed on a player's birth certificate. Once he passes the thirty-year mark, the question of retirement raises its irrelevant head. One day a player is twenty-nine and in his prime, the next he is thirty and being asked: 'Any thoughts on retiring?'

Journalists seem to be obsessed with it. After virtually every big match, you will read a retirement story from the losers' dressing-room. Some poor devil who isn't even fully dressed is asked has he any thoughts about packing it all in. He has devoted his entire life to getting this far but just because his team has lost he is asked about retirement. Meanwhile, over in the winners' dressing-room, the word 'retirement' is never mentioned. The world can seem a very lonely place after losing a big game and retirement seems a logical option, especially if a player is thirty-something and conditioned into believing that he has one foot in the sporting grave. As often as not dressing-room pledges don't last and a few months later the 'retired' one is back in business. Quite right too.

If the birth cert had mattered to me, Brendan Lynskey would never have enjoyed the extremely productive extension to his career from 1984 on. He was thirty at the time and, as he had never commanded a permanent place on the Galway set-up prior to then, critics thought we were mad to include him in our plans.

You must examine the reasons why he hadn't held down a regular place up to then. Basically, he was being asked to replace John Connolly. Now I cannot think of two players with different styles and the idea of Lynskey doing Connolly's job was ridiculous. Just as asking Connolly to do Lynskey's job would be crazy.

But, in the Galway team of 1985 onwards, Lynskey's target-man/take the punishment/spray the ball around talents were crucial. We had a forward line of runners and passers so we needed an anchor man. Lynskey fitted the bill perfectly and I couldn't care less what age he was.

Just as a player is never too old, he is never too young for senior hurling either. Joe Cooney is a typical example. He was only a few months past his nineteenth birthday when we brought him into the senior squad in 1984 but even then he was strong and durable and well able to look after himself. Minding players until they reach a certain stage of maturity doesn't work. In fact, it often leads to a loss of form or interest, or maybe even both.

Chapter 20
'NOW FOR THE TWO-IN-A-ROW'

Winning changes everything but not immediately. It took some weeks for it to change me after the 1987 All-Ireland final. I had said I was quitting as team manager and I intended to stick by it. I would get out at the top. Galway played a Rest of Ireland selection in a match in aid of GOAL the week after the final and I stayed away from it.

I felt bad about that because it was in aid of a very worthy cause, but I reckoned that if I turned up it would be an acknowledgement that I was about to change my mind. Anyway, I wasn't missed. The whole thing was a celebration. It was about the Galway fans coming to see their team playing on home territory for the first time since winning the final.

A good crowd turned out and everybody enjoyed themselves. Even GOAL Director, John O'Shea, had no complaints and that's saying something. O'Shea is not one who is given to shades of grey when expressing an opinion. He would be quite likely to walk up to a player who had just won an All-Ireland final and say, 'You know something, you're the worst full-back/midfielder/centre-forward ever to win an All-Ireland medal. Oh and by the way, I want you on Wednesday evening to play a match for GOAL. Be there. I'm not interested in excuses'.

O'Shea was working for the *Evening Press* at the time and would ring up players or officials anytime after seven o'clock in the morning. Fine, if he just wanted information, but he was also fond of giving his own opinion, which often went on the lines, 'How in God's name can you play that stiff? He's a woeful hurler'. The subject of his ire might be a player for whom you had the greatest respect, but it didn't matter to him. If he had a point of view, he would express it.

I always had far more respect for his work with GOAL than for his views on hurling! As for listening to his opinions at 7.30 in the morning… what a way to start the day! Still, I liked him and helped out in his GOAL activities anytime I could. He is straight and does remarkable charity work in the Third World. Most players feel the same about him and he virtually always gets a full turn-out for his GOAL matches. Even players who have got the O'Shea verbal lash will ignore it once a game is under the GOAL banner. Indeed, those games have now become an automatic part of the post All-Ireland scene. They are a good idea as not only do they raise money for the Third World, they also give the fans a chance to see their heroes back home in a playing environment days after the All-Ireland triumph.

O'Shea wasn't the only caller in the weeks after the 1987 final. In fact, the phone never stopped ringing. Was I really resigning as manager? Why bow out now after hanging in there through the disappointing years? I think Phelim Murphy and Bernie O'Connor never believed I would resign. They suspected that however determined I was to quit, it would be impossible to get out after making the breakthrough.

'We'll win the two-in-a-row, you know,' said Phelim one night during another of our late sessions. 'And the three-in-a-row,' chimed in Bernie. Talk about psychological pressure. They both said that if I resigned, they would go too. Brendan Lynskey was also talking of retiring. I'm not sure whether Phelim and Bernie would have quit had I retired, but they sounded serious about it.

The average age of the team was still only twenty-four years. People tended to forget that. The squad had been around at the highest level since 1985, so there was a general assumption that it was a very mature team. Age-wise, it wasn't. Take Conor Hayes, Sylvie Linnane, Steve Mahon and Brendan Lynskey out of it, and it was an incredibly young team. Even of that four-ball, Sylvie and Brendan were the only ones over thirty years old.

Still, I felt so drained after the 1987 final that the thought of climbing back up on the treadmill didn't appeal to me, initially at least. I have always said that players win games, coaches lose them. Players get the credit for success – and rightly so – but when a team loses, the management invariably comes in for criticism. That's all part of the game and it didn't bother me, but sometimes you get the impression that people think their team should never lose a game. When it happens, somebody has to be blamed. More often than not, it's the team management.

When I took over with Phelim and Bernie, we made up our minds that whatever else happened, we would not publicly blame the players. In all our years, we never singled out a player or a particular line and tried to scapegoat them for defeat. The same does not apply to other managements, some of whom are quite prepared to take the glory while dumping the responsibility on the players when things go wrong.

The Galway players knew where they stood with us on that one. The loyalty clause only came into force outside the dressing-room door. Inside, there were no holds barred. The talking was straight and often a little colourful when the occasion demanded. There could be no ducking under the ropes, either by players or management. We were loyal to the players and we expected the same of them. It's easy for players to blame the selectors or the coach when they really should be looking into their own hearts.

In recent years, some counties have had examples of 'player power', attempting to dictate who should be in charge of them. It simply does not work. Managers chosen by players are in an impossible position as they feel beholden to the squad. It can blind a manager to the reality of what he has to do.

I am not saying that a manager should be aloof and remote from the players. Far from it. He must get to know them as individuals and has to deal with them as such. You cannot treat every player the same way. Some need to have their backsides kicked all the time, while others need constant encouragement. It's vital to get to know them well so that you can work on the different personalities. A manager should never get too close to the players, though. By all means, do everything you can for them but a line must be kept there all the time. Familiarity can breed more than contempt. It also creates a climate for the gradual erosion of discipline.

The weeks after the 1987 final were hectic and gradually my resistance to continuing as manager was worn down. Technically, the management's three-year term was up, but our re-appointment would be a formality as far as the Hurling Board was concerned if we were interested in continuing. Phelim and Bernie kept saying that the hardest work was done and that the experience of winning an All-Ireland final would bring the team on a lot. I believed that too, although I wasn't so convinced about the hardest work being done. In the end the lure of the two-in-a-row challenge won out.

I was back for the Railway Cup, which was played over a weekend in Ennis in early October. We beat Ulster easily in the semi-final and then beat a good Leinster team in the final by 2-14 to 1-14. It really had turned out to be some year. The All-Ireland, National League and Railway Cups were all safely in Galway's possession. We were to add the Oireachtas trophy to the list by beating Wexford early the following summer.

Galway's great year was reflected in the All-Stars team when Conor Hayes, Ollie Kilkenny, Pete Finnerty, Steve Mahon, 'Hopper' McGrath and Joe Cooney all won awards, with Cooney also taking the Texaco Hurler of the Year Award.

It was good to see so many Galway players getting awards, even if I always had my doubts about aspects of the All-Star scheme. Far too much is decided by the All-Ireland final. Let's face it – a good quarter-hour in the All-Ireland final is worth a lot more than a consistent season's work when it comes to the All-Star selection. That's wrong.

Winning an All-Ireland works wonders for a team. Two things happen. Players become a lot more confident in their own ability, while the opposition, although bursting to put one over on the champions, have that little bit more respect which can sometimes undermine them.

We coasted through the 1987/88 League. The celebration trail was endless, but we had a fairly sensible bunch who knew how to mix business and pleasure. We remained unbeaten in our four pre-Christmas games. Quite how, I'm not sure as the lads were on the social whirl virtually every night.

We beat Kilkenny by two points in Nowlan Park (Sylvie was brilliant that day), drew with Tipperary (0-7 each) on a horrible day, scraped home (2-15 to 2-12) against Limerick in Ballinasloe, hammered Clare (3-14 to 2-3 in Pearse Stadium) and finished off with a 2-9 to 0-15 draw against Cork, also in Pearse Stadium. The match against Tipperary in November was significant enough in its own way. It was played in Semple Stadium and Tipperary were determined to end the year with a win over us. Either way, it had been a great season for them, having won the Munster title after a sixteen year gap and it would have crowned the year if they had avenged the All-Ireland semi-final defeat by Galway. We were equally determined to concede nothing to them, so the League fixture looked certain to have more bite than usual.

Unfortunately, the weather made an unwelcome intervention. The game was played in a non-stop deluge, turning it into a complete lottery. It finished level, 0-7 each, which was just about right in such awful conditions.

Our end of year competitive record read: Played 13, Won 10, Drew 3, Lost 0. Did Galway hurling fans ever think they would see the day when their team would capture the 'Triple Crown' and remain unbeaten all year long? I doubt it.

By now, there was almost a family-like atmosphere among the team. The inhibitions and the insecurities which had niggled away for the previous few seasons were well gone. We were at peace with ourselves. We were top of the pile and, based on the relative strengths of the opposition, had every chance of staying there for some time.

Our first League game of 1988 underlined the extent to which Galway hurling had progressed. We lost by a goal to Waterford in Dungarvan and it was the talk of the country. It was the first time we had been beaten in a competitive game since losing to Westmeath in Loughrea fifteen months earlier.

Waterford fans were as happy as if they had won the All-Ireland itself. It was understandable. We had beaten Waterford by sixteen points in the previous year's League semi-final. They had recovered well, however, and their win in Dungarvan set them up for a League semi-final place.

Losing to Waterford was not, in itself, serious for us. Of far greater significance as far as I was concerned was the bad ankle injury which Steve Mahon suffered. It was to keep him out for most of the year. We drew with Wexford in the final Division One game to set up a quarter-final clash with Offaly, who had taken full points from their seven games in Division Two.

They were well psyched up for that game and beat us through a late Mark Corrigan point. We led by six points in the first-half, but Offaly gradually came back into it. We lost Joe Cooney with a nasty head injury, which probably proved decisive. It's water under the bridge now but I was very, very unhappy with the circumstances surrounding that injury. Suffice to say that the stroke which did it was, shall we say, careless.

The defeat proved a blessing in disguise in many ways. It jolted us all back down to earth. We had forgotten what it was like to lose a big game but the Offaly defeat quickly reminded us that the gap between us and the rest was very narrow, if indeed there was a gap there at all. We probably needed that. When a team is going well, there is a tendency to free-wheel a little and overlook minor problems.

Tipperary exploited our absence and made a very definite statement of intent by winning the League title, beating Offaly fairly easily in the final. It was an important win for Tipperary. They now had a national title to add to the 1987 Munster crown and it was pretty clear that their graph line was still on the up. Another successful Munster campaign would drive it higher still. They were a team to be watched.

Chapter 21
'Save Your Excuses for Others'

By the summer of 1988, we were as close to a family unit as any squad could be. Of course there were little internal rivalries and frictions, but they are always there in every squad. Provided they don't grow and fester, there is nothing to worry about.

The panel was strong and, even more importantly, well-balanced. We had twenty-two or twenty-three players who could fit in on any given day, without disrupting the game plan. Players had come to rely on each other. Anybody who let himself down was letting the side down.

Our summer programme usually started around 7 June. Players were still training with their clubs on Tuesday and Thursday nights and I would take them on Mondays and Wednesdays. Very often, they would have a club game on a Sunday, followed by a challenge game with Galway in the evening.

As the weeks passed, the club activity tapered down and our training stepped up to four nights a week, plus Saturdays. Each player was given a training schedule at the start of the campaign. His life was to revolve around that. Excuses could be given to other people – Galway hurling came first on the days and nights we needed them.

That sounds easy in practice, but we are talking here about working people, not full-time professionals. As players started to get married and move upwards in their jobs, the pressures and responsibilities grew on all fronts. Still, there could be no deviation from the training schedule, without a damn good reason. The players knew and accepted that. On the day Gerry McInerney got married, for instance, the panel had to leave the reception in Hayden's Hotel, Ballinasloe to train in Duggan Park. We let Gerry off (Wasn't that nice of us!) but I ran the legs off the rest of them!

This sort of intense pressure isn't unique to Galway. It's experienced by every successful team – and some unsuccessful teams too – and is noticed only by those who are closely involved. The demands on players are fierce but in such a competitive world, it's the only way to succeed. That's why players can never be too well looked after, as far as I'm concerned. They are the people who keep the GAA alive and vibrant, even if there are those in the Association who regard them as scarcely more than necessary irritants.

I don't want to labour the point, but all you have to do is look around Croke Park on All-Ireland final day to see what I mean. Lads in green jackets scurry around, telling the players what to do, where to go, when to come out of the dressing-room etc. They are only doing their jobs, but it can be awful annoying, especially when you see the clipboard brigade barking out the orders.

I get the impression that, to them, All-Ireland final day is all about presentation and protocol. Yes, they have a part to play, but ultimately the players must come first. They are hustled out of the dressing-room twenty minutes before the throw-in, whether they like it or not. That may suit some, but not others, but as far as the GAA is concerned, the players' feelings don't come into it.

There is far too much pomp and ceremony before an All-Ireland final. I am convinced that many a good performance got choked between the dressing-room door and the throw-in because of all the hanging about. It's ludicrous to have players out on the pitch twenty minutes before the start. There are all sorts of distractions which can eat away at the concentration. In order to minimise them, I always had a policy of gathering the players around me as close as I could to the start.

I would stand in the centre, tossing the ball to each one in turn. It might have looked comical, but there was a point to it all. The aim was to get each player focused totally and completely on the ball. That was what really counted once the game started. Control that and you control the game. Other teams get in a huddle with their arms around each other while either the team manager or the captain give a last-minute pep talk. I didn't favour that – as far as I was concerned the ball was the medium and was all that mattered. The time for talking and urging was over. By then, the task is to calm the players down, not to whip them up any higher.

I never paid a whole lot of attention to the lists of 'do's' and 'don't' which Croke Park issues prior to the All-Ireland final. One, though, really annoyed me. That was in 1990 when we got an instruction to wear an all-maroon outfit for the final against Cork. Apparently it was designed to differentiate between Cork and ourselves for black and white television, so the plan was that Cork would wear their usual red jerseys and white shorts and we would wear all-maroon.

We had worn all-maroon against Cork in both the 1985 All-Ireland semi-final and the 1986 final so it seemed about time Cork were asked to change. Why shouldn't they wear all-red for a change? We weren't into doing the GAA authorities any favours after what happened in 1989 anyway, but rather than make an issue of it, we decided to ignore them in 1990. We would wear maroon and white as usual. The stewards could hardly start pulling the togs off our lads as they raced out on Croke Park.

I don't know whether the Games Administration Committee made any attempt to fine the Galway County Board for that. I'd prefer not to know. And if they did I hope the Board told them to go take a jump. Why should we always be the ones to change? Were they afraid to ask Cork to wear all-red?

Such peripheral issues were all irrelevant as we got down to serious training for the 1988 All-Ireland championship. We did a lot of physical work, but usually with the ball to break the monotony. Some of the training games were as tough as the real thing.

Our squad was around thirty-strong so we used two full teams. Competition for places was fierce and any young lad who started to make an impression was quickly introduced to the facts of life at the top. The likes of Steve Mahon or Ollie Kilkenny would gladly turn a young pretender upside down if the occasion demanded. Players were proud of their positions and didn't want new challengers emerging.

It was good for all concerned. I loved to see the more established players getting the run-around (provided it didn't last, as that would mean their form had dipped) in training. It was the best-possible defence against complacency, a creeping rust which is always trying to force its way into teams. As for the young lads, a collision with someone like Mahon was a great test. It was going to happen in a match anyway, so it might as well happen in practice since training should always resemble a match as closely as possible. Otherwise, where's the point of having it?

I also had a special routine for announcing the team. The players were always the first to know and I would tell them at the end of a training session. I would gather the squad around and emphasise how important each and every one of them was before announcing the team. I would then let the subs go and gather the actual team around me closely. I go to each one of them personally, usually thumping him on the heart and emphasising how proud he should feel at being selected for Galway and how he was not only representing himself but also the subs who had just left, his family and indeed the entire county.

Our little huddle in the middle of Kenny Park may have looked comical to on-lookers but I did it for a very specific reason. I wanted to boil up the emotions and to make the players feel really good about themselves. I would also choose that moment to begin the real concentration on the match ahead. The team was now selected. The doubts about who would be in and out were gone and I wanted every player to leave that night with his vision totally on the game.

Our little ritual had a bonding effect in every sense as the players would all link arms as I went through the talk. At the very moment I had them on a high, I would call a halt and they would all sprint for the gate and up the little hill in Athenry, leading to the dressing-room. The crowd would clap them off the field, which made them feel even better about themselves. I know it might have looked tough on the subs who were let go that few minutes early, but it was in no way designed to make them feel like second-class citizens. No, the idea was to get the first fifteen on a focus countdown to the big game. I would deal with the subs at another time, outlining that their role was not merely as back-up but rather as the unlucky victims of a system which only allowed fifteen players to start. Their chance would come if they kept at it. Obviously that was not the case for all of them, but it's important to give subs an incentive to work for too. Basically, they must feel that they are an integral part of the scene, otherwise they will not be able to switch on in an instant if they are called in.

Steve Mahon was injured for the 1988 campaign, something which created a problem for us. He had been one of our anchor-men for years and would not be easy to replace, even if we did have a big squad to choose from.

We did a few variations in training that summer, including having 9 am sessions on Saturday mornings. It worked well as the lads had trained and breakfasted by eleven o'clock and were free for the rest of the day. I'm not so sure that they liked the early starts, but they were happy to have most of the day off. I was always an early riser myself, but got caught out one particular Saturday morning, much to the delight of the panel. We had trained in Athenry the night before and it had gone badly for some reason. I felt that there wasn't enough concentration and was in lousy humour at the end of the session. I let fly.

'Right, you dozy lot, see you here at ten to nine tomorrow morning. Don't be late,' I barked, before speeding out of Kenny Park.

Would you believe it? I slept it out the following morning. I broke every speed limit in the country between Woodford and Athenry, but didn't make it until about 9.15. To make matters worse, I had all the sliothars in the boot of my car, so they couldn't start without me. It was a beautiful morning and I sped into the ground in a cloud of dust to find the entire squad lying flat out in the centre of the pitch taking the sun. I was clapped all the way down the hill and into the pitch! So much for lecturing them about punctuality the night before. I let them off lightly that morning!

As the summer progressed, we were obviously keeping a watch on what was happening elsewhere. Tipperary, who had won the League, were going nicely in Munster, eventually beating Cork, but as we were due to meet the Leinster champions in the All-Ireland semi-final, they weren't getting much of our attention. That could wait.

Kilkenny, who had been our great Leinster rivals for the previous two years, were beaten in the semi-final by Wexford, who, in turn, were beaten by Offaly in the final. Deep down, I was delighted with that, for while people kept talking about Offaly being our bogey-team, I was convinced that we wouldn't have a whole lot of trouble with them that year. It was one of those strange hunches one gets from time to time. I felt that our team would be way too mature for them and that we owed them a beating after the 1985 All-Ireland final.

Also, Offaly had beaten us by a point in the League quarter-final earlier in the year. A lot of our team felt very aggrieved at the manner in which Joe Cooney was injured that day. He took a terrible belt across the face and, to say the least, we were not happy about it. All in all, Offaly needed to be taught a lesson and we had plenty of motivating forces to help us along.

First, we had to pop over the quarter-final hurdle, which we did, beating London by 4-30 to 2-8. We weren't at full-strength that evening, lining out without Gerry McInerney, Steve Mahon and Brendan Lynskey, but it didn't matter. We played Michael Coleman at wing-back, which wasn't his best position and he didn't make any great impression.

Lynskey was caught up in a suspension controversy around then but, thankfully, it was sorted out for the semi-final against Offaly and we played him at midfield with Pat Malone. Offaly had reached the League final earlier in the year, losing to Tipperary, and while they had won the Leinster title in good style, their team looked unbalanced.

They played Pat Delaney and Eugene Coughlan at centre-forward and full-forward respectively. This pair had been at centre-back and full-back when they won their All-Irelands in 1981 and 1985. I felt if we got our game anywhere near right, we would win fairly well.

I suppose I should not have been so confident. Galway and Offaly had met in two All-Ireland finals and two semi-finals in the previous eight seasons and the score stood 3-1 in Offaly's favour. Add in the fact that they beat us in the previous spring's quarter-final and they had every apparent reason for optimism.

Offaly always love playing Galway. We are very close neighbours and since the start of the 1980s our paths have crossed many times. They would feel that they have a better chance of beating Galway than say, Tipperary or Cork, while Galway always believe that if things go right, they will beat Offaly. Current form has nothing to do with it – that's just how the counties see each other.

We beat them in 1988, pretty easily too, but not without discovering some defensive and midfield problems which had to be sorted out before the final. Martin Naughton gave one of his best-ever performances for Galway, scoring 1-5. One of his zig-zag runs which took him right down the pitch was breath-taking. In fact, there wasn't a more thrilling spectacle in hurling than Naughton in full flight.

Noel Lane wasn't far behind him scoring 1-4, although it wasn't to be enough to guarantee him his place for the final. We won by 3-18 to 3-11. It should have been a far more decisive win but we leaked two giveaway goals in the final minutes. Pat Delaney scored both, leaving the Galway defence with an embarrassed look. Conor Hayes was very definitely helping in enquiries as to how they came to be conceded.

Still, we were back in our fourth final in-a-row and yes, Tipperary were waiting for us. They had beaten Antrim by eight points in the other semi-final to set up one of the most-talked about finals for years. Tipperary had not played especially well against Antrim, but we knew that hardly mattered. Tipperary would never admit it, of course, but ever since beating Cork in the Munster final, they were thinking of the All-Ireland final. They never considered that Antrim might upset them. They played accordingly, just doing enough to reach the final.

Earlier, they had shown signs of a rapidly growing maturity against Cork in the Munster final. The match was in Limerick and I went along to have a look at it. Cork were really determined to avenge the previous year's defeat and quietly fancied themselves to do it. But Tipperary started with a flourish and looked to be out of sight at half-time.

However, Cork recovered and came right back into contention, but Tipperary kept their nerve and pulled away again to win well. It underlined how well they were developing. They would be very hard to stop in the All-Ireland final, not just because of their rate of improvement but because the momentum behind them was incredible. A year earlier, it had been more of the enthusiastic, hopeful variety, but now it was very much a confident roll. The whole of Tipperary, and indeed much of the hurling world, were convinced that their All-Ireland hour was at hand.

Chapter 22
THE PSYCHING GAME

Two weeks before the 1988 All-Ireland final, a magazine produced a two-page article under a banner headline: CLASH OF THE YEAR – FARRELL v KEATING. It depicted our rivalry as a world boxing title bout, fought over twelve rounds. It even featured pictures of us both with our heads super-imposed on boxers' bodies.

It carried a round-by-round scorecard, based on our various experiences, strengths, weaknesses, squads, etc. It was all only a gimmick (I came out a one round winner!) but it characterised the texture of that final, which was seen as a series of personal duels, rather than simply Galway v Tipperary.

Farrell v Keating, Hayes v English, Kilkenny v Fox, Keady v O'Connell, Cooney v O'Donovan. Depending on your angle, you could take just about any duel and decide it was the most crucial of all. It was that sort of final.

Attempts were made to dig up imaginary animosities between 'Babs' Keating and me. They didn't exist. In fact, I would regard him as a good hurling friend. When it comes to Galway or Tipperary we would tear each other apart, metaphorically speaking but, away from that, I have great respect for him and his achievements. I would like to think that he sees me in the same way.

We had worked together with the Galway team which reached the 1979 final and got on quite well. We were both living in Dublin at the time ('Babs' still does) and we travelled up and down together.

He had been brought in to coach the team in '79. I was there as trainer. He was the senior figure. He had a hatful of All-Ireland medals and was regarded in Galway as a Messiah brought in to save us. It was seen as a good move at the time as there was nobody inside with any experience of big-time success. Privately, I believed that you didn't have to be a top-class hurler to coach the game, but my theory on that one would not be put to the test until 1980. The senior players on the Galway team wanted 'Babs' in 1979 and they got him.

By the time the 1988 All-Ireland final came around, we were both high-profile managers, so it was inevitable that the comparisons would start. It made obvious copy for journalists. Deep down, I suppose, I wanted to put one over on him. It was nothing personal. It was just that I was sick to the teeth of all the Tipperary hype. The county's hurling awareness, which borders on the arrogant when things are going well, had been reawakened. The supporters managed to create an aura which suggested that God himself had decreed that Tipp would win the final. Some of them were even referring to Nicholas English as 'God'.

I was told later that RTE had been preparing a special feature on Tipperary all year to show how they won their first All-Ireland in seventeen years. Everywhere you turned it was Tipperary... Tipperary... Tipperary. We were the defending champions but we seemed to be no more than bit-players to the great blue and gold show.

There were two distinct challenges awaiting us after we reached the final. First, we had a fair bit of fine-tuning to do with our own team and second, we had to counter-balance the hype emanating from Tipperary. It was important to let people know that we were in the final too because sometimes a team can sniff an air of inevitability. There was more than a sniff around that August. The world and its mother, father, aunt and second cousin seemed to think our number was up.

Back in Athenry, I set about chipping away some of Tipp's gloss. We learned that they were training in secret, claiming that the crowds were so big that they could not get anything done otherwise. I found that extremely encouraging. My view was that if they had problems dealing with big crowds in training, what chance had they of coping with 64,000 screaming spectators in Croke Park on All-Ireland final day? I also figured that the glamour and glitz was getting to the team.

Once a team goes into secret training, all sorts of rumours start. We were told that the Tipperary subs were using Galway jerseys in practice matches, presumably to form a mental picture of the maroon and white in the first team's eyes. I turned that to our advantage too, telling our lads that the subs were kitted out like that to give the first team a feel of beating the maroon, something they weren't used to. It showed how respectful they had become of colours which once meant little or nothing to Tipperary.

I mean, really, could you imagine the Tipperary teams of old wearing Galway jerseys in training? Can you imagine them training behind closed doors either? Others read more into the secret training. I was warned by people who claimed to know that Tipperary were practising a revolutionary drill which would blow us off the pitch. Minds can become very fertile around All-Ireland final time, so it was a question of taking all in and letting most of it out again. I was amazed by the secret training routine. Even if they were finding it awkward to cope with the big crowds, all they had to do was vary the venue from night to night, without announcing it. As for the revolutionary tactics, they never materialised. Mind you, if Tipperary had beaten us we would have had to swallow all sorts of nonsense about what they had done behind closed doors.

Then, of course, there was the Tipperary captaincy affair. Tipperary still use the old-fashioned system of choosing a captain, whereby a representative of the county champions automatically gets the honour. It can never be a satisfactory situation since it often means that a player who is struggling to hold onto his place has the added burden of being captain. Either that or a newcomer can be asked to lead the team out on his debut.

Cappawhite's Pa O'Neill was Tipperary captain that year, but was dropped for the All-Ireland final. John Leahy, who had come on for O'Neill in the semi-final, held onto his place at left half-forward with Aidan Ryan switching to left full-forward. Nicholas English took over as captain. It caused a lot of bitterness in parts of Tipp as the rumour went round that O'Neill was being dropped to ensure that English, who was the county's folk-hero at the time, would be the man to bring the McCarthy Cup back to Tipperary. I'm sure that's not true (there isn't a selection committee in the world who would jeopardise a team's chances for such flimsy reasons) but once a rumour gets started, it's hard to kill off. That particular rumour still runs in parts of Tipperary every time the 1988 final is mentioned.

I was delighted by it at the time. It was another plank in the psychological build-up. 'Guess what, lads, Tipp are changing their team to ensure that if they win, English will bring the Cup back. How about that? Are you listening, Conor Hayes?' It was enough to send our lads into motivational orbit.

While we were able to turn the spotlight on Tipp's perceived problems, we also knew that deep down we had some of our own to sort out. We had beaten Offaly comfortably in the semi-final, but we were not convinced that the balance was right. Not only that, but Conor Hayes had not played well at full-back. How would he cope with an in-form English in the final? Come to think of it, the entire full-back line had leaked against Offaly.

There were plenty of people in Galway who wanted Hayes dropped.

They would never admit it afterwards, of course, but the selectors were repeatedly told that playing Hayes was like handing the McCarthy Cup to Tipperary. It was an awful insult to a player of his calibre and I can state categorically that we never once considered dropping him. That wasn't out of misguided loyalty but simply a matter of judgement, based on a number of factors.

Hayes was always a man for the big occasion. He was also a very good thinker on the game. Without ever mentioning English we knew that Hayes would be psyching himself up for the final, not in a wild, panicky way but in a controlled, appraised fashion. Hayes knew that many of the supporters who had praised him to the skies a year earlier, were now shaking their heads and muttering, 'He's finished'. All his great service would have counted for nothing if English gave him the runaround in 1988.

Hayes also knew that prophets of doom had scripted his obituary prior to the 1987 final. Liam Fennelly would run rings around him. Well, he didn't. Apart from one slip, Hayes kept a tight rein on Fennelly.

We decided straightaway that the defence would be the same as that which played Offaly. Rumours went around that we were considering putting Pete Finnerty in as a man-to-man marker on English. That wasn't true either. We didn't fear English so much that we were going to disrupt our entire defence. Besides, that would have meant dropping Hayes, something which was never on the agenda. No, we would stick with the defence we had and hope that they improved in training. That was often the case between semi-finals and finals and 1988 was no exception.

Midfield was another matter. We had lost our long-time anchor-man, Steve Mahon through injury and had played Brendan Lynskey alongside Pat Malone in the semi-final. It had worked OK for a while, but we felt it wasn't the partnership required to beat Tipperary.

Besides, we needed Lynskey's individual brand of power and distribution in attack. But at whose expense? Once again, our thoughts went back to those late night think-ins fifteen months earlier, when we reached the conclusion that we needed a big name on the bench to bring on as a sub. It had worked perfectly in 1987 when Noel Lane and PJ Molloy, two of the most respected attackers in the game, had come on against Kilkenny and brought a mature order to the youthful endeavours around them. The super-sub requirement, plus the need to have Lynskey in the attack, made up out minds. Lane would be left out.

To the hurling world at large, Lane was not the obvious choice to make way for Lynskey. Far from it. He had scored 1-4 in the semi-final. Now I'm not sure if it ever happened before, but I doubt very much if any forward who scored 1-4 from play in a semi-final was left out for the final. But that was Farrell, Murphy and O'Connor for you – likely to do anything. Ninety-nine per cent of Galway fans would have chosen Lane, probably ahead of Anthony Cunningham.

We still weren't finished with surprises. Tipperary were playing Joe Hayes and Colm Bonnar at midfield. Both were good ball-movers, but we reckoned that Pat Malone would do enough of that for us. We felt we needed strength and aggression and we had it in the form of Michael Coleman.

He had been on the team for the 1986/87 League and played in the final against Clare. He had a stinker. He looked very raw and we didn't hold on to him for the '87 championship campaign. In fact, I think he watched the final from Hill 16. In hindsight, it was a mistake to leave him off the panel in 1987. What he needed was coaching because he had many of the right attributes like courage, strength, determination and honesty. But then coaches, like players, learn as they go along too.

He came on a lot in 1987/88, hurling superbly at centre-back with his club, Abbeyknockmoy. We brought him back into the panel and actually played him at wing-back against London in the '88 quarter-final. He wasn't a success there. His style wasn't suited to wing-back and we should never have put him there in the first place. He lost out for the semi-final.

Coming up to the All-Ireland final, the idea of playing him at midfield took root. We felt that, despite his lack of big-time experience, the occasion would not get to him. Besides, he was going very well in training. All we wanted him to do was to play as he would for his club. It might sound like a tall order to pluck a player from obscurity and put him straight into an All-Ireland final, but you can do that with some people. Coleman was one of them.

Once again, it was fiercely disappointing for Tony Kilkenny. He had been left out for the second year in a row, not because he was playing badly, but because we felt somebody else (in this case Coleman) gave us more options.

We usually chose the team in Phelim's or Bernie's house on a

Monday night and would meet again on Tuesday to review it. We met in Hayden's Hotel at around 4 pm on the Tuesday before the All-Ireland (we had switched the training to Ballinasloe to suit Keady and Lynskey, who were coming down from Dublin) and went through every angle again.

We knew we would face a barrage of criticism when the team was announced. We could have played safe by choosing the team which started against Offaly, but we had never been afraid to trust our hunches so why start now?

A big crowd turned up in Duggan Park that evening, not just to hear the team but to sniff after any spare All-Ireland tickets. Keady and Lynskey were late for some reason, which scarcely left us in the best of humour. There were several journalists there, waiting for team news. Once again, I had to break the bad news to Lane and Kilkenny that they were not on the team. Kilkenny was understandably disappointed but Lane was positively devastated. He would have walked onto any other team that year, yet here he was being told that there was no room for him on our team, despite scoring 1-4 in the semi-final. One could understand if he had let the air out of our car tyres on his way out of Duggan Park. Instead, I think he adjourned with Peter Murphy to Larry Murray's pub in Loughrea to toast the selectors! All told, it was an edgy sort of evening.

After I had announced the team to the panel, Phelim released it to the press. When the session finished, the journalists were waiting for us as we came in. Within seconds our dressing-room was invaded by reporters. It was one of the very few times I felt irritated by the press. The last thing we wanted was a posse of reporters descending on Michael Coleman, who was confused enough after just learning that he was to play in the final. But quite naturally the press were only interested in the surprise packet, who was self-consciously sitting in the corner, trying to figure things out.

Looking back on it, there was a funny side. Most of the national newspaper journalists wouldn't have known Coleman if he came up and belted them across the head. Of course, they couldn't let that be known. So they hung around sheepishly for a few seconds, trying to figure out where Coleman was. Eventually, they worked the puzzle out and descended on him.

I was angry. 'Tipperary wouldn't let ye in to see them training and we can't even shower and change in peace,' I muttered to nobody in particular. Really, though, I could hardly blame the press. Coleman's selection was the story of the night. Especially since it meant that it was at Lane's expense. Having got their quotes from Coleman, the journalists dashed from the dressing-room to the nearest phone to relay news of a selection which would prove most controversial.

It was hard on Lane. To this day, I'm sure he cannot understand why he didn't start either the 1987 or 1988 finals. But the fact is that he scored what turned out to be the winning goals in both, unlike 1985-86 when he started both finals and made little impression.

Coleman's selection was the talk of the county and beyond all week. Obviously it had a high risk factor, but there are times when you have to take chances. It also had the advantage that it kept Tipperary guessing. The last time they would have seen him was in the 1987 League final, which didn't go his way at all. Now here he was being brought in at midfield, indirectly replacing a man who had scored 1-4 in the semi-final. I could imagine 'Babs', Donie Nealon and Theo English pondering over that at training. They would either interpret it as a ploy to be watched or a sign of panic. Probably the latter!

They made a few changes themselves. Apart from dropping Pa O'Neill, they completely re-jigged the defence, with only Bobby Ryan selected in the same position as for the semi-final. I was encouraged by that. I reckoned that they were choosing their team with our attack in mind rather than simply on the basis of who was best in the various positions.

Once again, I felt that our subs' bench could be our trump card. Our top six subs were Peter Murphy, Michael Earls, Tony Kilkenny, Noel Lane, Pearse Piggott and Gerry Burke. It was an impressive lineup. Tipperary were living in dread of Lane's arrival. He liked playing against them and was now very much the super-sub. It was a frustrating role, but it had its advantages. He would be coming on at a time when opposition legs were tiring and also he was under no pressure to deliver. A sub can hardly be blamed if a team loses. However, he can be hailed a hero if they win, something which Lane experienced both in 1987 and 1988.

The days leading up to the 1988 final were very tense. On the one hand, we felt under no real pressure, in the sense that we had already won an All-Ireland final and that no team has a divine right to win a second. But we also knew that we were sitting on the edge of history as far as Galway hurling was concerned. Gradually, that became the over-riding emotion. Besides, we badly wanted to beat Tipperary in an All-Ireland final just to prove our true pedigree.

Chapter 23

THROUGH A NEW FRONTIER

Tipperary were out first. Those who saw their arrival onto Croke Park for the 1988 All-Ireland final say it had a profoundly dramatic impact. It was an emotional explosion by a county which was back in Croke Park for a senior final for the first time since 1971.

I had warned our lads to ignore it. Blue and gold are strong colours and are difficult to overshadow, but this was Galway's fourth consecutive final, so I reckoned they could handle the preliminaries fairly comfortably. By now, they were good at getting the focus right and blotting out all distractions.

The days before had gone well. There was no apparent sign of fraying nerves. There was an icy resolve about the squad which was very obvious even on the way to Dublin on Saturday afternoon. The Ashling Hotel was packed as usual on the Saturday night, so the players dispersed in little groups around the place.

Although I am a non-drinker, I had no rules against a player taking a pint or two the night before a game. Maturity comes from within, not from inflexible rules imposed from outside. By this stage I felt the players knew the behavioural parameters well. A player who doesn't know how to behave the night, or indeed the nights, before a big game is no use to you anyway. The lads had their own routine and I had no problems with that.

There was an incredible atmosphere on the morning of the game. You could sense it everywhere. I reckoned that the whole occasion would be harder on Tipp than us. 'Babs' had experienced it as a player but he could not absorb all the pressures for his squad. Our lot had been through it all so often that I felt that they would not lose nearly as much by way of nervous energy in the preliminaries.

On our way into Croke Park, a Tipperary fan galloped over to me and shouted: 'You're for it today, Farrell, you cocky bastard. I've been reading all that shit in the paper about how you don't rate Tipp. We'll show you.' I hoped that the Tipperary players and management felt the same. I had been doing a column in the *Sunday Press* all summer and never missed an opportunity to tell people that I had seen nothing capable of beating Galway. The days of being over-generous to opponents and playing ourselves down were gone. I wanted Tipperary to believe that we were dismissive of them.

In a way, we were. Respect for opponents is one thing, but it must be kept in very close check. Dwell too long on the opposition and you undermine yourself. Yes, we talked about certain aspects of Tipperary's play in our team talks, but always in a negative way. Instead of saying, 'Nicholas English or Pat Fox are very good at this or that so watch them,' I would say, 'Tipperary's only real plan is to get the ball to Fox and English – curb that and they are in trouble.' At all times, I wanted our lads to feel superior to Tipperary.

Tactically, we had worked out our strategy in detail. All that was left to be decided by luck was who would win the toss. Tipperary did and jumped right into our laps by opting to play against the wind. We would have taken it had Conor Hayes won the toss. It wasn't a big deal as far as were concerned but we believed that if we had the wind in the first-half, we could establish a pattern whereby Tipperary would be chasing the game rather than fitting into whatever groove they had worked on. The room for error is far greater when you are chasing the game.

Defining the precise advantage which experience gives a team can be difficult but Conor Hayes, who was playing in his sixth All-Ireland final, gave a classic example even before the start. The lads in the green jackets were scampering here, there and everywhere as usual, making sure things went to schedule. Two of them were despatched to bring the captains together for the throw-in.

Nicholas English trotted over the second he was asked but Hayes, cute as a fox, fiddled around for while pretending to be tying his lace. Then he ambled over and had a quick word with Sylvie. It left English swishing his hurl impatiently waiting for Hayes, who eventually sauntered over casually as if to say, 'I'm here now, we can have the toss'. The old dog for the hard road! Hayes had made a very definite statement to English, even before the ball was thrown in. 'You're new to this, boy, and it's not like anything you have ever experienced before.'

The strategy to counteract English was quite simple. Hayes was a brilliant reader of a game. The plan was to keep English going out from goal as much as possible. Hayes wasn't as quick as English but compensated by reading the angles brilliantly. His mind was very quick indeed. He was a fiercely proud player and, deep down, he had been stung by criticisms of his performance against Offaly and by the general perception among neutrals that he was going to be 'skinned' by English.

Hayes thought an awful lot about how he would approach the duel with English, who was being hyped to the skies. Really, there was no way English could hope to deliver on the expectations some Tipp people had mapped out for him. A year later, he scored 2-11 against Antrim in the All-Ireland final, but a lot of Tipp fans thought he would do that in 1988. It was never a possibility.

Hayes was accused afterwards of dragging and mauling English, but he did what any good full-back would do in similar circumstances. He took English's space every chance he got. There is a subtle difference between that and mauling an opponent. He made life as uncomfortable as he could for English but as for doing it illegally, obviously the referee didn't think so. Anyway, did English get any more special attention than Joe Cooney and Eanna Ryan got at the other end? I don't think so. Besides, what was Hayes supposed to do? Stand back and let English have a field day.

I greatly resented suggestions that Hayes had 'horsed' English out of the game. If anything, Hayes was too gentle as a full-back all through his career. His nation-wide popularity rightly owed much to the fact that he was such a sportsman, but there were days when I wished that he had a bit more brute force in him. But that was not his style.

As the game warmed up, we quickly noticed that Tipperary midfielders, Colm Bonnar and Joe Hayes, were lying back deep on our puck-out with the wind. The signal was sent to John Commins not to give the puck-out full power but instead to drop the ball a bit shorter for Pat Malone and Michael Coleman to run onto. Commins could place a delivery on a 5p piece and we got an ocean of ball that way. Amazingly, Tipp didn't cop onto it and often left Malone and Coleman with an incredible amount of space.

Still, they were hurling well enough until we put on a spurt in the second-quarter to go 0-9 to 0-3 ahead. One of those points was knocked over by Hayes from a free. Tony Keady was our long range free-taker but on this particular ball, Hayes asserted his captain's prerogative to take the free himself. Keady was looking over the bench as if to say, 'What the hell is going on here?' Hayes pointed it and jogged casually back to stand alongside English. Advantage Hayes. English was the one supposed to be doing the scoring.

A few minutes later, Galway won a free in roughly the same position.

Hayes stayed put this time and beckoned Keady to take it. He scored too. Asked later why he hadn't taken the second one, Hayes replied mischievously: 'I reckoned there was no point putting my 100 per cent record on the line.' Point taken, in every sense! It was a typical example of Hayes thinking on his feet. His game was going well so he decided, as captain, to press home the advantage and chance the long range free. Pointing it sent his stock soaring even higher. After that, he handed the job back to Keady.

Tipperary came back at us before half-time and they admitted later that they felt confident that our 0-10 to 0-6 interval lead would not be enough against the wind in the second-half. I wasn't as worried as the Galway fans seemed to have been afterwards. We were hurling well enough and had plenty of experience of playing against the wind.

Sometimes it can be easier to play against the wind. You have to be more precise in everything you do but, if you achieve that, you can get a good momentum going. With Malone and Coleman, who had adapted magnificently to the challenge in his first major championship game, going so well at midfield, Tipp despatched Aidan Ryan out as a roving corner-forward. It was a move we had anticipated.

Presumably, Tipp thought that Sylvie (Linnane) would follow him, thereby leaving a gap in the corner where they could feed the ball for English to run onto. I had instructed Sylvie to hold his position when that happened. Let Aidan Ryan go where he liked – the lads outside could cope with that. Ryan didn't just go deep, he went way, way back. On one occasion he actually popped up in his own full-back line and got a right ear-bashing from the Tipp backs.

Sylvie's job was to be a 'sweeper', playing either in front of Hayes and English or sweeping in between them as cover. There were certain risks involved in that gamble but with Ryan making no real impression outfield, it worked beautifully. Sylvie cleared several balls from the centre, both in front of, and behind, Hayes and English. Quite naturally, English's confidence dropped as the game progressed. It wasn't going his way at all and it really must have been terribly frustrating for him. I was surprised that Tipp didn't give him a roving commission once it became apparent that he was getting no ball inside. It was worth a gamble, especially as there was little between the sides through the second-half.

Ollie Kilkenny was giving the performance of a lifetime on Pat Fox, 'sitting' on him for every second and even when Fox got possession he was forced into impossible angles by Kilkenny, who also got in a few crucial blockdowns. Kilkenny's contribution to that final tended to be over-looked afterwards but it was very, very significant. I always rated Fox extremely highly and while all the focus was on English that year, Fox was every bit as much of a threat. Like Hayes, Kilkenny was brilliant in those situations. Some corner-backs are flashy and like to burst out to make long clearances. Kilkenny was more of a marker and, very often, was hardly noticed. The great thing from our perspective was that his opponent wasn't noticed either.

Of course, it was our half-back line which really broke Tipp's hearts. Peter Finnerty, Tony Keady and Gerry McInerney were unbelievable. Keady's second-half performance was as good as anything seen for years in Croke Park as he stood firm under an aerial bombardment. It was a truly magnificent performance, one which later earned him the Texaco Hurler of the Year Award. Once again, Tipperary played literally into our hands, with Ken Hogan's wind-assisted puck-outs repeatedly dropping on our rampant half-backs. No effort was made to vary the approach, despite its apparent failure.

Finnerty was in his element too, bursting out time after time to clear the ball and showing the kind of determination which helped dissolve Tipperary's resistance. Declan Ryan had some good moments against McInerney but, typically of 'Mac', he never let them upset him and stepped forward to score two vital long range points. They were truly inspirational scores from a man whose striking is unlikely to appear in the purists' text book.

Luck was with us too. Paul Delaney, normally good on long range frees, was off target a couple of times. Commins made a smashing save from Pat Fox and John Leahy actually had the ball into the net, but the referee adjudged that he had been fouled before he took the shot and awarded a free in.

However hard they tried, Tipperary could not draw level and that crucial psychological edge always rested with us. We also had a major advantage in the calibre of subs at our disposal. We were able to inject the massive experience of Noel Lane and Tony Kilkenny into the proceedings. Lane did terrible damage in the full-forward line. We left himself and Eanna Ryan as a two-man full-forward line and, time after time, they won possession and held the ball up until the support arrived. Lane was brilliant at that. Not only did it set up several scoring chances, but it also wasted valuable seconds as he juggled with the ball out in the corner, waiting for reinforcements to arrive. He really was a heart-breaker for Tipperary.

He clinched victory with a goal, ironically off a Tony Kilkenny clearance, beating Conor O'Donovan and clipping the ball past Ken Hogan. Tipperary's day of woe was completed when English drove a penalty over the bar in the closing seconds, to leave them four points adrift, 1-15 to 0-14.

'Had I been in from the start, I would have scored four goals,' Lane said to me that night. Perhaps, but one was enough, especially when it proved to be the winner.

A feeling of relief set in when Gerry Kirwan sounded the final whistle. Now there could be no doubts about it. This Galway team had proved its greatness. We had created history by becoming the first Galway team to win two hurling titles back to back. Another frontier had been flattened. There was a special satisfaction about beating Tipperary in such a close game. The days when Galway always lost the close calls were gone.

As far as we were concerned Galway were every bit as much a hurling power as Tipperary, Kilkenny and Cork. We had lost two finals before winning one, so we had no particular sympathy for Tipperary. They would have to learn the hard way, like everybody else. Besides, the county had presumed far too much going into that final.

Later on in the year, 'Babs' Keating was quoted as saying that our tactics were questionable in that final. The implication seemed to be that we had sledged the resistance out of Tipperary. I was aggrieved by that and fired back in a newspaper interview. I did it to maintain the team's good name. The problem with an accusation like that is that it tends to stick and becomes subconsciously ingrained in people's minds. I couldn't care a toss what most people thought, but I suspected that referees might become that little bit more wary of us in 1989. My fears proved to be well-founded.

Still, at the end of 1988 God was very much in his heaven as far as Galway hurling was concerned. We had lost the Railway Cup final to Leinster in Casement Park in October, but it didn't matter a whole lot. For not only had we won the two-in-a-row, we had also remained unbeaten in our four League games and were heading into 1989 with a song in our hearts. It had the haunting air of 'Three-In-A-Row'. Little did we know then of the trauma which awaited us.

I had planned to resign after the final. I genuinely wanted to get out, but once again the pressure to stay came on. I eventually agreed, probably because the prospect of completing the treble was too appealing to resist. There was something magical about the prospect of winning three-in-a-row. Galway footballers achieved it in the 1960s and it had left an indelible mark on Galway people's consciousness.

Towards the end of 1988, a number of hurling people questioned the fairness of a system which allowed Galway directly into the All-Ireland semi-finals. We were seen as being some way ahead of the rest and I could understand how it galled people that such a strong county as Galway should be in a privileged position. My answer was the same then as now. Introduce the open draw and everybody will start off from the same base. It wasn't our fault that we had no Connacht championship.

Chapter 24

THE KEADY AFFAIR

Former English champion jockey, Johnny Francome, once said that when things are going badly in racing, it's a mistake to think that they won't get worse.

His words kept spinning round in my head as I drove home after training one Sunday evening back in July 1989. Galway were buried waist-high in the murky quicksands of the Tony Keady affair at the time. We were working furiously to wriggle free of them when… bang! We were hit by another savage blow.

We were having a routine, low-key game in training, with no apparent dangers to anybody. When Martin Naughton sailed up to fetch a puck-out, we were looking forward to watching another of his darting runs down the wing. Not this time.

He fell to the ground, roaring in pain. 'Nocko', as I used to call him, was not one for dramatics. He always had been one of the quieter lads and we suspected straightaway that he was in serious trouble. We were right. His knee was badly damaged. There was absolutely no question of him playing in the All-Ireland semi-final against Tipperary. Keady was already ruled out, having been run over by the GAA's latest hobbyhorse. Playing in America without proper clearance was a mortal sin in the GAA's eyes for a time around then. What was that about things getting worse?

The summer of 1989 was one of the most traumatic periods in the history of Galway hurling, a time in which the GAA authorities showed how petty they can be when they put their minds to it. To this day, I can never forgive them for the mean, heartless way they treated Tony Keady and, indeed, Galway.

The season had started out so encouragingly. We had carried on from the All-Ireland success of 1988 and remained unbeaten right through the League. Not only that, but we had kept our great rivals, Tipperary locked in a tight psychological grip by beating them in a fantastic League final in April.

It meant that they still hadn't beaten us in League or Championship since their re-emergence in 1987. They had been without Pat Fox and Nicholas English in the League final, but we were far from being fully tuned either. Yet we beat them by 2-16 to 4-8 in a thrilling game. Our morale was sky-high. Beating them in the League final was important. Once you get a run on a team, it's crucial to keep it going and we certainly had Tipp on the run at that stage.

We had beaten them in the 1987 All-Ireland semi-final, drew with them in a subsequent League game in Thurles, beaten them in the All-Ireland final in '88 and again in a League game in Ballinasloe in March '89. Now we had bested them in a League final as well.

Admittedly the margins were narrow each time, but they were always our way. I know that Tipperary were very encouraged by the fact that they came within two points of us in the League final, despite being without Fox and English, but it didn't worry us. That game was in late April, by which stage Tipp were far more advanced in terms of fitness as the Munster championship was only weeks away. We had coasted through the League with virtually no training and were no more than seventy-five per cent of the way towards peak tuning.

The three-in-a-row outlook was good. Galway and the All-Stars went to the US shortly afterwards. I didn't travel because, by then, another US tour held no great appeal to me. My only interest in the tour was that the Galway lads would enjoy themselves, prior to putting everything else out of their minds in the quest for the three-in-a-row. It was going to be an exciting, challenging, possibly ever historic summer for Galway hurling.

I was never a great one for GAA politics and when I heard some weeks later that Tony Keady, Aidan Staunton and Michael Helebert were in trouble for allegedly playing illegally in New York, I thought, so what? They hadn't been sent off, or anything, so it couldn't amount to much. Not half!

The American scene had always been a minefield in terms of deciding who was legal and who wasn't. If you wanted to choose an All-Star team, all you had to do was call into Shannon Airport any Friday evening. You could have selected two fine teams in the departure lounge as hurlers and footballers travelled Stateside for the weekend junket. It was all good, clean fun. If there were clubs in American daft enough to fund weekend trips, so be it. Players get little enough for their efforts and a weekend in New York holds a lot of appeal for some players.

The GAA authorities made occasional noises about it, but never really sorted it out, largely because many of those running Gaelic

Games in the US didn't give a flying fig about Croke Park edicts. They ran their own independent republic. Besides, the GAA here didn't know exactly what to do. They wanted to bring some order to the weekly migration, but didn't want to upset New York too much.

It was Keady's and Galway's wretched luck that the Croke Park powers choose 1989 to make a clumsy, obstinate stand. Keady, Staunton and Helebert were each suspended for two games by the New York Board in June, following allegations that they had played for Laois against Tipperary without the proper clearances. Keady, who was the central figure because of his high-profile, always insisted that he didn't know he was doing anything wrong and that he was told by GAA officials in New York that they had cleared everything for him.

We thought that the two-match suspension, which didn't mean anything here anyway, was the end of it until stories started appearing in the newspapers that the GAA's Games Administration Committee were not happy with the way the New York Board had handled the case and that they were investigating it. We still weren't too worried. At worst, we reckoned it would be warnings all round.

We had no idea the GAA were going to be so personal about it. The upshot was that in early July, Keady and Co were suspended for twelve months. We couldn't believe it. They weren't guilty of clobbering an opponent over the head or breaking into the Croke Park safe or peddling All-Ireland tickets on the black market. No, all they had done was play a hurling game in New York. Yet, they were banned for a year because bits of paper weren't signed in triplicate or some such bureaucratic nonsense.

The minute I heard the severity of the sentence, my heart sank. We could appeal, but Galway's record of getting concessions in Croke Park was not great. Correction, it was downright awful. A year earlier, Brendan Lynskey had been suspended for three months after playing in some mickey-mouse seven-a-side competition. He was eventually cleared to play in the championship after an appeal to Central Council, but not without some worrying days and a real fight.

Lynskey, who was living in Dublin at the time, had played in a seven-a-side tournament run by the Offalyman's Association. He was sent off and was subsequently suspended by the GAC. Our argument was that, as proper sanction had never been granted for the tournament, it did not have official status and that the GAC had no power to deal with disciplinary matters arising from it. How could they suspend a player for being sent off in a tournament which they didn't even know was taking place? Well, they did, and it took an appeal to Central Council to get it rescinded. It was a slap in the teeth for the GAC as Central Council upheld our appeal, 29-6.

That might have looked like a great victory for Galway but, in truth, it wasn't. We should never have been there in the first place and I'm convinced that when Keady came back before Central Council a year later, some members thought, 'Oh, no, not Galway again'. The Lynskey case may well have coloured their thinking, even if they did uphold his appeal.

A marker had been put down. Galway would have to watch their step. Galway might have done a great deal for hurling as the West's only real power, but that didn't seem to count for much in the corridors of power.

As the weeks dragged on, it became apparent that diplomatic channels were getting us nowhere with the Keady affair. Appealing to the Management Committee looked a complete waste of time, since it was most unlikely that they would overturn the GAC's decision. We felt we had some chance if we could get the appeal before Central Council, which was far more broadly based, having representatives from all thirty-two counties.

Towards the end of July, the *Irish Press* ran a story that Galway were considering withdrawing from the All-Ireland semi-final in protest at the way the Keady affair had been handled. It was something that Phelim Murphy and Bernie O'Connor and myself had discussed. We were so incensed about the whole thing that we felt something needed to be done to keep the Keady affair on the agenda.

Once the boycott threat was mooted, it became a major story. Several newspaper reporters turned up in Kells when we played a challenge game against Antrim on the Wednesday week before the semi-final. We confirmed that, as far as the selectors were concerned, the threat to withdraw was a genuine option. It was the front page lead on the following day's *Irish Press* and all hell broke loose.

Deep down we knew that we could do no more than threaten to withdraw, not without the backing of the County Board anyway. In fairness to them, they could not support a boycott as it would have meant that every football and hurling team in Galway would be suspended for a year. But had that not been the case and if I were the sole decision-maker, I would have pulled out of the semi-final. Phelim and Bernie felt the same. There is no doubt in my mind about it. That might look drastic but there are times when one has to stand up and be counted. What the GAA were doing was wrong. Maybe not in terms of their rule-book (although that was questionable, given that as far as we were concerned they had not applied the rules to the letter of the law), but writing a rule into the official guide does not make it morally or ethically sound.

The Management Committee gave us a mini-concession when they decided to call a special meeting of Central Council for the Tuesday night before the semi-final to hear the appeal. I have no doubt that they did that because of our threat to withdraw. The last thing the GAA wanted was an empty Croke Park on semi-final day (think of the revenue they would have lost) and despite their public comments, they did not know how far we were prepared to go. We thought we had a fair chance of winning the appeal, on the basis that the Central Council had a nation-wide representation and that most of the members knew damn well that players from their own counties had been as 'guilty' as Keady and Co only they had not been caught.

Unfortunately, we also knew that some of the top echelons of the GAA wanted the Keady suspension to stand. They always denied that they saw him as a big fish, whose suspension would serve as warning to the smaller fry, but I never accepted that. The manner in which they pursued the case supported my theory.

Frank Burke, Jimmy Halliday and Joe McDonagh represented Galway at the Central Council meeting and made splendid submissions. The problem was that enough delegates were not prepared to go against the original GAC decision and the appeal was thrown out on a 20-18 vote. There was even a call to have the meeting held in camera but it was beaten on a 22-13 vote. I found it extremely distasteful that there were thirteen members who didn't even want the public to know what happened at the meeting. So much for democracy.

What made the whole thing farcical was that five members of the Games Administration Committee, who had suspended Keady and Co in the first place, were also on Central Council. Effectively they were hearing an appeal on their own decision.

From any viewpoint, that was unfair. A few years later, the GAA were forced to change their rules on who was eligible to vote on an appeal. It took a court action by Waterford County Board chairman, Eamonn Murphy to bring about the change. That's the sort of thing which drives me mad about GAA officialdom. A five-year old child could see that their procedures were defective, yet it took a High Court judge to convince them that this was the case. How, in all fairness, could you allow people who had already made up their minds to sit in and vote on an appeal against their original decision?

I would love to have asked the twenty Central Council delegates who voted to keep Keady out of hurling for a year if they knew of anybody in their own counties who had played illegally in the US and got away with it. It's easy to be self-righteous when you are dealing with a player from another county. Besides, did they think that the punishment fitted the 'crime'?

We trained in Athenry on the night of the meeting and we were sitting in the Mart canteen, having a meal when the phone rang. Phelim Murphy took the call and I knew instantly from the look on his face that we had lost. He gave us the thumbs down sign by way of confirmation.

One of the most irritating aspects of the Central Council meeting was the fact that we did not even get the support of all the Connacht delegates. That was hard to take. We were not appealing for clemency for a player who had hit his opponent. All Keady had done was to play the game he loves, yet he could not rely on the full support of his own province in the appeal.

As Galway are the only Connacht county flying the hurling flag at the highest level, one might have expected more support but no, he could go to hell as far as some from the West were concerned. It confirmed, I suppose, that overall the Connacht Council sees itself primarily as a football Council. It's something Galway hurling should always bear in mind.

Two months later, GAA Director-General, Liam Mulvihill said in an interview that if Galway had not gone for a full pound of flesh and sought to have the suspensions cut, Central Council might well have agreed. We didn't need Keady for the League – we wanted him for the All-Ireland semi-final. Besides, if the GAA thought his 'crime' merited a year's suspension why should they cut it? Galway were arguing that the suspension was flawed from the start, as the objection to Keady had not been lodged for ten days after the game. The rules state that it must be lodged inside seven days. All of which goes to show that the GAA can find a way around their own rules when they get the bit between their teeth.

Some time later, it emerged that there was a doubt about Paul Delaney's eligibility for Tipperary, arising out of some transfer problem with a London club the year before. Tipperary left him out of the All-Ireland final team, possibly fearing an objection if they had played him.

Personally, I doubt if there would have been. It most certainly would not have come from Galway. We were well aware of the circumstances of the Delaney case a few days after the semi-final. It was well inside the time limit to raise an objection, but we had no intention of doing so. There was no way we would attempt to inflict the sort of pain Keady had experienced on another player. Nor indeed would we have done anything to damage Tipperary's chance in the All-Ireland final. We had a great rivalry with them but it never extended beyond the playing fields. It was a pity that Delaney was denied the chance to play in the 1989 final and there was nobody more delighted than me to see him winning an All-Ireland medal in 1991.

The Keady-Delaney controversy dragged on because deep down everybody knew that a few players had been sacrificed in the interests of regularising the position regarding weekend junkets to the US. A few months later, the GAA calmly announced that an amnesty would be given to any player who came forward and admitted that he had played illegally in America.

It was laughable, really. A few months earlier, the GAA were telling Keady and Co that they couldn't play for a year – now they were inviting players to 'turn themselves in' in return for an amnesty. Not only that, but players were granted an amnesty without their names being made public. In fact, you had the crazy situation where players were suspended and reinstated on the same night, without having their names released. Any wonder Galway people have never forgiven the GAA authorities?

Interestingly too, the GAA took no action against the officials in New York who had persuaded Keady and Co to play there. If there was a case to answer, surely they were more guilty than players, who simply wanted to hurl. But no, the Croke Park authorities ran for cover on that one, stating that it was a matter for the New York authorities. The GAA punished the players but washed their hands of any responsibility in relation to the officials who had caused the problem in the first place. Were they not all GAA members, subject to the same rules? Apparently not. All in all, a dark and dingy episode in the history of the GAA.

Had we withdrawn from the semi-final, it would have blown the whole fiasco sky-high. We would have got little support for such a strong stand but there are times when you have to stand alone, especially when you believe in what you are fighting for. Frankly, I don't believe that the GAA would have accepted our withdrawal. I believe that somehow they would have come up with a compromise. After all, the gate receipts from the All-Ireland semi-finals that year amounted to £343,000. With respect to Offaly and Antrim, at least £275,000 was generated by the Galway-Tipperary game. Can you imagine the GAA allowing that sort of money to slip away?

GAA Director-General, Liam Mulvihill, made an oblique reference to the whole affair in his annual report some months later. He defended the GAA's right to impose heavy suspensions for playing illegally on the grounds that it was a premeditated offence whereas an on-the-field incident was not. Premeditated? Does anybody seriously believe that Tony Keady said to himself when he left on the All-Stars' trip, 'I'm going to play illegally in New York before I come home'.

Liam Mulvihill also wrote that there was an onus on officials to accept discipline as they would expect others to accept it from them. Fine, if the discipline is based on fair play. When it's not, as was the case in the Keady affair, then nobody is under an obligation to accept it. On the contrary, they are duty-bound to oppose it. No rule book can prevent people from fighting for justice.

Chapter 25

CHAOS IN CROKE PARK

One of the great ironies of the 'Keady Affair' is that Tony's absence was not solely responsible for our 1989 All-Ireland semi-final defeat by Tipperary. The accompanying sideshow was a minor distraction (although not to the extent some commentators suggested), but Keady's actual absence was not as significant as many thought.

Let's put it this way. We didn't spend the entire summer moaning to each other about it at training sessions. It was something which was simmering away in the background but in no way did it intrude on our preparations. We suspected for some time that Keady was unlikely to be playing and had planned accordingly. Sean Treacy was his obvious replacement at centre-back and we were quite happy that he would do a fine job. Treacy had played at left half-back in the League final against Tipperary but, with Gerry McInerney back from America, switching Treacy to the centre was the best option. Having said that, we would have chosen Keady had he been cleared on the Tuesday night before the semi-final. After all, he was first choice centre-back and had played brilliantly against Tipperary in the previous year's All-Ireland final.

Some players might have been effected by all the controversy but not Keady. He is the sort that if 50,000 spectators turned out to see a game, he would be wondering why it wasn't 55,000 just to see him. His confidence was incredible. It was part of his personal game plan and it rarely let him down. He had continued to train with us right through the summer of 1989 despite his suspension, so we had no doubts about his fitness. It was tough on him, not knowing whether he would be eligible but he put in a good campaign and was as fit as the rest.

Still, Treacy slotted in well at centre-back, playing soundly from start to finish. He even pointed a long range free (a Keady speciality) early on and generally came out of the game very well. The absence of Martin Naughton and Noel Lane was to prove far more damaging than Keady's unavailability. Naughton's pace up the wing had always been a vital part of Galway's attacking strategy. Not only did it spread panic into defences, it also created room for his colleagues. When a whole defence is running backwards, the forwards have every advantage. Naughton was brilliant at making that initial break.

With Naughton gone, we would have turned to Noel Lane to start. We had used him as a super-sub in the previous two years but we needed him from the start for this game. We would have re-jigged our attack to slot him into the corner. Tipperary hated the sight of Lane. He had scored a goal against them in each of the two previous championship games and generally out-witted them. But he was gone too, with a long-term injury, so we selected Ray Duane, a gifted but enigmatic player.

He had played a blinder on the minor team which lost the 1986 All-Ireland semi-final to Offaly and had been on the senior panel for some time so we felt that he had to be given his chance. It didn't work out. Ray never got into the game as we had hoped he would, although he was unlucky on a few occasions. We were criticised afterwards for playing him but what do you do with a player like that? You have to give him his chance sometime. He had been a brilliant minor and had all the skills but never quite managed to express them at the highest level. That was a great pity, both for him and Galway.

Probably never in GAA history did an All-Ireland hurling semi-final generate so much interest. A sell-out crowd of 64,127 turned up at Croke Park for the Offaly-Antrim and Galway-Tipperary double header. With respect to Offaly and Antrim, at least eighty per cent were there for the Galway-Tipp clash. The atmosphere around Croke Park that day was electric. All the more so when Antrim shocked Offaly in the first semi-final.

Given the 'Keady Affair', there was always going to be a special tension about that semi-final but with Galway and Tipperary having established themselves as the top two teams in the land over the previous two seasons, there was a sort of Muhammed Ali-Joe Frazier backdrop to further fuel the fire. This really was a winner-take-all match. Had we won, we would have been set fair for the historic three-in-a-row. Had Tipperary lost to us for the third consecutive season, it might well have knocked the heart out of that particular squad.

By now, Tipperary were in their third season at the top and were getting better. They were also more experienced at handling big day pressures. We expected that we would have to be at least on a par with 1988 form to beat them. As it turned out, we would not have had to be that good, because Tipperary didn't play all that well apart from a glorious spell in the first-half.

Eanna Ryan gave Galway a great start with a goal in the first minute. It was a typical piece of Ryan trickery, sneaking in where nobody was looking to poke the ball over the line. We led by 1-1 to 0-1 after five minutes. So far so good. What happened after that will never be forgotten in Galway, or Tipperary for that matter. We went a full seventeen minutes without scoring while Tipperary knocked over point after point. We were all over the place. Our full-back line was in trouble, although in fairness, they were being subjected to incredible pressure, because we weren't competing enough further out the field. It was one of the most disjointed periods I can recall the Galway team of that era producing. Nothing went right.

After their 1988 experiences, Tipperary had abandoned the idea of playing Nicholas English at full-forward, opting instead for Cormac Bonnar with English in the corner. Bonnar, English and Pat Fox were causing us all sorts of problems. Tipperary should have been out of sight but somehow we managed to hang on. It was instinct, I suppose. Our team had been together a long time and had a nose for survival even through the worst of storms. Eanna Ryan poached another typically opportunist goal just before half-time and, amazingly, we were only two points behind, 0-11 to 2-3 at the break.

We were blessed to be so close. But once we were, I felt that we had a great chance of winning because sooner or later it was inevitable that we would raise our game. We weren't going to hand our title over without a fight. We felt quite confident coming out for the second-half. Tipperary knew that they had produced some great hurling, but they were still only two points ahead of us. I reckoned that, if and when we raised our game, the doubts would come flooding back for Tipperary.

Something we hadn't bargained on was the influence Wexford referee, John Denton, would exert on the game. We felt at half-time that we were getting absolutely nothing from him.

Things got worse in every sense in the second-half. Pat Fox threaded his way through for a goal and a little later, Sylvie Linnane was sent off, allegedly for striking Nicholas English. It was a very harsh decision.

Linnane's offence was hardly any more serious than that of the Tipperary player who struck Peter Finnerty with his hurley in the first-half. The culprit escaped without even a booking! Eanna Ryan was hit off the ball early on and that offender escaped with a booking. Any wonder we were incensed when Linnane was sent off?

Even with Linnane gone and a six-point deficit to face, I felt that we could still win. We brought Finnerty back to corner-back to mark English while Michael Coleman, who had plenty of experience of half-back play, came back to right-half and Joe Cooney went to midfield to partner Pat Malone. That left us with five forwards. Tipperary were in front but there was no great conviction about them. It was as if they were looking over their shoulders, waiting for a Galway surge. That happens to teams in those sort of circumstances. We had beaten Tipp in all the 'majors' over the previous seasons and they had a deep-rooted respect for us. They knew right well that, even with fourteen men, this game was far from over as far as Galway were concerned.

When our comeback came, it was full of the awesome fire and power which that Galway squad could muster. Cooney got on top at midfield and our attack, although out-numbered, were using space sensibly and kept chipping away at Tipp's lead. Once again, we were to feel the painful slap of the referee's hand. 'Hopper' McGrath could hardly be described as a dirty player. In fact, if I were to compile a list of honest, genuine, sporting players, 'Hopper' would probably top it. His name would never be found in a directory of 'hard men'.

So when he launched himself awkwardly into a tackle on Conor O'Donovan ten minutes from the end, I remember thinking: 'Hopper, what a stupid thing to do, you're giving the Tipp defence (which was creaking under the pressure at the time) a soft free out'. O'Donovan went down and play was held up for a while as he got attention.

John Denton ran over to McGrath, and sent him off. We couldn't believe it. Neither could 'Hopper', whose frustration levels reached boiling point as he passed by John Leahy on his way of the pitch. Leahy said something to him and 'Hopper' lashed out at him. It was completely out of character and shows just how crazy things had become.

I remain convinced that we would have beaten Tipperary if McGrath had not been sent off. We had coped with Linnane's absence, but now we were down to thirteen men. Still we kept plugging on. Eanna Ryan, who was revelling in the challenge, was flattened as he galloped through. The offender escaped with a booking.

We came within two points of Tipp with three minutes to go. They extended the lead to three and were hanging on grimly as the game ticked into injury time. Given all the second-half stoppages, we thought there was at least three, if not four, minutes of injury time but no, the referee played less than a minute. Tipperary 1-17 Galway 2-11. Our title was gone.

My immediate reaction was one of disgust because I felt that we had not got a fair deal anywhere along the line. Tipperary were understandably euphoric. Not only had they beaten their bogey team but they had also qualified for the final against Antrim. They never admitted it, of course, but Tipperary felt all along that they would dismiss Antrim with relative ease in the final. It turned out that way too.

It takes time for a defeat like ours to sink in, but there was no escaping the questions. Within minutes, reporters were pounding on our dressing-room door, asking what had gone wrong? How did we feel? What did we think of the referee? Bloody hell, how did they think we felt? As for the refereeing, well they saw the game, let them make up their own minds. That's what they were being paid to do.

I made a few choice remarks about the standard of refereeing, knowing well that they would probably land me in trouble with the GAA authorities but not really caring. All the GAA bosses were in Croke Park that day so they had seen for themselves. As far as I was concerned, John Denton did not have a good day. It was a view shared by many others, as the newspaper reports testified.

'Galway will argue for many a day that they were beaten by the referee as well as by their greatest rivals of recent times. That may seem to be a harsh criticism of John Denton who, like all referees, had an unenviable task in a contest of this importance. But it must be said that several of his decisions were dubious and most of them were in favour of Tipperary' ... Paddy Downey, *Irish Times*.

'Denton himself could have been censured for an inept performance. He blew for fouls which no-one but himself saw, ignored blatant fouls and made other decisions, which were baffling. From an early stage, he was struggling to maintain control and proved to be a burden on the players, the Galway side especially'... Donal Keenan, *Irish Independent*.

'From a distance, Galway may be depicted as wretched losers who lost all dignity with their crown, but they are entitled to a fairer postscript. For it must be said that John Denton yesterday looked like a man they had offended grievously. From start to finish, this supposed voice of reason had clearly lost his way.... Vincent Hogan, *Irish Independent*.

'He ('Hopper' McGrath) was the second of the players to be sent off by a referee who didn't fully exert his authority on the field and didn't inspire confidence off it'... Jim O'Sullivan, *Cork Examiner*.

'Galway have good reason to feel aggrieved with some of John Denton's refereeing decisions but in the overall context they only have themselves to blame for they over-reacted'… John Guiton, *Tipperary Star*.

Clearly, I wasn't alone in believing that the referee didn't have a good day! Interestingly, both Vincent Hogan and John Guiton are natives of Tipperary, yet they acknowledged that Galway had reason to be unhappy.

GAA Director-General, Liam Mulvihill, said the following week that there were 'several incidents of a complete lack of discipline both on and off the field and that is something which will have to be examined'. Well, Holy God, as Miley from Glenroe might say! What about Galway's grievances? Did anybody in authority care to listen? I presume I was being cited for a 'lack of discipline'. I must have been, as I was subsequently suspended. I greatly resented that. I deal with disciplinary matters virtually every day of my working life, so I have some experience on the subject. Believe me, discipline comes from respect and you cannot force respect out of people by waving a rule book at them. Especially when you don't always adhere to the rules which you have set down. No, you have to earn respect.

It was mischievously suggested afterwards that Galway had gone into that semi-final in the wrong frame of mind and that we lost our heads once the game started going against us. I was personally criticised for making too much of the 'Keady Affair' rather than playing it down and getting on with the training.

My good friend, Joe McDonagh wrote in a magazine article last year that the 'hopes of a three-in-a-row evaporated due to over-concern with off-the-field activities'. No they didn't. Joe and I go back a long way together but we would be coming at things from different angles in terms of GAA administration and bureaucracy. Let's put it this way, it's unlikely that I will be the next President of the GAA! Joe probably will and I have no doubt that he will make a great success of it. Joe would favour the diplomatic role in any controversy. So would I if I thought it would work, but it most patently failed in 1989, which is why we threatened to withdraw from the semi-final. No, Joe, 'over-concern with off-the-field activities' did not cost us the three-in-a-row.

The fact is that we did play down the Keady affair in training. What we did publicly had other motives behind it. We wanted to highlight how ridiculous and unfair the whole thing was. We trained all along on the assumption that Keady would not be playing and had the Central Council over-turned the suspension, it would have been a bonus. But we would not be human if we didn't feel that we were being got at for some strange reason. The claim that our public expressions of outrage over the treatment of Keady and Co cost us the game is simply not true.

A year earlier, we had to fight like hell to have Brendan Lynskey reinstated after being sent off in a seven-a-side tournament in Dublin. The Games Administration Committee handed him a three-months, suspension despite the fact that there were major question marks over whether or not the competition was officially constituted in the first place. For whatever reason, we were not popular in the corridors of power.

By an amazing coincidence, the Meath football team, which also won the two-in-a-row in 1987-88 were in the same boat as far as the GAA hierarchy were concerned. They never got the credit they deserved and when they were beaten in the 1989 Leinster final, I suspect that some very prominent GAA officials were chuckling gleefully under their hands.

Once it became clear that Keady was not going to be eligible, we tried to turn his absence to our advantage, claiming that it was us against the rest. We didn't know how true that really was until semi-final day.

The sending off of 'Hopper' McGrath compounded our frustration. With McGrath gone, we felt that we had to beat Tipperary, the Games Administration Committee, the Central Council and the referee. No, I'm not being paranoid but I will ask this question, 'What other county got such treatment from officialdom in recent years?' None that I can think of. Even Meath footballers never had as many boulders placed in front of them.

I am not suggesting that there was a 'get Galway' campaign out there. It seems to me that the problem is one of isolation. We are on our own in Connacht, something which is very obvious when you examine how Galway referees fare when it comes to big-match appointments.

Galway have won All-Ireland finals at all levels in recent years, yet none of our referees ever get near the big games. It's not as if they are officiating at a lower level on the club scene either. After all, Kiltormer and Sarsfields have won the last three All-Ireland finals, so the county must be doing something right.

The standard of refereeing is as good in Galway as anywhere else – maybe even better – but the GAA authorities either don't accept that, which is a disgrace, or ignore it, which is an even bigger disgrace.

Unlike the other traditional hurling counties from Leinster and Munster, Galway referees do not have anybody batting for them at the highest level and, consequently, they are left on the sidelines. It's all wrong.

Galway referees don't have a Connacht championship in which to advertise their talents. Leinster and Munster generally stick by their own referees so it's impossible for a Galway referee to get any profile during the summer months. Come the autumn and the Games Administration Committee will appoint the referees who have been performing at the highest levels in Leinster and Munster.

That may seem logical enough, but why don't the GAC appoint more Galway referees for League games? Come on down, lads, and take a look at the standard of refereeing in Galway. You will be surprised how good it is.

It was very easy to blame us for over-playing the Keady hand coming up to the 1989 semi-final. The loss of Naughton and Lane was equally significant, but there was nothing we could do about that. We continued to highlight the Keady affair because of the apparent injustice of it. If highlighting injustice is wrong in some people's eyes then I'm glad I am looking through my own.

Speaking out may not make you popular among the GAA's top echelons but so what? I would prefer to say my piece and face the Games Administration Committee's music than sing dumb and try to live with cowardice. After all, the GAA belongs to all its members, not just those who know the way to committee meetings in Croke Park. Sadly, a lot of people seem to lose sight of that very, very quickly.

CHAPTER 26
COULD THIS SEASON END, PLEASE?

I thought long and hard about resigning as team manager after the 1989 All-Ireland semi-final. I was already two years over my original term and I was thoroughly sick of the way we had been treated by the GAA over the Keady affair.

I was back before the Games Administration Committee a few weeks after the semi-final to answer charges of bringing the GAA into disrepute for comments made after the Tipperary game. The whole thing was a charade but I had to go through with it.

Frankly, I was past caring. They could accuse me of anything they liked – I really didn't give a damn. It would be a sad day if any sports organisation could take away the right of free speech and I wasn't going to be gagged. The GAC suspended me for two months but, as in 1986 when I was also banned for speaking my mind, it didn't make any difference to me. The suspension was virtually up by the time the National League started.

It was an amazing scenario really. At one stage seven Galway players and two officials stood suspended. Phelim Murphy escaped a ban for his comments, but was warned about his future conduct!

Tony Keady, Michael Helebert, Aidan Staunton were all banned for playing in New York. 'Hopper' McGrath and Sylvie Linnane were suspended after being sent off against Tipperary, while Steve Mahon was suspended after being dismissed in a junior game and Brendan Lynskey was banned for comments made to a newspaper on the day of the All-Ireland semi-final.

Bernie O'Connor and I were also suspended so, all in all, Galway hurling looked in a turbulent state in the autumn of 1989. We were being depicted as raging mavericks by the GAA authorities. Presumably, they never once looked into their own hearts and asked: why has this happened? It wasn't as if we were a confrontational lot, always looking for trouble. Our disciplinary record was as good, if not better, than most other counties, yet here we were locked tightly inside the GAA's punishment bay, where the quality of mercy was very definitely strained.

Frankly, I believe that deep down the GAA authorities knew that we had reason to feel bitter but they could never admit it. They were tied up in their own bureaucracy, which acted as a shield against the real world, a world where a squad of players wanted to train and play and win without outside interference.

My first reaction was to distance myself from it and spend my time outside the wire, away from all the pressures and the pettiness. Gradually though, my attitude changed. Why the hell should I let small-minded decisions force me out? Galway hurling meant more to me than that. So did the players who had brought such honour to Galway and to hurling. Besides, I didn't believe that we had lost the All-Ireland title. It was more a question of having one hand tied behind our back and trying to play with the other.

I felt no resentment towards Tipperary when they won the All-Ireland final. Far from it. If Galway were not destined to win the title, I felt that Tipperary deserved it, after two bitter disappointments in 1987-88. As it happened, the final turned out to be an anti-climax as Antrim's lack of big-time experience completely undermined them and they were beaten by eighteen points.

Antrim's achievement in reaching the All-Ireland final probably didn't get the accolades it deserved because of the controversy after our game with Tipperary. We had played Antrim in a challenge game in Kells on the Wednesday week before the semi-final and they had shown absolutely no sign of the raging torrent of ambition they were to unleash against Offaly. That wasn't very surprising, I suppose, since both the Antrim and Galway players had dashed to Kells after work and got straight out of cars and onto the pitch. Still, we won so well that it was difficult to envisage Antrim making up enough ground to beat Offaly. Somehow, they did.

I was delighted for Antrim manager, Jim Nelson, in particular. He had always believed in Antrim hurling and, at long last, he had been rewarded. I had a great relationship with Nelson and indeed the Antrim players. Like ourselves, they were outsiders, looking in on Leinster and Munster.

In fairness, they had it much tougher than us. The isolation factor was a big problem for them. They had to travel long distances, even to get challenge games. At least in Galway, we were near the mainstream action. We were conscious of Antrim being sort of kindred spirits of ours, and, where possible, Galway always facilitated them with challenge games. We established quite a bond down through the years and it's something I believe will always be there.

We missed Antrim's great win over Offaly, having gone into the dressing-room to prepare for our semi-final. On our way onto the pitch, we could hardly believe it. Antrim officials and players were celebrating in the tunnel and they could hardly have been any happier had they got the McCarthy Cup. That was their All-Ireland final.

Without in any way being disparaging, I think both Tipperary and Galway knew that our game would be the 'real' final. It was most unlikely that Antrim would have beaten us either as we were even more experienced than Tipperary.

Besides, it was very hard for Antrim to keep the lid on things before the final. Whenever a new team reaches an All-Ireland final for the first time, there is an inevitable explosion of hype and, try as they will, it is not easy for the players to escape it. That was especially true in Antrim who were not expected to reach the final.

Our sad experiences that autumn had a strange sort of effect on the squad. After the initial frustration had lifted, we decided to give it another go and to dedicate everything to regaining the All-Ireland title in 1990. The Railway Cup, so often our rallying force, was held in Wexford in early October and, without even mentioning to each other, we decided to have a right go at it.

Between injuries and suspensions, we were well below full-strength, but pride can be a great motivator. In fact, we were without eight of the team which started against Tipperary in the semi-final, plus of course, Keady, Naughton and Lane.

We won the competition in dramatic circumstances. We beat Leinster by 1-19 to 2-15 on the Saturday and had two points to spare against Munster, 4-16 to 3-17 on the Sunday. I suppose we saw it as some little satisfaction as Munster had six of the Tipperary team which won the All-Ireland final. Our team that day was: John Commins, Dermot Fahy, Sean Treacy, Sean Dolphin; Peter Finnerty, Michael Coleman, Pat Higgins; John Hardiman, Tom Monaghan; Anthony Cunningham, Joe Cooney, Michael Kenny; Gerry Burke, Syl Dolan, Eanna Ryan.

The 1989/90 League was nothing more than an irritant after that. The squad had grown weary of events on and off the pitch and we wanted to fast-forward right up to August 1990 and the All-Ireland semi-final. Of course, we had to wait but, try as we might, we couldn't lift ourselves for the League.

In fact, it was a total disaster. We lost the opening game to Cork by two points and then flopped to Dublin in Pearse Stadium. We were four points up with six minutes to go, but Dublin finished with a sprint and beat us by four points. We beat Limerick well in Ballinasloe and then headed for Thurles for the final game of the year against Tipperary.

It was being billed as a grudge match but it was nothing of the kind. Winning or losing would prove nothing for either side. Winning would not bring back our All-Ireland crown. Losing would not take the McCarthy Cup away from Tipperary. It turned out to be a low-key affair, which Tipperary won well, 1-14 to 0-11. Deservedly so.

None of the ugly undercurrents which had raised their mischievous heads in the All-Ireland semi-final surfaced. Limerick referee, Terence Murray, did a good job on it as usual. I always liked Murray as a referee. I found him tough but sensible and he invariably managed to mix common sense with the letter of the law. That's what makes a good referee. Wexford's Dickie Murphy is in much the same boat, but unfortunately good referees are in short supply generally.

We were delighted to hear the final whistle that evening, not just because Tipperary were beating us well but because we wanted to bring the curtain down on what we regarded as a miserable season. We had won the League final, the Railway Cup and the Oireachtas final but by Christmas 1989, they didn't count for much. Our entire year had been dedicated to retaining the All-Ireland title. The three-in-a-row was the real goal and we hadn't got it. The other titles, nice and all as they were, were tasteless by comparison.

That shows how much things had changed in Galway hurling. In 1975, winning the League title sparked off a huge celebration. In 1980, the Railway Cup success was regarded as a fine achievement. Now we had won the two of them in the same year – plus the Oireachtas – and we felt the season was a failure. Nothing wrong with that, of course. Ambition is a sign of positive thinking.

There was no escaping the sense of loss in Galway hurling at the end of 1989. We would have accepted it had we lost our title in ordinary circumstances. But we hadn't. Forces outside our control had a mischievous hand in it. That made it very galling as the three-in-a-row would have been something special. It has only been achieved seven times in hurling history and never by a county outside the top three, Cork, Kilkenny and Tipperary. It's a very difficult thing to do. Take Kilkenny, who have won twenty-five All-Ireland titles. They have won just one three-in-a-row (1911-12-13). They have had some great teams in the meantime, but the three-in-a-row has eluded them. Tipperary have won the three-in-a-row twice but have not done it since the 1950s; while Cork completed their fourth three-in-a-row success in 1978. So it terms of greatness, it stands as a real monument to a side. Galway were good enough to achieve it in 1987-88-89, if we were left alone.

Our first League match of 1990 was against Kilkenny in Nowlan Park. They hurled us off the pitch, eventually winning by 5-12 to 0-10. We could not have been flatter had a dozen bulldozers spent the week running all over us. Excuses? We hadn't any, we were plain terrible. By now, surviving in Division One was becoming increasingly tricky, even after we beat Antrim in Ballinasloe.

Eventually, we found ourselves needing to beat Wexford in New Ross to avoid relegation. A year earlier we had hammered Wexford in a League game in Tuam, but a lot had changed. Besides, we had always found it hard to take points out of Wexford and this was no exception. We were a point up with a few minutes to go but they levelled and then Jimmy Holohan knocked over the winning point from a 'seventy' in injury time.

We didn't know it at the time but the Tipperary team were all gathered around transistor radios in Nowlan Park on the same day. They had gone into the match against Kilkenny level with us on points. They drew with Kilkenny in a game which finished a few minutes ahead of ours.

As they came off the field they were told we were a point ahead – a result which would have sentenced them to relegation – but they got a late reprieve when Wexford bounced back to beat us. We were relegated and Tipp stayed up. Such is the thin line between Divisions One and Two.

Apart from the initial shock of being relegated, we weren't too worried about it. We had enjoyed good League runs in the previous five years and it was inevitable that we would have one rotten season. Besides, a spell in Division Two never does any great harm as all the top sides have shown.

We knew even at that stage that, bar any great discoveries on the club scene through the summer, we would be heading into the championship with much the same squad as in 1989, so being out of the League so early wasn't a major problem. That year, for instance,

Kilkenny went on to win the League but were demolished by Offaly in the first round of the Leinster championship.

It's amazing how quickly things can turn around. We had gone right through the 1988/89 League season without defeat. Twelve months on and we had lost five of seven League games. Deep down, though, we knew that there was still plenty of spirit, plenty of ambition and, most of all, plenty of hurling left in the squad. What we needed was a summer training campaign to get us back on track.

CHAPTER 27
'A GOOD TEAM SHOULD NEVER LOSE A SEVEN-POINT LEAD'

Ask Conor Hayes about his best ever performance in a Galway jersey and he is quite likely to tell you that it was the 1990 All-Ireland final. But he was on the subs' bench. Exactly!

Nobody was more amused than Hayes by the hero-status he acquired after Cork beat Galway in that final. He had lost his place after a nightmare All-Ireland quarter-final against London and had not regained it. Galway conceded five goals in one of the most astonishing finals seen for years and immediately word went out: 'Had Hayes been at full-back, none of this would have happened'.

Many Galway fans suddenly developed a dose of amnesia. Some, who had whispered in my ear after the 1988 All-Ireland semi-final that unless we dropped Hayes for the final, Nicholas English would have a field day, now saw things in a different light. 'Hayes was always a man for the big day. No way would five goals have gone in had he been playing'.

I cannot say whether or not they would have. But I can say for certain that I have absolutely no regrets about leaving him out of the team. Nobody in Galway has more respect for him than I have, but the Conor Hayes of 1990 was not the Conor Hayes who had played so splendidly for Galway through the 1980s.

Hayes' status as a person of real character was underlined by his attitude to the 1990 final. He could easily have rowed in with the view that he should have been playing and criticised the selectors, especially after Cork's remarkable comeback. But to his credit he took it like a man and I actually read one interview where he said that while he would love to have played, he would probably have picked Sean Treacy ahead of himself, had he been a selector.

Hayes just wasn't firing right that summer. For most of his career, he suffered a lot from back problems. He was a long way below his best both in the 1989 League final and the All-Ireland semi-final against Tipperary. Frankly, I think his time had come and I'm not sure his heart was in it in 1990. Still, he was a proven winner so we decided to play him against London in the quarter-final to see how he would go.

With Sylvie Linnane out of commission, we switched Peter Finnerty from wing-back to corner-back, put Sean Treacy at left full-back for the injured Ollie Kilkenny and drafted Pat Malone back to right half-back in place of Finnerty. Tom Monaghan partnered Michael Coleman at midfield. It was an experimental line-up but then a game against London should have left us with some room to try a new formation.

The match was in Ballinasloe on the Sunday evening after Galway had lost a Connacht football final to Roscommon in Dr Hyde Park. It was a beautiful evening and despite the fact that Galway were well fancied to beat London, a massive crowd turned out. We won alright, by 1-23 to 2-11, but it was a most unsatisfactory performance. Any Offaly spies who were in Duggan Park must have been very optimistic about their semi-final prospects as they left that evening.

Conor Hayes wasn't the only one who played poorly but we were especially worried about him. Finnerty had not looked very happy in the corner either and Malone was needed back at midfield. We dropped Hayes and Monaghan for the semi-final and brought in Dermot Fahy and Ollie Kilkenny as corner-backs in a re-shuffled defence which had Treacy at full-back. The good news in attack was that we had Martin Naughton back for his first championship match in two years. I suppose the main focus in the semi-final was on Sean Treacy and he performed solidly in an easy win over a listless Offaly side, so there was no question of recalling Hayes for the final.

Offaly never hurled in that semi-final. They were stuck to the ground and we had the game won at half-time when we led by 1-9 to 0-3. We eventually won pulling up by 1-16 to 2-7, with 1-2 of Offaly's total coming in the last six minutes.

We had worked very hard in 1990. Having been knocked out of the League early on, we knew we had to put in a great summer effort, which we did. I always tried to vary the approach and in May 1990, we brought the squad away for a full-time weekend stint in Carraroe. We went there on the Friday night and I had them out for a jog in a local field before eight o'clock the following morning. The grass was long, but I kept them at it for an hour. Back up for breakfast and then down for a ninety minute hurling game. After that we watched a video and then went out for another session. The squad were dead on their feet that night.

The whole idea was to bring body and mind together for another campaign. We just weren't looking for the players' time – we needed them mentally and psychologically too. When a squad is together a long time, it is important to keep recharging them. The youngsters who came into the squad back in 1984 were now mature adults. Very few of them had their own cars back in '84 but now the trappings of success were all around. That's as it should be, but it's vital for a manager to keep a firm grip in those situations. Otherwise, the more experienced players, bloated by success and awards, will try to start calling the shots in a subtle manner. The second a manager hears the shots being called, he has either got to shout louder or get out. He can never, ever allow himself to be dictated to by his players. Listen to them by all means, but be very careful not to heed the wrong signals. That was a philosophy under which I always operated.

One of the problems we had around 1990 was that there weren't many newcomers forcing their way onto the panel. Meanwhile, we were losing players at the other end. Apart from Hayes, Sylvie Linnane had a groin strain all year and Brendan Lynskey had been out of side through illness and injury.

On the plus side, Noel Lane, who had missed most of 1989 through injury, was back on the panel and playing well. We had to dispense with our policy of using him as a sub and chose him at full-forward. Joe Rabbitte had come through on the fringes and was the sort we needed to throw in that year. We played Offaly in a challenge game in Joachim Kelly's home club, Lusmagh, earlier in the summer and Rabbitte did very well against Eugene Coughlan. He looked a real find, but he ran into problems with a burst appendix, which disrupted his training for weeks, so we couldn't consider him. That was a pity. He was just the sort we needed to be coming through at that stage. In fact, Rabbitte's absence may well have cost us the All-Ireland final. He was new and fresh and exciting and would have been an unknown quantity against Cork.

Cork had regained the Munster title, dethroning Tipperary in the process, so the All-Ireland final was a real 50-50 affair. Still, unlike 1986, I felt that this time we had the forwards, who were good enough to beat them. As it happened, the forwards were good enough, but the backs were not. We leaked a goal in the first minute (Why did we always seem to do that against Cork?) but Joe Cooney master-minded a recovery, which gave us control long before half-time. Ten minutes into the second-half, we were leading by 1-17 to 1-10 and apparently coasting to another title.

In the following nineteen minutes we conceded 4-3 in the sort of nightmare collapse which still haunts all concerned. Theories abound as to why that happened, most of them conceived in the glib school of analysis.

THEORY 1: The Galway full-back line was chaotic without Hayes' calming influence. How come then that it had held out for forty minutes? No, there was more to it than that, notably the quality of ball the Cork full-forward line was getting.

THEORY 2: Galway were over-confident after going in at half-time leading by 1-13 to 1-8, having outscored Cork by 1-8 to 0-2 in the second-quarter. Absolute rubbish. What exactly does over-confidence mean? That you don't mark? That you take things easy? That you shoot wides? The idea of over-confidence setting in during an All-Ireland final against Cork is like saying that a sprinter would ease up if he got ahead of Linford Christie.

THEORY 3: Joe Cooney, who had given an unbelievable performance in the first-half, ran out of steam. Not true. He didn't disappear in the second-half any more than his colleagues. The pattern changed. Cooney wasn't getting nearly as much good ball up to him, unlike the first-half when he destroyed Jim Cashman. What was he supposed to do? Gallop back and pick it up in his own half-back line? Cooney had done enough earlier to win the match for Galway. He carries absolutely no responsibility for our defeat.

THEORY 4: Cork manager, Canon Michael O'Brien, gave his team such a roasting at half-time that they were afraid to come back in as losers. I have no idea what he said but he must have been pretty infuriated nine minutes into the second-half because it still wasn't working. Besides, what would the critics have said about the Cork management if Galway had won? Imagine the criticism they would have got for not switching Cashman off Cooney, who scored 1-6 from play in the first-half.

As far as I'm concerned there was no great mystery involved in Cork's comeback. Most games have periods when one side or the other are in control. Ours came in the second-quarter and early in the second-half and, while we made reasonably good use of it, Cork took greater advantage of theirs later on, certainly when it came to scoring goals.

Once again, though, a number of decisions went against us. Eanna Ryan had the ball in the net in the first-half, only to be whistled back and awarded a free. I can never understand why a referee does that. Surely if a player is fouled and he still manages to score, the advantage should go his way. Whistling him back for a free-in is no advantage, especially when he has scored a goal.

Two crucial decisions also went against us in the second-half. Tony Keady was fouled, but got no free. He lost the ball and Tony O'Sullivan pointed. Then, of course, there was the famous incident where Ger Cunningham made an incredible save with his face from a Martin Naughton blaster. The ball bounced off Ger and over the endline.

He went down injured but the umpire, who was standing a few feet away, signalled a wide. Unbelievable. It was such an obvious '65' that even the Cork players were mystified. Why didn't the referee over-rule the umpire? From the puck-out, Cork got a point. That decision cost us a possible point off a '65', while Cork scored at the other end. A two-point difference in the space of a few seconds. Little things like make all the difference.

Noel Lane was unlucky once or twice too. He scored four points but with even a modicum of fortune could have had at least two goals. But there's nothing you can do when Lady Luck sets out her stall. She had given us most of the breaks in the 1987-88 finals and this time she was redressing the balance. That said, Cork deserved their victory. Any team which scores 5-15 deserves to win.

Our finishing tally of 2-21 would have won all the previous All-Irelands going back to 1971 but it wasn't enough this time. The game was rightly hailed as a classic, but that meant nothing to us. Far better to be involved in an 0-3 to 0-2 game and win than delight everybody in a high-scoring thriller and lose.

I'll spare his blushes by not naming the Cork official who put his arm around me at the post All-Ireland lunch on the Monday and whispered, 'Cyril, a good team should never lose a seven points lead'. I felt like punching him, the arrogant sod! Instead, I simply replied: 'It could happen to any team, even Cork'.

Ten months later, Cork lost a nine-point lead to Tipperary in the second-half of the Munster final. What was that about a good team not losing a seven-point lead? How about losing a nine-point lead? It proves one thing. You can never make categorical statements like that. Not in hurling, anyway, where goals come so rapidly.

Losing the 1990 final was a real sickener. Had we won it, some of the sour taste of 1989 would have disappeared. As it was, we were left with an even uglier taste. I definitely should have quit after that final. In a sense, it was the end of an era and I should have known that. But, to be honest, there was no mad rush for the team manager's job. There is a misconception that there are dozens of people out there queuing up for these sort of jobs. Very often that is not the case.

Certainly back in 1990, I wasn't aware of any would-be managers dying to take over Galway. Nonetheless, that wasn't my problem and I should have stood down. It's only in hindsight that you notice little things and looking back I have to say my enthusiasm was on the wane.

I had been going virtually full-time since the autumn of 1984 and, however hard you try, it's impossible to guard against staleness. It manifests itself in little ways. I started thinking to myself, 'Maybe we have enough training done, or maybe we won't start the training programme as early'. I might even have been making allowances for certain players. That's what happens when you are with a group for a long time.

When I first came in 1979 and 1984, I was ruthless in terms of training. Even the older players who might not have felt up to the punishing grind had to go through it or drop out. There were no allowances.

I'm not saying I started making conscious allowances in 1991, but I suppose my own candle was beginning to burn out too. It's difficult to motivate others when you are not fully motivated yourself and, in some ways, I wasn't properly tuned in in 1991. Let's put it this way, I would have done things differently now that I have had a break and a chance to look back.

We were in Division Two of the League that winter and, while we had a few scares, notably against Laois, whom we beat through a late goal by sub, Gerry Keane, we won promotion and qualified for the play-offs. We beat Ulster and Munster to win another Railway Cup and then headed for Thurles to play Kilkenny in the League quarter-final. We looked well on our way to winning when Joe Rabbitte got a goal to put us five points up with twelve minutes to go.

But we collapsed in the closing minutes and Kilkenny scored 1-4 to win by 2-11 to 2-9. We tried to disguise it as best we could, but it was a big disappointment. The writing was appearing on the wall in large, ugly letters. We were losing altitude, rapidly. Four months later,

Tipperary wiped us off the pitch in the All-Ireland semi-final. By then, the scene had gone stale. We started with only eight of the two-in-a-row team. We had Peter Finnerty at full-back, a move which didn't work and, overall, we were easy pickings for Tipperary. They were 2-3 to 0-1 ahead in fifteen minutes after Cormac Bonner and Michael Cleary had cut through our defence and Tipp eventually won by 3-13 to 1-10. It's only in hindsight that you realise it, but the truth was that an era had ended after we lost to Cork in 1990. Being so close to it, we didn't actually spot it.

The squad was breaking-up before our eyes. It was time to stand down. Automatic replacements were waiting that year. Galway U-21s had won the All-Ireland final, with great wins over Cork and Offaly, which was a welcome boost at the end of a disappointing senior season. As many of that team represented the future of Galway hurling, it was appropriate that those in charge of them would be promoted to senior management. Jarlath Cloonan, Gerry Holland, Sean Kelly, Tommy Grogan and my own clubmate, Mick Fogarty took over.

I felt a great relief after leaving the scene in 1991. For the first time in years, I could go to a club match in Galway and enjoy it for itself, instead of looking for players who might make it to the senior squad. Believe me, after a long spell in charge that was a real luxury.

I did not have to sit down and think up some new way to approach the season. Now I could stand back and enjoy hurling, purely for its own sake.

Chapter 28

'IF YOU HAD YOUR MOUTH OPEN, YOU'D HAVE CAUGHT THE BALL'

Comedian Max Boyce once had a song about Paul Ringer, a former Welsh international rugby forward. Ringer was a hard man, whose version of rugby regularly brought him into conflict with the ruling classes.

He got himself sent off in one international match at a time when rugby referees were ridiculously tolerant of violent behaviour. He had over-stepped the mark, good and proper and paid the ultimate price. It's different nowadays. Rugby referees tend to be far more strict and will send a player off without any hesitation.

Boyce's was a very witty song and had a recurring punch line: 'Paul Ringer took the blame'. He listed everything from rising inflation to rising damp and chimed in at the end, 'Paul Ringer took the blame.' Had Boyce heard of Sylvie Linnane, he could have re-released the song in Ireland, replacing Sylvie for Ringer.

Sylvie had an abrasive style. He also had red hair. It was a dangerous combination. Red heads stand out and, if they put a toe out of line, they are noticed and remembered. Referees seem to open a special file, catchlined 'red-heads'. Sylvie was a tigerish little devil from the first day he took a hurl in his hand. He was also a tough player, one who gave or expected no favours. Over the years, he acquired a reputation for being a hard man and paid a heavy price for it.

He became something of a marked man as far as opposition and referees were concerned. No, he wasn't always blameless, but his reputation in no way reflected the truth about him. In his early days, he might have strayed off-side once or twice but as his career progressed, he shed the impetuous side of his nature to a large degree. Still, he had a name as a bad boy and had to live with it. In fact, I'm quite convinced that he was paying for past sins when he was sent off in the 1989 All-Ireland semi-final, an incident which greatly upset him.

Sylvie inspired a love-hate relationship. I recall one particular game against Offaly in Tullamore at a time when feelings were running pretty high between the counties. Sylvie had been involved in a few incidents in a game where personal animosities broke out all over the place. At the end Offaly fans wanted to dispense their own form of justice on one of Gort's most famous sons.

Some of the Offaly players, realising what was happening, came to Sylvie's assistance as he was making his way to the dressing-room. Padraig Horan still tells the story of how he got a few belts across the head from Offaly fans, who were incensed that he had intervened on Sylvie's behalf.

Those who take a surface view of hurling possibly remember Sylvie for the wrong reasons. I remember him as one of the best backs of the 1980s, a player of great skill and touch. In fact, his skill level was phenomenal but tended to be over-shadowed by his competitive edge. He had great wrists, as anybody who played him in squash will testify. Above all, though, he had an incredible determination. Even in a game of darts, he would do anything to win.

Sylvie's talents were typified by the smooth manner in which he made the transition from wing-back to corner-back. It might seem an obvious move for a player as he gets older, but not every wing-back can do it successfully. In fact, only a few do it really well and Sylvie was one of them. There is a whole different approach required but Sylvie coped superbly with life in the corner.

He really was some character. His fearless temperament meant that he got more than his fair share of belts and cuts. He took them without complaining and tended to have little sympathy for fellow-players who suffered similarly. Once, back in the '80s, Niall McInerney got a nasty cut to the head in an Oireachtas semi-final. It needed about fifteen stitches. Mac was in the corner of the dressing-room feeling sorry for himself but Sylvie had no sympathy.

'It's about time, Mac. You've got away without a scratch for ages. The rest of us (meaning himself) get it all the time,' remarked a very unsympathetic Sylvie.

Another time in training, Peter Murphy was taking penalties against Sylvie, John Commins and Conor Hayes. Murphy was a great striker of a ball. He didn't hit it particularly hard, but he could put a fierce spin on it, which made it very tricky to deal with. On this particular occasion, it smashed straight into Hayes' mouth, dislodging a few teeth. Poor Hayes was left spitting out blood and teeth and generally feeling miserable. Sylvie checked the damage and shook his head. 'Know what, Hayes, if you had your mouth open, you'd have caught the ball'.

Then there was the day in 1985 we were playing an open draw match against Armagh in Trim. We were winning well and there was a fairly leisurely atmosphere to it all. Pitches were wet that spring, so there was plenty of mud flying. Galway Hurling Board chairman, Tom Callanan, was walking around the back of the goal near Sylvie's corner, all dressed up in his Sunday best. Play was at the other end of the field but suddenly Sylvie swished his hurl and left poor Tom covered from head to toe with the best of Meath mud. A startled Tom turned to see where the flying avalanche had come from, only to see a very innocent looking Sylvie staring intently up the field!

Conor Hayes was a rock-solid anchor man and, like Sylvie, made an immense contribution to Galway hurling. He was very popular all over the country, mainly because of his great sportsmanship. He was also an outstanding captain. He would probably have been made captain earlier had he been living in Galway. However, he was based in Cork which more or less ruled him out, until the autumn of 1986.

One of his great assets was his capacity to think on his feet, on and off the pitch. That manifested itself in various ways, but one particular instance stands out. It was after the 1986 League final, which we lost to Kilkenny. I had brought Hayes up to take a second-half penalty at a stage when the match was sprinting away from us. It was a wet, miserable day and I needed somebody with a strong drive and a good nerve. Hayes was the man and he duly planted the ball in the net.

He was asked in an interview about it afterwards and he said that he had been practising penalties for weeks. That was certainly news to me but even in defeat he wasn't going to make the mistake of conceding anything. The fact was he hadn't been taking penalties. Not in training anyway and I doubt very much if he was practising them on his own out in Kiltormer.

Hayes had a great capacity to reason things out. He knew his limitations but, equally importantly, he knew his strengths. So when the whispering campaign was underway prior to the 1988 All-Ireland final suggesting that he should be dropped, it merely served as a rallying force for Hayes. Not in a loud, abrasive way but in a quiet, measured manner. He knew that people were predicting a wipe-out for him against Nicholas English but he turned that to his advantage. He had hurled in a lot more finals than English and reckoned that his big-time experience would count for something. He was very proud of his performance in that final, although he was never the sort to give the two-fingers to the critics who wanted him discarded. I remember him getting on the coach after that final. He was one of the last to board and he stood at the door for a few seconds grinning. 'Bring on Carl Lewis, I'd out-sprint him any day'. It was his way of saying: 'I showed them all, didn't I'.

Hayes would never have been recognised for his speed, but he scored in positioning and in anticipating play. He was a brilliant reader of angles. He also had a safe pair of hands.

He was very popular among the players and was particularly good at bringing the players together if there was any friction in training. Over the years that was inevitable. It's impossible to have total harmony among a big group, but Hayes was an expert at calming things down and getting his colleagues to concentrate on what they were really there for. The rest looked up to him.

He was also excellent in dealing with the media. That took a lot of pressure off the other players. Some players have no problems doing interviews while others hate it. I encouraged players to talk to the press if they were asked but to be careful about what they said. It worked quite well. Hayes, as captain for so long, dealt a great deal with the media and took it all in his stride.

He was unlucky in that he had to live with an on-going back injury for most of his career. It sometimes prevented him from achieving the levels of fitness we would have liked, but there was nothing he could do about it. If he pushed it too hard, he might have missed an awful lot more games than he did.

Hayes was a good judge of his own form. He never once complained about having been left off for the 1990 All-Ireland semi-final and final, although it was fiercely disappointing for him. He could easily have got the sympathy vote after the '90 final by claiming that, had he been playing, Cork's comeback would not have been so devastatingly successful. But he didn't. He was too loyal for that sort of easy point-scoring.

Nor did he make any big deal about his contribution to Kiltormer's All-Ireland club success in 1992. He was way below his best against Cormac Bonner in the 1989 All-Ireland semi-final and had to wait almost three years to put the record straight. But he did it in style in that epic three-match club semi-final saga against Tipperary champions, Cashel King Cormacs, marking Bonner out of the game on each of the three days. That was deeply satisfying for him, as was the win over Birr in the All-Ireland final, which meant that he had won All-Ireland medals in all grades except minor.

So impressive was Hayes' form in the 1992 club championship that he was invited back on the Galway panel. He declined, probably wisely, because there is a world of difference between club hurling in February-March and inter-county hurling in summer. Hayes knew that better than anybody. Besides, he had no more frontiers to cross. He had achieved everything he wanted in hurling. A comeback might only have damaged his reputation as one of the best defenders of his era.

Hayes' Kiltormer colleague, Ollie Kilkenny, was a very under-rated corner-back. He was utterly committed and was very much a team man. He couldn't care less if he didn't hit the ball once in the whole game, provided his opponent didn't get near it either. Others could do the flashy stuff. His ambition was to have the corner-forward 13 walking off the pitch feeling thoroughly miserable afterwards.

Like Sylvie, he knew no fear and crossed the pain barrier without even thinking. He broke a finger playing Offaly one time and we assumed he wouldn't be fit for the next game. He came to me at training one evening and said that he would be fit to play. 'But you won't be able to catch the ball,' I replied. 'Don't worry about that. I don't need to catch the ball. I won't let you down.' Some spirit!

His brother Tony, together with Michael Earls, were the two best readers of the game on the entire panel. Earls was a very good full-back but was unlucky that his career coincided with Conor Hayes reign. But when it came to assessing a situation, Earls was brilliant. So too was Tony.

To this day, I'm sure he cannot understand why he wasn't chosen for the 1987 and 1988 All-Ireland finals. He had done nothing wrong either year. It was just that we felt other options (Pat Malone in '87, Michael Coleman in '88) suited the game plan better. But he took it like a man and came on in both finals.

John Commins forced his way onto the team in 1986. He had been the minor goalie in 1983 and maintained his rate of progress to such a degree that we decided he had the edge on Peter Murphy in 1986. It was a close call, but we felt that Commins' innate confidence would bolster the defence. He also had a better puck-out than Murphy.

Commins repaid our faith in him. He had a mixed sort of game in the 1986 All-Ireland final, but was outstanding in both the 1987-88 finals. In 1986, he had been beaten four times against Cork but underlined his growing maturity by coming all the way upfield in the second-half to smash a penalty to the net. A week later, he repeated it in the U-21 final in Thurles against Wexford. That score convinced me that Commins had a great nerve. We needed a goal and he delivered as if it was the most routine chore in the world.

It looked around then as if Commins would be the Galway goalie for the next ten years but, after a somewhat shaky final in 1990, he lost out to Richie Burke. Such is life for a goalie. You really are only as good as your last save and with more and more young keepers emerging in Galway, there is no room for error. Still, Commins can look back on his spell with undiluted satisfaction. Keeping a clean sheet in All-Ireland finals against Kilkenny and Tipperary is a pretty impressive record to look back on.

Finnerty, Keady and McInerney! They became the most talked about half-backs of the 1980s and, in many ways, characterised the spirit and soul of the two-in-a-row team. Peter Finnerty never even wanted to be a wing-back. He had been a full-back at minor level and I think that's how he saw himself when we brought him into the senior panel. But wing-back was available and I told him that he could make it his own if he worked for it. It took him a good while to settle into it but, once he did, he was superb. It was mind over matter as far as Pete was concerned. He would go through an opponent rather than around him and while that was energy-sapping, it also knocked the stuffing out of opponents. He was utterly fearless, too, and seemed to respond to getting a belt. Often, in fact, his best performances came when he got a rattle early on.

Finnerty's style has a high burn-out content. A player can only produce that level of determination and intent for a certain number of seasons. It takes a heavy toll physically. A switch back to the full-back line (à la Sylvie) seemed an obvious move, but it never worked out. He didn't settle at full-back or corner-back and never revisited the great heights he had set at wing-back. Still, his contribution to Galway's glory spell in the 1980s will never be forgotten.

Keady was a class player. He was equally good left or right and could turn on a 10p piece. I had liked the look of him when I saw him playing for the Galway U-21s against the seniors in a challenge game in Pearse Stadium in 1984. I made a note that if I ever came back as team manager, I would have him at centre-back. He tended to mark space rather than his man, but was so good under the dropping ball that few centre-forwards could beat him.

He thrived on confidence and needed to be told how well he was playing. Once he was happy with his own game, the sky was the limit. He would knock over frees from eighty yards range as if it were dead simple and, in fairness, you could bank on him to score the pressure ones. Lots of players will point frees if their side are seven points up or seven points behind but the really good marksman won't flinch when he is facing the vital one with a minute left and his side a point behind. Keady was in that category.

But, God, could he be infuriating in training. I think he used to do it to wind me up, but he would go through a session, hitting all the frees wide. He would have this deadly serious look on his face as free after free went just left or right. I would suggest a few adjustments, usually to no avail. After a time, I decided it was as well to leave him on his own. I would pretend to be doing something else while keeping an eye on him and, often as not, he would suddenly find the range and lash them all over the bar. To this day, I suspect he was shooting them wide to annoy me and I could almost see his tongue sticking out at me once I turned my back. The main thing was, though, that come the pressure free in Croke Park, I could rely on him.

Keady and Brendan Lynskey were working in Dublin for much of the glory years and shared a house in Phibsboro. They worked well off each other but there were times when they nearly drove me mad. They used to devise the most comical reasons for not coming down to training. In fairness, they didn't miss a whole lot of sessions but there were a few occasions when they didn't make it. That's when the inventive minds got to work. They once swore to me that they couldn't make it for training because a fallen tree had blocked the road outside Maynooth and by the time it was cleared, it was too late to continue the journey. There wasn't a puff of wind around Athenry the same evening!

Despite their strange ways, I knew that they were looking after themselves in Dublin. They liked to give the impression of men-about-town who didn't take their hurling seriously but that was far from the truth. An incident after the 1988 All-Ireland semi-final win over Offaly illustrates the point.

They went their own way after the game, saying they would see us for training during the week. It was the August Bank Holiday weekend and I stayed in Dublin that night. About three hours after the match, I was driving down the North Circular Road when I spotted two familiar figures jogging along. Keady and Lynskey! They had their own special circuit which they ran, and here they were out for a run a few hours after an All-Ireland semi-final.

That was a side of them very few people knew about. Deep down, they were very, very determined. Later that night, they were holding court in The Merchant pub on the quays. They were back to their clowning ways, letting on to be half-drunk. What nobody knew was that they had been out for a run just before they came in. Very few players, in either hurling or football, would have done that.

Lynskey loved The Merchant. It became a sort of HQ for Galway hurling fans and there was always good fun there. One night, Lynskey was telling anybody who was prepared to listen that his role with Galway did not involve scoring. His instructions were to get the ball and lay it off to forwards who could score. He was the original target-man and prided himself on a good eye, a good hand and a good sense of vision, once he won possession. Ned O'Shea, proprietor of The Merchant, was amazed.

'Are you telling me that you're a full forward but that you're not supposed to score. What sort of coach have you got at all?' Ned is a Kerryman and the idea of a full forward not being asked to score was complete heresy. Mind you, there was no actual rule preventing Lynskey from scoring! We were always delighted to see him score but, all things being equal, it was better policy to have him setting up scores for the opportunists around him.

Lynskey never got the credit he deserved outside of Galway. But then people didn't understand what exactly his role was and tended to judge him on his lack of scoring power. Lynskey could never be described as a classic striker of the ball, but he had a great many other talents which were just as important in our attacking set-up.

He had never really commanded a regular spot on the Galway team up to the end of 1984 when we took over. He was in and out of the squad up to then and thought his chance had gone. After all, he was thirty years old then. I never believed in assessing a player's worth through his birth certificate and the fact was that we needed a Lynskey-type to be the focal point of the attack. He was fiercely strong and had a great eye for the ball. He also had a good sense of what was happening around him and with so much speed and skill in our attack, his job was to set up possession for Cooney, Naughton etc. He did it splendidly.

I suppose the ultimate tribute – if you could call it that – was paid to him in the 1986 All-Ireland final when Cork singled him out for 'special' treatment. They identified him as the main play-maker in our attack and lashed into him accordingly. That they got away with it is another of the sad mysteries which surrounded that final.

The first time Gerry McInerney came to my attention was as a shy, quiet minor in the summer of 1983. 'Mac' was, and still is, a man of few words. But put a hurl in his hand and he comes to life in a very positive way. His strength was obvious from his minor days, as was his ability to catch a high ball. His striking was never his strong point, although people forget that he scored two vital long range points in the 1988 All-Ireland final.

He became something of a cult figure around 1987-88 when he made his annual trips home from the US to play for Galway. He took to wearing flashy, white boots which, coupled with his long, flowing hair, made him very noticeable on the pitch.

His near contempt for the opposition always amazed me. The quality of opponent was completely irrelevant to him. In fact, he wouldn't have recognised most of the big names in the 1987-89 period as he spent nine months of the year in America and hadn't the slightest interest in what was happening in Kilkenny or Cork or Tipperary. If I mentioned some aspect of an opponent's play which he should watch closely, he would just grunt as if to say: 'Don't be bothering me with that stuff, who the hell is this fella anyway? I never heard of him'.

Steve Mahon was another who had endless belief in himself. I knew him since the successful U-21 campaign in 1978 and always regarded him as one of the team's anchor-men. He was an old-fashioned midfielder, who grafted very hard. He wasn't a particularly good marker, claiming that it was up to his opponent to worry about him. It worked fairly well and hardly a game went by when he didn't pop up and score a vital point or two.

If you wanted to test the team's mood, Mahon was a good barometer. If Mahon was pessimistic, then you knew things were going badly. He believed that things would come right on the day and he had absolutely no doubts about his ability to make that happen. So if he was feeling down, I knew things were bad.

Mahon and his likes represented the new age of Galway hurling. They had endless confidence in themselves and weren't haunted by memories of the bad old days. Winning the 1978 U-21 final really was critically important in that development. Now we had a situation where the senior team was going reasonably well, while the underage scene was vibrant. When Galway won the U-21 final back in 1972, things were different. The senior revival still wasn't underway so inevitably the confidence levels in the county were lower. In 1972, for instance, Galway seniors were beaten twenty-seven points by Kilkenny in the All-Ireland semi-final and a year later, London knocked Galway out of the championship. That had all changed by the end of the decade.

Steve Mahon and Pat Malone were a great midfield partnership. Malone did an awful lot of valuable, if unseen, work. He also had a great temperament. He was a very effective midfield operator and would have made an equally good centre-back. In fact, people tend to forget that he was at centre-back when Galway won the All-Ireland minor final in 1983 and the U-21 final three years later.

It says something about the All-Stars' selection system that he didn't win an award until 1993. But then players like Malone always suffer in that type of situation. He is a quiet man on and off the pitch and would not have got to know many journalists. Sad to say, that counts when the All-Stars are being selected.

Michael Coleman took over Mahon's role in 1988 and did it very effectively, even if he was a different type of player. Coleman tended to be more of a marker than Mahon, but wasn't as good at snapping up the long range points. Coleman was a typical example of a player who got his rewards through sheer hard work. He was very raw when he first came on the scene but had tremendous strength and determination. He improved rapidly once he got in among good players and his skill level rose accordingly. It really was asking an awful lot of him to slot in for the 1988 All-Ireland final but, after a shaky start, he adjusted magnificently. It was a day for big men in every sense and Coleman came through in great style.

We will never know for sure but I believe that Galway's trophy cabinet could have been even better adorned were it not for the sad way in which both Eanna Ryan and Martin Naughton were forced out of the game through injury. Eanna was only approaching his prime when his career was ended due to an ear injury sustained in a club game in 1990. A couple of seasons on and Martin had to call it a day because of a recurring knee problem.

They were very different players but together, they formed a lethal left wing combination. Naughton was like your old-fashioned soccer winger, who loved to scoot down the line. He had blistering pace which very often enabled him to beat his man. Straightaway, that gave us an advantage. We now had the extra-man and a great many scores were engineered off Naughton's speed.

I could never understand the attitude of Cork coach, Johnny Clifford, who commented prior to the 1987 All-Ireland final that Naughton wasn't 'my type of player at all. He tends to lose touch with his colleagues and also fades out of games'. I rated Naughton much higher than that. Johnny did us a favour with those comments, just as he had done with his remarks that Gerry McInerney would be a weak link that day. Both Naughton and McInerney had plenty of motivation going into that game, thanks to Johnny!

If Eanna Ryan was a soccer player, he would have been a real goal poacher. Although he could hurl anywhere from midfield in, I always thought he was at his most lethal at corner-forward. He had a predator's instincts and always seemed to be in the right place at the right time. He was also very skilful and had the most delicate of first touches.

One goal, in particular, stands out. It came in the 1989 League semi-final against Dublin in Croke Park. The ball was driven across from the Hogan Stand side towards Hill 16. It dropped on the edge of the square and Ryan connected even before it touched the ground. Spotting that the Dublin goalie was coming off his line, he half-chipped, half-sliced the ball, angling it artfully into the net. A truly magnificent score. He was more than a goal poacher, of course. He was also a very effective midfielder and while he wasn't big, he was very durable and was difficult to knock off the ball. It really was a pity that his career was brought to such a premature end. He was a huge loss in the 1993 All-Ireland final, for instance, when Galway had no poacher who could capitalise on the breaking ball around the Kilkenny goal.

When it comes to evoking contrasting views, no Galway hurler was as adept at it as Anthony Cunningham. Critics claimed he had nothing only speed, while supporters felt he was a fiercely unlucky player. I tend to fall into the latter category. He had the rather unfortunate distinction of having been taken off in four All-Ireland finals, but it would be wrong to assess his career purely in those terms.

He had blistering speed and fitted in very well when our hand-passing game was in full flow. His first touch was a problem though and the harder he tried the worse it seemed to get. There were days when he came so very, very close to having a blinder, only to be let down by his first touch. We were criticised for remaining so loyal to him when picking All-Ireland final teams but, frankly, we were going on form every time. Besides, he was always more likely to play better at the start than if he was brought on as a sub.

Noel Lane was different. I know that he will never understand why he wasn't started in the 1987-88 All-Ireland finals but the truth was that in the 1985-86 finals he hadn't got into the games at all. It was as if he seized up and didn't do himself any sort of justice because he really was a most gifted player but, unfortunately, he showed few of his real talents in the 1985-86 finals.

It seemed to me that he handled the pressure better in his 'first coming' back in the late 1970s-early 1980s. He was the ideal man to have as a super-sub. Apart from giving his colleagues a lift when he came on, he had a sufficiently impressive reputation to worry the opposition. Most important of all, he had the skill and brain necessary to adapt quickly to the pace of the game. That is a real talent, believe me. Some players take time to settle when brought in as a sub. Lane didn't need that. He could go straight out and switch on.

He will probably never forgive the selectors for leaving him out in 1987-88 but the fact is that he has two All-Ireland medals from those years, having made vital contributions in both. Would he have done as well if he had been chosen from the start? We will never know, but we had to go on past experiences.

Lane showed his real manliness by the manner in which he accepted those decisions. He told me in no uncertain terms that we were wrong but that was the end of it. There was no more whinging or complaining. He put the disappointments behind him and concentrated on his super-sub role. I'm quite sure that every time he was brought on, he was fired by a determination to show the selectors how wrong we were in the first place. That was exactly what we wanted to happen.

He was fired by a deep personal pride too, as I found out early in 1990. He had missed much of 1989 with a back injury (it had been bothering him for years) but I still felt he had a lot to offer. The full-forward position was very much open going into 1990, so we decided to invite him back on the panel.

I drove over to his house a day or two after Christmas to ask him back. An All-Ireland final seemed an awful long way off on a raw

December night, but I told him that if he was prepared to make the effort, the full-forward berth was there for the taking.

He hesitated for a while but his wife, Carmel, encouraged him to give it another go, so he agreed to rejoin the panel. We started training in a gym in Galway around 20 January. I paired off with Lane for some of the exercises and was amazed to find him in such good condition so early in the year. One night, I was glancing through the gym's record book and what did I find? Yes, the bold Noel had been using the gym for a full two weeks before the organised squad sessions had started. It was typical of him. If he was going to give it another go, there would be no half-measures and he was determined to have a head start on the rest when the official sessions started.

PJ Molloy's contribution to the All-Ireland double was also significant. He wasn't even on the panel when we won the 1987 League title but forced his way back in during the summer. PJ knew that his role would be as a sub and he was delighted with that. He got a great kick out of winning the '87 final, having come in as a sub for Cunningham in the second-half. He was a great influence on the younger lads that year. His dedication was an example to all while his experience was invaluable. There is a world of difference between bringing in a Noel Lane or a PJ Molloy as opposed to a youngster who is on the fringe of the panel. Experience is vital in those circumstances, while the opposition are also likely to be more aware of players with a proven pedigree. The roar which went up when we sent on Lane and Molloy in 1987 was a rallying call to the rest of the team. Kilkenny had no subs of that calibre to boost their effort. Both Molloy and Lane were, of course, key forwards in the 1980 success also.

'Hopper' McGrath was one of the quiet men of the team, but was none the less effective for that. He had a near telepathic relationship with Joe Cooney which yielded several great scores and generally he had the capacity to pop up and score a vital point. More often than not, his scores came at crucial times. If we had gone seven or eight minutes without scoring, the chances were that 'Hopper' would be the man to end the dry run. Or if the opposition were on a good run, he would sneak a point from the half-chance.

I have always held that a team is only as good as its subs, a theory which is certainly borne out by the Galway two-in-a-row success. We were very lucky to be able to call on subs like Lane, Molloy, Tony Kilkenny and Gerry Burke. Burke came in as a sub in the 1988 All-

Ireland final and was a regular right through 1989. We were lucky too that we had others of the calibre of Peter Murphy, Pearse Piggott, Michael Earls and Tom Monaghan waiting on the wings.

Murphy was a rare breed in that he could either play in goal or in attack. Piggott hurled all over the place for us but just couldn't make any position his own, while Earls had the bad luck to be vying for the same spot as Conor Hayes. Tom Monaghan was one of those players who always looked likely to force his way into the team but he never actually achieved it. We were particularly disappointed when we brought him in as a sub in the 1990 All-Ireland final against Cork. He never adapted to the tempo of the game. It was a great pity because he was a very talented player who never quite produced it on a consistent basis.

Ray Duane was another who fell into this category. He had skill to burn and would look magic in training but, for whatever reason, he rarely did himself justice when presented with opportunities on the team.

One of the striking features of the two-in-a-row team was the bond which grew among them. Inevitably, you will have different personalities on a squad, but it's very satisfying if you can get them all thinking broadly on the same wavelength. There is a certain amount of luck about that. It's like any group of players which come together. What makes one great and another mediocre? Very often, there is a lot more to it than mere talent. Proper attitude, personal ambition, determination and loyalty are all vital ingredients and I was very lucky to have a squad which possessed the lot. Even more importantly, Galway hurling was lucky to have them.

One of the curious things about our double success was that it was achieved in the same years as Meath were winning the two-in-a-row in football. I had a special affinity with Meath football, having coached Skryne in 1984. I was living in Dublin at the time so there was little travelling involved. I enjoyed my spell with Skryne. It was a proud, ambitious, well-organised club which was not unlike Galway hurlers in that they were always coming close to winning the county title without actually doing it.

Liam Hayes and Colm O'Rourke were their 'big two'. There were very different personalities but each contributed a lot in his own way, just as they did for Meath for so long. I could see from my spell there that the basic structures of Meath football were sound and it certainly didn't surprise me when they made the All-Ireland breakthrough in 1987. Skyrne made the championship breakthrough in Meath too, although it took them longer.

Sean Boylan's involvement with Meath footballers increased my interest in them. Sean is really a hurling man, but has been an outstanding success as Meath football manager. We had a fair bit in common, in that neither of us were top class players. I think we proved that you don't have to have All-Ireland medals to coach winning teams.

Amazingly, Galway hurlers and Meath footballers ran parallel in a number of ways. Apart from winning the two-in-a-row in 1987-88, neither of us reached the final in 1989. We were back in All-Ireland deciders in 1990, where we both lost to Cork.

There was another similarity between us. Neither Galway nor Meath were very well liked by the GAA authorities. Galway had regular clashes with them while Meath were in the dog-house after a few of their players refused to accept their All-Ireland medals from the then GAA President, John Dowling, in 1988. I doubt very much if either Galway or Meath would have won many votes in a poll among GAA officialdom for the most popular All-Ireland winners of all time. But then we weren't playing for GAA officialdom. At all times, we were doing our best for our counties. That's hardly a crime is it?

After watching Sean Boylan enjoying so many successes with Meath, I often wondered how I might have got on as a football coach. I would have liked to coach football, just to see how I got on. It offers more tactical options than hurling in that it is much easier to hold possession in football and a team in possession is a team in control. There were some informal soundings one year as to whether or not I would be interested in taking over the Galway football team, but I wasn't keen. Too many things appeared all wrong to me and I was not prepared to become involved in a set-up in which I had no great faith.

CHAPTER 29
MISSION IMPROBABLE

Wexford people have always been among my favourites. They possess a compelling zest for life, without taking it, or themselves, too seriously. The 'sunny South-East' description is as apt for their disposition as it for the weather.

Not surprisingly, they have a great attitude to hurling. Years of living alongside a domineering neighbour has not dulled their ambitions one bit. On the contrary, Kilkenny's triumphs have merely heightened Wexford's resolve to down them next time out.

Too often though, Wexford have seen a win over Kilkenny as an end in itself. Beat Kilkenny and the season is deemed a success, even if no titles are brought home. It reminds me of Galway years ago when putting up a brave show in an All-Ireland semi-final was regarded, if not as a reason for celebration, as certainly a source of consolation.

For years, Wexford were the only real threat to Kilkenny in Leinster. In fact between 1965 and and 1979, they met in every Leinster final with the exception of 1969 when Offaly made it to the final, losing narrowly to Kilkenny. Kilkenny, it must said, generally held the upperhand but Wexford could always spring a surprise when least expected. They took special delight in unseating Kilkenny if they were the reigning All-Ireland champions. They achieved that in 1968, 1970 and 1976 when they demolished an outstanding Kilkenny side which was hot on the three-in-a-row trail. It was one of Wexford's greatest Leinster triumphs, a 2-20 to 1-6 win against a team which had reigned supreme for the previous two years. In fact, Kilkenny might well have been going for four-in-a-row that year had their 1973 campaign not been devastated by injury problems.

Nobody would have thought back in 1977 that Wexford were about to enter a championship desert. But the introduction of the open draw, allied to Offaly's improvement relegated them to third place in Leinster. Still, Wexford were always capable of the big shock and struck again in 1984 when a Tony Doran goal ended Kilkenny's three-in-a-row ambitions in the Leinster semi-final. Wexford seemed set to end the barren spell but hurled poorly in the final, giving Offaly an eight-point start before launching a spirited comeback, which eventually fell short by a single, infuriating point.

It was all so very disappointing. It was as if they couldn't move on to higher peaks, once they conquered one mountain. Yet, despite the annual disappointments, Wexford fans remain among the most loyal in the country. They travel in force everywhere, waiting and longing to have something to celebrate. Per head of population, and bearing in mind the number of disappointments they have endured, they are probably the most loyal fans in the country.

Wexford acquired a reputation as being All-Ireland champions only in inconsistency. The problem with that is that once a team loses some games it felt should have been won, personal insecurity sets in. That, in turn, feeds off itself and players start looking over their shoulders, as if waiting for trouble, even when things are sailing along smoothly. That has often happened Wexford.

I came across Wexford quite a lot during my spell with Galway and knew most of their players well. We always found them very difficult to beat. In fact, they probably took more League points off us than any other team during the 1980s. Even when they didn't, it was always a very tough struggle, especially down in Wexford. In fact, I can only remember one game which we won very easily. That was in Tuam Stadium in March 1989, when we beat them by thirteen points on a wet, windy day. It was one of the few times – if not the only time – we played in Tuam, but Phelim (Murphy) was into spreading the hurling gospel at the time and felt we should play at least one League game in the North of the county, where hurling is not all that strong in playing terms. We were going very well and had not lost a competitive game for twelve months at the time.

When Joe Shaughnessy, Martin and Pat Quigley and the Supporters' Club asked me to join Wexford as coach in the spring of 1992, I was caught between two minds. My first reaction was to view Wexford as game, but persistent, losers who could not be injected with a winning culture in a few short months. On the other hand, I liked Wexford, liked the players and as the arm-twisting got progressively more severe, I decided, 'What the hell, let's give it a go'.

Phelim Murphy and some other close hurling friends thought I was mad – and told me so. My reputation would suffer if Wexford were beaten. How could I achieve anything in few months? What about the travelling? Why bother after having achieved so much with Galway? All very sound advice, but I had decided to give it a shot and, stubborn sort that I am, I wasn't for changing. I left for Wexford with Phelim's blunt words ringing in my ears: 'Farrell, you're mad'.

I didn't do it for the money. I heard all the rumours about how I was making a fortune out of it. Some people would have you believe that I was being paid enough to buy a luxury apartment in Barbados. It's amazing how these sort of stories sprout. The national pastime of surmising about other people's business is alive and well and thriving in GAA land, especially when a coach drives across a county boundary.

Yes, I was paid expenses and I make no apology for that. Was I expected to drive a round trip of 250 miles from Woodford to Gorey (Wexford did most of their training there that season) a few times a week for nothing? Believe me the driving, especially the return leg late at night, was no fun. Anybody covering those distances deserves to be compensated.

If I wanted to make money out of coaching, I would have chosen an easier route. I would simply have taken up one of the many offers which came in from clubs over the years. There is far more room for private enterprise on the club circuit than there ever will be on the county scene. Altogether, it's much easier since the pressures are less intense and, if you want, you can skip from club to club. The GAA powers get themselves very excited from time to time about allegations that inter-county team managers are being paid. A small percentage may be, but it's nothing compared to the money paid out by clubs. So if money was my motivation, I would have set up a deal with a club, away from the spotlight and the pressures.

I did not join Wexford for the money but because I saw it as a challenge. They had been on the fringes of the big-time for several seasons and I suppose I thought my experiences with Galway might be helpful in opening a few doors for them. Besides, I wanted to see what it would be like to deal with a whole new scene. I was curious about that.

In hindsight, I was wrong. I was trying to do in three months what it had taken three years to do in Galway with a great side. Mission improbable became mission impossible and Wexford were well beaten (3-16 to 2-9) by Kilkenny in the Leinster final.

To be honest, we were lucky to get past the first round against Laois. There was a lot of hype going into that game in Carlow and it seemed to effect Wexford more than Laois. Jimmy Holohan was sent off after fifteen minutes and we never really got into any sort of pattern. I had been on to Jimmy to impose himself a bit more from a physical viewpoint. He was a strong man but didn't always use it. I'm not sure whether or not he took my advice too literally. Anyway, he was sent off, pretty harshly it must be said, because he was anything but a dirty player. His absence left us with a big gap, one which thankfully the Laois defence indirectly filled by losing concentration.

Laois manager, Paddy Doyle, devised a clever plan to make use of the extra man, playing possession hurling and exploiting the overlap extremely well. It was one of the few times I have seen the extra-man used so expertly. Had 'Babs' Keating or Ollie Walsh devised it, it would have been hailed as revolutionary, but because he was a low-profile manager in charge of a low-profile team, few seemed to notice. I did because it had Wexford on the back foot for ages. Laois had an ocean of possession but shot some terrible wides. Our defence played well too and we hung on in there, very luckily at times. We were eventually rewarded when the Laois backline made a series of mistakes which gifted us the winning goals in the second-half. I would have to say that Laois contributed enormously to our safe passage out of Dr Cullen Park that day.

Playing with an extra-man can be very difficult. In theory, it should be a great help but, in actual fact, it often results in a dilution of responsibility among players. Take six backs marking five forwards. The forwards will be constantly thinking how they might find space while sub-consciously the backs will say: 'We have an extra-man, we can't be caught out'. They very often are because a thinking player is better than two on automatic pilot.

The quips from the Laois crowd that day were very amusing. A small section of them kept chanting at me to, 'F*** off back to Galway', choosing to forget that their own manager, Paddy Doyle, was a Tipperary man!

By then I was beginning to have doubts about the wisdom of my move. I was getting on well with the players and selectors but it seemed to me that that Wexford's ambitions were not as single-minded as they should be. The club scene dominates to a large degree in Wexford and unlike most other strong hurling counties, many of the squad were playing football as well. They were on the go all the time. I tried to get through to them that if they hoped to win a Leinster final, inter-county hurling would have to dominate their entire lives. It wasn't easy because the clubs tend to make incredible demands on their players in Wexford. If they weren't playing hurling they were out on the football fields.

I remember one night a few players came to me and explained that they could not make training on the following Saturday morning because they were playing in an eleven-a-side competition. It was a gold-watch tournament and their club wanted them. They played in it every year. I told them that they could always buy a gold watch but that a Leinster or All-Ireland medal could never be bought. Better still, we would buy the gold watches for them!

Don't get me wrong. I found them great to work with (you would never find more genuine players than the likes of George O'Connor, Martin Storey, Liam Dunne, Eamonn Cleary and Jimmy Holohan, all of whom have given incredible service to Wexford) but the squad as a whole were products of a system which was more geared to club rather than county activity. I'm not saying they neglected the county scene. It was more a question of not being allowed to give it full concentration because of club games.

That is not an unusual scenario in a county which is not enjoying much success. The club becomes all-important, often to the detriment of the county team. The trick is to successfully combine the two, because nothing boosts club hurling like a successful county team. Wexford appear to be unconvinced on that, which is a pity.

We ran into trouble early on when Liam Dunne got a bad ankle injury in April. He was a key figure in our plans. His loss might not be as serious in another county but when your panel is limited, you cannot afford to lose a player of Liam's calibre. He worked very hard to be right for the Leinster final (he always turned up for training even when he could hardly walk) but we couldn't risk him in the starting line-up. I always operate on the policy that a player who is not fully tuned up for a game should not be played, irrespective of how much talent he has. Dunne came on as a sub in the final and did OK but that does not alter my views. It would have been wrong to start him after being out for so long.

Dublin were disposed of in the semi-final but we weren't hurling well. I needed a lot more time to work with the team, but it simply wasn't there. Coaching takes time. You just cannot ride into a camp and make wholesale changes overnight. First you have to get to know the players on an individual basis. You then have to spend time working out ways of improving their skills and finally you have to devote time to working with them over a lengthy period.

Going into the final I knew that my presence in the Wexford camp was a motivating force for Kilkenny, who were still smarting after that double defeat by Galway in the 1986-87 championships. Kilkenny admitted as much afterwards. The last thing they wanted was to see me coaching a Wexford side to beat them in a Leinster final. They played accordingly.

Kilkenny produced as good a hurling as I have seen for years in the opening twenty minutes of the final. It was marvellous to watch, unless you were either a Wexford man or a Galway man who had been brought in to give a crash course in winning. Wexford missed an ocean of chances and, in the end, were soundly beaten. Significantly, Kilkenny went on to win the All-Ireland final that year.

I felt very sorry for the Wexford players and selectors and indeed the Supporters' Club, all of whom had put so much into it. In a sense, I suppose, I felt I had let them down even if the odds were all against me. I got on well behind the scenes with the selectors, Martin Quigley, Dave Bernie and Jimmy Furlong, all of whom are excellent hurling men, even if sometimes I thought they were too conservative with their selections.

They were inclined to look on certain players as being too young and others as being too old. Personally, a player's birth cert never bothered me. He could be nineteen or thirty-nine. Provided he did what was required, I couldn't care less.

Eamonn Cleary was a prime example. He spent much of his career as a sort of fall-guy in Wexford. He had played all over the place back in the 1980s before finally settling at full-back, where he won an All-Star award in 1989. His form slumped a bit in 1990, possibly because now that he was an All-Star he felt he should perform like one rather than simply playing his own game. Still, it seemed to me that when things went wrong, Cleary took more than his fair share of blame. It was the story of his career.

We brought him back to play at centre-forward in 1992 and he did a fine job, not as a prolific scorer but as a ball winner and a ball-mover. In fact, he was one of the few to do himself justice in the Leinster final.

Players like that have plenty to offer in every county but tend to get discarded too soon. Cleary was very dedicated and saw the extension of his career as a bonus which was much appreciated. He played as if every game might be his last.

I enjoyed my few months in Wexford but in hindsight, I probably should never have taken the job. There are no crash-course solutions in sport and I would have needed at least a year to work on the Wexford squad. I didn't have enough time to devote to the sort of intensive training, coaching and assessment which are vital in the modern game.

I left Wexford feeling that the county was very hungry for success but that it would not achieve it unless there was a radical re-evaluation of the internal structures. Success comes from the bottom up, so it's vital to keep the production lines to the senior side clean and efficient.

Wexford's lack of success at underage level is disturbing for them. Not all good underage teams make the senior grade, but it's still imperative to have them coming through. Wexford haven't been producing enough top class minor or U-21 teams and that has shown at senior level.

They need to get their underage structures right – and in fairness they are working towards that now – otherwise they won't reach a stage where not only will they make the breakthrough but also have the back-up to sustain it. The problem is that young Wexford players grow up thinking as losers. The seniors have failed to win one final from seventeen attempts (All-Ireland, League, Leinster championship) since 1977, which really is a most horrible legacy to hand on to young talent.

There is no short-cut solution for Wexford. The only way forward is to invest in the future. It may take five to ten years to yield the fruits but it will be worth it. The emphasis must be on the young players. It's difficult to accept that Wexford have not won an All-Ireland minor title since 1968 or an U-21 title since 1965. Indeed, they have not been winning very many underage titles in Leinster either. Until such time as they do, the senior sideboard will be bare.

I have been asked several times if my heart was really in the Wexford job and how would I have felt if they had won the Leinster final and qualified for an All-Ireland semi-final clash with Galway. Yes, my heart was very much in the Wexford job. It wasn't the same as coaching my native Galway, but I had given a commitment to them and the satisfaction came in seeing improvement in certain areas.

As for a possible match against Galway, I hardly thought about it. I was long enough in hurling to know that you don't start planning for an All-Ireland semi-final until such time as you have actually qualified, especially when you have to beat Kilkenny to get there. But if Wexford had qualified to meet Galway, I would have used everything I knew about the Galway lads in an effort to beat them. Nothing personal, but when you are in charge of a team, your loyalty is with them. Or at least it should be. Obviously I wouldn't have got the same delight from winning an All-Ireland with Wexford. It would have been a different sort of satisfaction altogether.

I knew after the Leinster final that I could not continue with Wexford, even if they wanted me. The travelling was a killer and to do the job properly, it would have been necessary to run a strong winter campaign with training a few times a week. The prospect of a cross-country run on January nights was not appealing.

Within two months of finishing with Wexford, I was approached by Offaly. They wanted me to take over as team manager for the start of the 1992/93 League. They were determined to get an outsider, believing in the belief that he could do better than one of their own. Kilkenny's Dermot Healy had presided over the 1981-85 All-Ireland double while Longford's Eugene McGee had managed the football side which won the 1982 All-Ireland final. In the circumstances, their 'foreign' policy on managers was understandable, but only up to a point.

Part of the reason that unsuccessful counties bring in outside managers is that they have nobody inside with any experience of winning. That was behind Galway's decision to bring in 'Babs' Keating in 1977 and 1979 and Offaly's move for Dermot Healy. Things are different in Offaly now. They have a whole string of players with a history of All-Ireland success.

They made a very good case to me, pointing out that they had as good a young squad as any county in the country. I couldn't argue with that but something didn't seem quite right.

Padraig Horan, who had made an immense contribution to Offaly's breakthrough as a player, had been manager of both the senior and U-21 sides in 1992 and I knew that he had effectively been squeezed out. That was Offaly's own business but I didn't like the undercurrent which accompanied it. If they could do that to a man who had given so much to the county as a player, they would hardly hesitate to drop an outsider if he didn't deliver. Horan's experience was always at the back of my mind, even after having several meetings with the Offaly delegation. They did their best to persuade me to take the job but I didn't really want it. My heart wasn't in it, so I thanked them for their interest and said 'no thank-you'. I have never regretted that decision, despite Offaly's success this year. Undeterred, Offaly persisted with their 'foreign' policy and persuaded Limerick's Eamonn Cregan to join them. In fairness, it worked out well and they now have the McCarthy Cup.

Chapter 30

STICKS AND STONES

We all like to be liked. If you can be popular too, all the better. A word of advice. If you are in the popularity game, don't take up team management. In fact, if your skin is not as thick as an elephant's hide, don't take it up.

Who is the first to be criticised when a team loses? The manager! It goes with the territory. Players get the credit, managers get the blame. Fair enough, I suppose. But God help any sensitive soul who wanders into team management. He will get some shock.

In my early days in charge of Galway, I was aware of criticism. I wasn't overly sensitive, but I noticed it and tried to analyse whether it was justified or not. I was deeply disappointed by the reaction to the 1981 All-Ireland final defeat, for instance. It was as if we had almost gone out of our way to open the gates for Offaly, while the stories about rows in the dressing-room were mischievous to say the least.

For a county which had not won a whole lot up to 1980, Galway quickly learned how to be very critical. The team management were savaged after the 1986 All-Ireland final, as if it were some sort of terrible shame to lose two All-Ireland finals in a row. One would have thought that a county like Cork, which was far more accustomed to success, would have found it more difficult to cope with two consecutive final defeats, but the squad escaped the bitter word after losing to Kilkenny for the second time in 1983.

I met Jimmy Barry-Murphy at the post All-Ireland reception the following day and, while he was deeply disappointed at the way Cork played, he was already talking optimistically about the following year. He was right, of course. Cork came back in fine style to win the Centenary All-Ireland title.

People have very short memories. You're a hero one day, a villain the next. That goes for players too. Two particular instances stand out. The fans who wanted Big Mike Conneely dropped after the 1980 All-Ireland semi-final carried him shoulder-high a month later after the win over Limerick. We talked about that on the evening of the final and I remarked to Mike: 'Don't ever forget who your friends are'. He didn't. Nor would any other player want to because they really are only as good as their last game.

I could have opened a Hurling Advice Bureau after the 1988 All-Ireland semi-final such was the volume of opinion being offered on what we should do with Conor Hayes. 'Drop him' was the most favoured option among the self-appointed advisers. A few weeks later, he was a hero after keeping Nicholas English in check in the final.

I grew immune to criticism during my second spell in charge. I couldn't give a flying toss what anybody thought. Thankfully, Phelim Murphy and Bernie O'Connor were the same. Just as well because otherwise we would have spent half the time pulling daggers out of our backs, especially in 1986 and 1990.

I know too that there were many who thought we handled the Keady affair badly in 1989 and that had we adopted a more diplomatic approach, we might have got a sympathetic hearing from the Central Council. Joe McDonagh referred to it in an article last year, claiming that the three-in-a-row hopes evaporated due to over-concern with off-the-field activities.

Joe obviously sees things from a different perspective. He will make a great GAA president when his day comes. I'm different. I was never one for playing power games with GAA officials. I speak as I find.

One of the reasons I always liked 'Babs' Keating was because of his willingness to speak his mind. It got him into trouble more than once but it never stopped him. In fact, his straight-talking was part of his charm. It was also good for Tipperary as it projected a lively, vibrant atmosphere from the county. 'Babs' really was larger than life and you need characters like him to liven up the scene.

With the media so tuned in to GAA affairs nowadays, it's very important to know exactly what you are saying and to whom you are saying it. In general, the journalists who write on GAA are extremely fair. They are not scandal-seekers, nor are they given to putting a spin on things. I always believed in a policy of being as open as possible with the media. I found it altogether more satisfactory than trying to work against them. In fact, I cringe when I hear of counties banning the press from talking to players prior to big games. All that succeeds in doing is giving players the idea that they are involved in something which is too important to be discussed in even the most routine way. I always advised players to be careful what they said. Otherwise I left it to their own judgement and generally there were no problems.

Coping with the media is an art in itself nowadays. There was a time when you would get to know virtually all the journalists in a short space of time, but as the coverage has increased, so has the number of journalists and it takes a little time to work out the angle they are coming from.

It's very easy to walk into the most innocent of traps. Let's take an example. If a journalist casually remarks to you: 'The Tipperary half-backs were very poor the last day, weren't they?' and you reply 'yes', without elaborating, the chances are the following day you will be quoted as saying: 'The Tipperary half-back line were very poor'. More likely than not it will be under a heading: 'X slams Tipperary half-backs'.

That gives the impression that you steered the conversation in this direction when, in fact, you simply responded 'yes' to a statement. Journalistically, there is nothing wrong with it. It's just that sometimes the wrong impressions can be given because only the answers are reported, not the questions. In general though, the media are fine in this country, certainly when it comes to sport.

Of course, dealing with the media is a two-way process. You can use them to your own ends too, if the occasion demands it. Players will not admit it but they are influenced by what they read in newspapers. Being human, they like to see their names in print as having played well. The trouble with that is that not all journalists are good judges and that very wrong impressions can be given. A well-known player will very often be reported as having played well simply because of his reputation, while a lesser-known player will be ignored.

Corner-backs rarely get man-of-the-match ratings, for instance, and if you look back over the Texaco awards winners, you will find at least a two to one ratio in favour of forwards. Backs, especially those who play on the wings, have to perform really well to get noticed.

Very early in my second spell in charge of Galway, I tried out a little experiment, just to prove to the players that they should not believe everything they read. I sent the word out that Sylvie Linnane had broken his toe. Sure enough, a report on the sad plight of Sylvie's big toe appeared in a few papers. I showed it to the players and said: 'See, it says here that Sylvie's toe is broken, so it must be'. Of course it wasn't.

OK, so maybe it was an unethical thing to do but it served its purpose. As far as I was concerned the only opinions the players had to worry about were those of the selectors. Provided we felt a player performed well it didn't matter what was written in the papers. Equally, good write-ups were no guarantee of immunity from criticism from Farrell, Murphy and O'Connor.

Journalists are no different to anybody else. The friendly player who co-operates with them always has a better chance of being given the benefit of the doubt, so his name will pop up as having played well on a regular basis. There is no great harm in that, except that the public believe what they read and a weak management can find it very hard to row against the public tide, even if some player is not performing well.

In general, it's easy enough to have a good relationship with the press, provided everybody knows the limits. GAA coverage has grown dramatically over the last fifteen years, which is good for the games. Journalists are always looking for new angles, so when we were asked by a journalist if he could stay with the Galway squad right through the 1987 All-Ireland weekend to report from the inside, it represented a brand new departure from the conventional coverage.

I had no objections to it. Neither had Phelim or Bernie while the team were far too concerned with the game to worry about it. We took the view that no journalist had been with us in 1985 or 1986 and we had still lost the finals, so where was the harm in allowing one in in 1987? As it happened, Galway won and everything was fine but what would have happened had we lost?

The critics would have had a field day. Imagine allowing a journalist into team meetings, the dressing-room and the dug-out! Any wonder Galway lost? What sort of a management have they? All of which goes to show that you can make any case you like, depending on whether a team wins or loses.

An interesting aside to that story is that the journalist who was with us had no pass to get either into the dressing-room area or onto Croke Park. We smuggled him into the dressing-room before the game but when he went to go out on the pitch before the team, he was stopped by a steward. 'No way through here, unless you have an official pass'. Whereupon, I handed him mine while the steward was not looking. That left me without a pass, but the steward let me through without it. Officious as they might be, the stewards would hardly prevent a team manager from getting out onto Croke Park.

One area which every team management has to deal with is criticism that they are not giving certain players or certain clubs a fair deal. There is very rarely any truth in that since every management's priority is to play the best players. But sometimes perception can become reality and unless you are very careful, these sort of stories take root. Either that or there are claims that selectors are favouring players from their own clubs.

That is one of the reasons I have always preferred a small management team. Three is the ideal number. Increase it to five and the risk of selectors dividing into two factions is far greater. I was very lucky to have Phelim Murphy and Bernie O'Connor with me. They were way above club loyalties. What's more, they didn't give a hoot what anybody said or thought of them. They had a job to do and they did it to the best of their ability.

CHAPTER 31

THE PICK OF THE PACK

Picture the scenario. Hurling has gone international and is operating a thriving transfer trade. Agents from all over Europe are in Ireland, trying to lure the best talents to Italy, Germany and Spain.

They are new to the scene. They are not quite sure what they want in a hurler and have asked you to draw up an identikit of what makes the complete player. What do you do? Spend days ringing around, asking experts for their opinion? Take various characteristics from our top players and try to piece them together?

I have a better idea. Simply, scoot back over videos of Joe Cooney, stopping off at the vintage parts. The international market would have no complaints because Joe Cooney is, as Chris Eubank might put it so modestly, simply the best. Joe may have slipped somewhat from the awesome heights he reached some years ago, but I have no hesitation in saying that he is the best hurler I ever came across. Yes, and that includes John Connolly.

It's important to qualify that. John Connolly was past his best by the time I became involved with the Galway team in 1979, so I am assessing him purely on the basis of my experience of him when I was manager. Whether or not Connolly was better than Cooney in his prime is a debatable point. It's impossible to adjudicate accurately on it since Connolly did not get nearly as many opportunities to play at the highest level. For much of his career, he was a star in a moderate team. Still, if I had to put my neck on the line and decide between Cooney and Connolly at their best, my instincts would come down on Cooney's side.

As far as I am concerned, Joe Cooney has been the best hurler to emerge anywhere in the country since I began senior coaching in 1980. He first came to my notice as a shy, quiet youngster on the Galway minor squad of 1983. I knew his older brother, Jimmy, very well from his playing days with Galway. Jimmy was a tough, determined, durable corner-back who would prefer to go through you rather than around you. He was out-going and forceful and was never short of a word or two.

Joe was very different. He was quiet, almost reserved, the sort who would let his hurling do the talking. There was a lovely light touch to everything he did, even as a minor. Sometimes, you look at a minor and you know straightaway that he is destined for great things. Joe fitted that bill brilliantly. Everything about him was natural. All that was missing was strength, experience and maturity which, of course, came with time.

The one single attribute which differentiates between Cooney and most others is vision. DJ Carey is possibly on a par with him in that department but is not as strong as Cooney. Joe could play anywhere. I have no doubt that he would have been equally good in defence or attack, or probably even in goal. His vision is remarkable. He sees openings which others don't and, when he has players around him who can respond, he is lethal.

It's fair to say that Joe Cooney has never played a really bad game for Galway. There have been times when he has not made as much of an impact as was expected of him, but that is simply because his standards are so high. The 1990 All-Ireland final illustrates my point. He gave a perfect performance during the first-half against Cork and had done more than anybody to turn an early deficit into a five-point lead by half-time.

I can still see Cork centre-back, Jim Cashman, banging his hurley off the ground in frustration as Cooney pulled off yet another of his amazing tricks. Later in the year, Jim was deemed to have been the country's best centre-back by the All-Star selectors, yet he was made look like a novice for thirty-five minutes by Cooney, who scored 1-6 from play.

The popular line is that Cooney faded in the second-half and that this was central to Cork's revival. Not true. Certainly, he was not as effective but then he was not getting the same quality ball he had enjoyed in the first-half. I would still rate that final as one of his best ever performances.

The great thing about Cooney was that he could adapt to any type of game. People claimed we were mad to start him at centre-forward against Ger Henderson in the 1987 All-Ireland final. Henderson would be too strong and too cute, we were told. But then there was a general misconception about Cooney's strength. He was a lot more durable even then than was generally thought and could cope with any sort of opponent. He did well on Henderson, whom I regard as the best centre-back of my era. A year earlier, Cooney had been sheer magic in the semi-final against Kilkenny.

His ability to anticipate the play, plus his uncanny awareness of where his colleagues were at all times, were central to our unorthodox attacking strategy that day. Having been involved in some of the earlier goals, it was appropriate that he should score a truly great one himself after executing the most delicate chip lift with his boot, which not only gave him possession in front of the Kilkenny goal but also beat a defender in the process.

His brother, Jimmy, said he often saw him practising the chip lift as a youngster and while it might have come off only once or twice in big games, it was something to savour when it did. If I had one criticism of Joe, it is that he tended to be too unselfish. There were times when I wanted him to hold possession and go for that little gap, rather than pass the ball out but then that was part of his nature. He never shed his modesty and always behaved as if those around him were as good as he was. Frankly, I don't believe that he realised the extent of his own brilliance.

Some critical Galway fans faulted him for his free-taking, claiming that he was too casual in his approach and that he nearly always missed one or two important ones in the course of a match. The point is that Cooney never wanted to be a free-taker. He was pressed into service because we had no real alternative. I reckoned that Joe's natural touch, combined with his coolness under pressure, would see him through and it did. Yes, he missed some but overall his strike rate was on a par with the best average throughout the country. In a Galway context, he was very good as, up to then, we never seemed to have a free-taker who could be relied upon to produce the scores in pressure games.

Given that Joe could play virtually anywhere, I have slotted him in at right half-forward on the Galway 'dream team' 1980-1991, a period in which I was in charge for all but two seasons. Choosing such a team is a tough task as I am drawing from two successful eras, although there is an overlap in players such as Sylvie Linnane, Conor Hayes, Steve Mahon and Noel Lane, all of whom were on the scene both in 1980 and 1987, when we came back with a new-look team.

I go for John Commins in goal, ahead of Mike Conneely. Commins' record of playing in two consecutive All-Ireland finals without conceding a goal speaks for itself. It is a rare achievement in hurling. In fact, prior to Commins' double shut-out in 1987-88, it had not been done since the 1950s. Back then, of course, games were only an hour long so Commins' record in two seventy minute games speaks for itself.

Big Mike was a fine goalie too, but I would have to side with Commins.

Sylvie Linnane, Conor Hayes and Niall McInerney could have slotted into any of the three full-back positions. Given his versatility, McInerney is unlucky to lose out but my trio are Linnane, Hayes and Jimmy Cooney. It's a very marginal call between Cooney and Ollie Kilkenny at left full-back, but Cooney probably had that bit more hurling in him. Kilkenny was a very tight marker but was not as inspirational as Cooney.

McInerney was as cute a back as ever caught a hurl and the fact that he cannot squeeze into the team is a tribute to the multi-talented duo of Linnane and Hayes. They really did stand the test of time in all types of conditions.

With Sylvie selected at right corner-back, Peter Finnerty is the obvious choice at right half-back. Sylvie was at wing-back in 1980, but once he moved back to the corner nobody came along to make right wing-back his own until Finnerty exploded onto the scene in 1985.

Centre-back and left-half? Tony Keady or Sean Silke? Iggy Clarke or Gerry McInerney? There was no better reader of a game than Silke. All things being equal, a good reader is worth anything because he anticipates things long before they happen. That was Silke's forte but Keady's sheer class and his incredible self-belief make him impossible to overlook for centre-back. He was a marvellously inspirational figure and while he didn't always mark his man as closely as I wanted him to, he usually managed to improvise. Keady's self-confidence was such that he always believed he was better than the opponent. Provided that is not overdone, it is a good philosophy to take into a big game. Both Silke and Keady were good strikers of the ball but Keady would have the edge on long range frees, especially under pressure.

Iggy Clarke was dreadfully unlucky to miss the 1980 All-Ireland final. That would have been his crowning glory. The fact that he missed one of the greatest days in the history of Galway hurling does not alter one fact. He was quite simply the outstanding wing-back of his era. There was a beautiful rhythm about everything he did and there was no sweeter sight in hurling than Iggy in full, graceful flow.

Gerry McInerney is a different type of player. More secure under the high ball, he is utterly fearless but lacks Clarke's poise and is not nearly as good a striker. Mac depends on his instincts and they rarely let him down. He can also be very inspirational. Definitely a man to have in your corner on a big day but Iggy's greater range of skills earn him the

No 7 shirt, ahead of Mac and Seamus Coen, who was a much underrated hurler. Coen had a number of plus points. He could play in a variety of positions and was absolutely brilliant if you wanted an opponent to be man-marked out of the game. You would hardly notice Coen in a lot of his matches but when you totted his opponent's score afterwards, you would find that very often he had drawn a blank. Ollie Kilkenny was also good at that sort of shut-out.

John Connolly would be pencilled in as top choice midfielder by most Galway people. If we were dealing with the mid '70s, he would be my first-choice too but I am starting from 1980, by which time John had lost altitude as a midfielder. By then, he was of more value as a full-forward. I know that he never agreed with me on that, but it's an opinion I have always held and I am not about to change it now.

The two best midfielders of my era were Steve Mahon and Michael Coleman. Mahon lasted right through from the late '70s to the late '80s and is an obvious selection. He was very much his own man and liked to let others worry about him. Coleman came onto the scene in 1988 but did enough from then on to make him No 2 ahead of Pat Malone and Michael Connolly. Coleman's strength and courage were his main assets early on, but he improved rapidly as a hurler once his confidence grew. Michael Connolly was one of the best captains we had and produced some outstanding displays, while Pat Malone's quiet unassuming way about the field was always likely to leave him unnoticed by the mass of hurling followers. Those close to the scene noticed and appreciated him. Still, I would have Mahon and Coleman as first choices.

There are all sorts of options in attack. I would go for Cooney at right half-forward with Brendan Lynskey in the centre and Martin Naughton on the left. The balance there is perfect. A ball-winner (Lynskey), a runner (Naughton) plus an all-rounder (Cooney). That means no place for the 1980 half-forward line of Frank Burke, Joe Connolly and PJ Molloy.

Molloy is probably the unluckiest to lose out as he survived to the second Galway era in the 1980s. I considered accommodating him in the full-forward line, but such is the competition for places in there that, reluctantly, I had to leave him out altogether. Choosing Lynskey ahead of Joe Connolly (and indeed Frank Burke) at centre-forward will surprise many but I believe that Lynskey was far more important to our successes in the 1987-88 era than is generally realised. He was a better ball winner than Connolly and while Joe was a great leader and motivator, Lynskey's overall value earns him the nod.

John Connolly gets the full-forward berth. His mere presence was enough to strike fear into the opposition's heart. Noel Lane is my choice at left full-forward. Yes, I know that we didn't choose him there, or indeed anywhere, on the All-Ireland final teams of 1987-88 but as I have explained elsewhere, there were specific reasons for that. As far as I am concerned, Lane was a brilliant talent, whose contribution to Galway hurling in three decades is well documented. The fact that he keeps out PJ Molloy is self-explanatory.

Eanna Ryan gets the No 13 shirt ahead of Bernie Forde and 'Hopper' McGrath. Forde had a brilliant final in 1980 and was still on the scene at the launch of the new team in 1985, but I believe Ryan's greater versatility was more valuable. Eanna could play anywhere from midfield in and had a goal poacher's instinct. It is a rare quality.

Overall, I think my 'dream team' is more than just a collection of individuals, chosen from an eleven-year period. It is the sort of team which could work together. The balance between markers, ball winners, stylists, and opportunists is about right. Come to think of it, I would love to be taking this team into an All-Ireland final.

GALWAY DREAM TEAM 1980-91

John Commins

Sylvie Linnane — Conor Hayes — Jimmy Cooney

Peter Finnerty — Tony Keady — Iggy Clarke

Michael Coleman — Steve Mahon

Joe Cooney — Brendan Lynskey — Martin Naughton

Eanna Ryan — John Connolly — Noel Lane

One of the myths which has grown up in hurling is that teams like Kilkenny, Cork and Tipperary are all technically better than the rest of us. That is inevitable, I suppose, as they have won seventy-six All-Ireland senior titles between them, compared with a combined total of thirty-one for all the other counties.

We are told that the 'Big Three' are all experts at ground hurling, as if it were the only pure brand available. Yes, it has its uses but is not nearly as effective as some would have you believe. Anyway if it were such a vital part of winning hurling, Kilkenny would never have taken twenty-five All-Ireland titles. Kilkenny players, more than any others, will always get the ball into their hands if they can. It is a policy which has served them well.

Your typical Kilkenny player wants to get the ball into his hand all the time. He likes to settle on it before laying it off. You will very rarely see a Kilkenny player pull on the ball along the ground unless it is very much a last resort.

Cork tend to be a little bit fancier. In terms of wrist work, they are probably the best of all, excelling in little flicks and passes. It makes their hurling very attractive to watch but their really good forwards will always take the ball into their hands too if possible. It is more conducive to precision finishing.

Tipperary play a more forceful, direct game. They were criticised in the 'Babs' Keating era for not having enough steel in them, which was ironic, given that previous Tipp teams had a reputation for being very, very hard. I never felt that the Tipp team of the 1987-94 period lacked physical fibre but, as with so many situations, perception becomes reality and once the word went around that they were slightly soft-centred, it stuck. The fact that it was not based on any concrete evidence was ignored.

Dermot Healy's arrival in Offaly led to a subtle change in their approach in the early 1980s. He brought the Kilkenny style with him and it worked well on Offaly. In fact, it still is working for them. Healy's role in Offaly's emergence as a real hurling power cannot be over-stated. Obviously he needed the players to achieve anything, but his switch of emphasis in terms of approach and tactics provided that little extra which Offaly lacked earlier on. Having said that, people like Andy Gallagher also did an awful lot to lift Offaly hurling.

Offaly's breakthrough in Leinster in 1980 and at All-Ireland level in 1981 created its own tradition in the county. The young lads who emerged later on thought like winners, something which was obvious in their glorious comeback when all seemed lost in the 1994 All-Ireland final.

Wexford have much the same style as Kilkenny and Offaly, only they tend to do things slower. In fact, that has been part of their problem over the past few seasons. Clare, Waterford and Limerick have more in common with Tipperary's direct style than with Cork's subtle touch.

Galway have a running, hand-passing style, something which I always thought suited us well. The player with the ball in his hand is in control. The player who pulls on the ball along the ground is not. Antrim have used Galway's style quite effectively at times but have a tendency to delay the pass too long. If you are playing a running game, then your timing must be spot on – otherwise you can get caught in possession.

Of all the teams I came across during my time with Galway, I have no hesitation in nominating the Kilkenny team of 1982-83 as the best. That team had everything, experience, craft, strength, confidence and an incredible sense of togetherness. I would rate them well ahead of the Kilkenny team which completed the double in 1992-93. Yes, that was a fine team (in fact, it may have a lot more to say for itself yet) but, man for man, the 1982-83 side was better.

Not surprisingly, I include four players from that team on my ideal selection between 1980 and 1994. (Incidentally I am omitting all Galway players from this selection, in the interests of objectivity.)

Kilkenny's Noel Shekhan is my choice in goal. Cork's Ger Cunningham, Offaly's Damien Martin and Jim Troy and Limerick's Tommy Quaid are all genuine rivals but none could match Skehan's unbelievable consistency or his capacity to produce the stunning block from point blank range.

My choice of Tipperary's Paul Delaney at right full-back will surprise some people but I always thought he was an under-rated hurler. He has a sure first touch and invariably puts hurling skill above all other considerations, which is a good sign of a corner-back. Kilkenny's Joe Hennessy is a credible alternative but I stick with Delaney on the basis that most of Hennessy's best hurling came at right half-back, although he switched to the corner late in his career.

Leonard Enright (Limerick) and Brian Cody (Kilkenny) would both have many supporters for the full-back position, but personally I would prefer Offaly's Eugene Coughlan for his sheer tenacity and consistent judgement. Kilkenny's swashbuckling corner-back, Dick O'Hara gets the No 4 shirt ahead of Pat Fleury (Offaly), Johnny Crowley (Cork) and John Henderson (Kilkenny).

Liam O'Donoghue (Limerick), Ger Henderson (Kilkenny) and

Tom Cashman (Cork) comprise my formidable half-back line. O'Donoghue didn't always get the credit he deserved but he had all the attributes of a great wing-back as far as I am concerned. Henderson was unrivalled at centre-back. At his peak, he had everything and played every game with his heart and his head. There were never any half-measures with Ger.

Tom Cashman was a delight to watch, wherever he played. When people talk about class, certainly in a defensive context, then they need look no further than Cashman. Midfield picks itself – Frank Cummins (Kilkenny) and John Fenton (Cork). It would be the dream combination. Cummins was strong, committed and consistent while Fenton had a lovely touch in the air and on the ground. Add in the fact that he was deadly from frees and you have an added bonus.

I know that my choice of forwards will surprise many, especially Nicholas English fans. I have not included him among my six best attackers, despite the fact that some saw him as the best forward of the 1980s – early '90s. It would be easy to slot him in somewhere, simply for the sake of paying tribute to his undoubted talents but I would regard that as an easy way out.

Yes, I have great admiration for English but, given the quality of players at my disposal I cannot fit him in. Right half-forward? I would prefer Cork's Tony O'Sullivan, whose deft touches were so effective. O'Sullivan's ability to winkle a score in little or no space, or when things were going badly for Cork, always impressed me greatly.

Left half-forward? English never played a whole lot there but even if he did, I would have Kilkenny's DJ Carey ahead of him. Carey's instinct, allied to his touch and timing, make him a truly special talent.

Nor can I find a place for English in the full-forward line. His team mate, Pat Fox, had a greater return in terms of scores-per-chances. Fox's eye for goal was unerring when he was at his peak. Wexford's Tony Doran, Kilkenny's Christy Heffernan and Liam Fennelly, Offaly's Padraig Horan, Cork's Jimmy Barry-Murphy, Ray Cummins and English are all vying for the full-forward spot. It's a magnificent seven in terms of talent, with my vote going to McKenna who, at his best, really was a dynamite full-forward.

English did most of his best work at left full-forward for Tipperary but once again, he loses out. This time, he is beaten by Barry-Murphy, who was one of the truly great opportunists of our time.

And what of centre-forward? My choice there will surprise many because he never won an All-Star award and was rarely talked of as a great player. Yet when you look back at the period in question, was there a better centre-forward around than Offaly's Brendan Bermingham? Personally, I doubt it.

Bermingham's role was thankless, in many ways. It hinged mainly on keeping the ball moving into the Offaly full-forward line and in breaking up play out in the half-line. He did it magnificently for a long time. He was the cable carrying the power to Offaly's bright lights in attack. Not surprisingly, the All-Stars selectors never noticed him. A player has got to be very prominent in an obvious sort of way to win All-Star approval. Bermingham wasn't but that should in no way detract from his influence on the Offaly attack in the 1980s.

Oddly enough, there are not a whole lot of alternative candidates. Outside of Galway's Joe Cooney and Brendan Lynskey, there have been few consistently good centre-forwards since the departure of Cork's Gerald McCarthy, who was one of the most gifted players I ever saw.

MY ALL-IRELAND TEAM 1980-94

NOEL SKEHAN
(KILKENNY)

PAUL DELANEY   EUGENE COUGHLAN   DICK O'HARA
(TIPPERARY)   *(OFFALY)*   *(KILKENNY)*

LIAM O'DONOGHUE   GER HENDERSON   TOM CASHMAN
(LIMERICK)   *(KILKENNY)*   *(CORK)*

FRANK CUMMINS   JOHN FENTON
(KILKENNY)   *(CORK)*

TONY O'SULLIVAN   BRENDAN BERMINGHAM   DJ CAREY
(CORK)   *(OFFALY)*   *(KILKENNY)*

PAT FOX   JOE McKENNA   JIMMY BARRY-MURPHY
(TIPPERARY)   *(LIMERICK)*   *(CORK)*

Chapter 32

PLANNING FOR THE FUTURE

I worry for the future of hurling. That may sound odd coming from somebody who lives in a county which is going well and where the structures are sound. But the truth is that nobody, or no place, is immune to change.

The warning bells have even been sounded in Kilkenny, a county with a hurling pedigree of the highest order. Nicky Brennan, a man closely involved with the sport all his life as a top class player and administrator, painted a distinctly gloomy picture at the 1994 GAA Congress. He is not the alarmist type, so if somebody like him from a hurling heartland is concerned about the game's future, it's time to take stock.

There is no point looking at hurling in isolation. It must be done as part of an overall review of where the GAA stands heading into the next century. That might sound rather vague but it's not. Putting it bluntly, the question has to be asked – does the GAA have a viable future in a changing world, or more specifically in a changing Europe? Does hurling have a viable future within a changing GAA?

The thought of an Ireland without the GAA and its games may sound unthinkable. That's understandable but the reality is that it will not survive purely on its own momentum. It has got to be pushed along in a vibrant, systematic, positive way.

The redevelopment of Croke Park is an example. Inevitably, there were criticisms when the GAA authorities committed themselves to a £120 million redevelopment plan. Especially so, when it emerged that they were building corporate boxes for the rich to indulge themselves on big match days.

Corporate entertainment is part of big-time sport the world over these days. It may have vulgar connotations in some respects, but it's a fact of sporting life. The GAA cannot remain immune from it. Nor should it, if it can tap the corporate sector for big money to help finance its affairs.

I have no objections to the corporate boxes in Croke Park. If company executives want to be seen in Croke Park on big match days, that's fine by me, provided loyal fans do not suffer. Maintaining a balance is the key here. When Croke Park is fully redeveloped, there will, in fact, be more tickets available to the ordinary fans than there were in the old stadium. That's what the GAA hierarchy tells us and we have to believe them – for now anyway.

So why then are ordinary GAA fans perturbed by the introduction of high-powered corporate activity in Croke Park? Simply because they see it as the erection of another row of bricks in the wall between themselves and the GAA authorities.

There is very much a 'them' and 'us' attitude between the GAA hierarchy and the ordinary member. Rightly or wrongly, there is a feeling that the hierarchy are aloof and distant. They are up there in Croke Park making all the decisions and they only come down amongst the minions for the odd function at Christmas or when we win an All-Ireland final.

I know the GAA's top brass will howl 'not true'. It's too late. That is the common perception and the GAA authorities only have themselves to blame. Individually, they are all nice, decent people but collectively, they have lost the common touch.

They are not good at promoting the organisation. There is a tendency to react to things rather than to initiate them. They are especially sensitive to criticism, even when it comes from people who are steeped in GAA tradition and who know the Association inside out. There is a distinct difference between them and the anti-GAA type, who can see nothing right in the organisation. Basically that is down to jealousy and should be ignored. The trouble is, the GAA seems to have difficulty differentiating between objective criticism from its own members and supporters and ridiculous attacks from outsiders, many of which are based on prejudice.

Surely it should be possible for an organisation of the GAA's size to have a monthly newsletter circulated through the clubs so that ordinary members are kept informed of what is happening at top level. As things stand, we have to depend on the newspapers for far too much information. In many cases, journalists elicit it through unofficial channels, simply because they are told very little of what is going on. Thankfully, they are very adept at discovering details of various meetings, but that is not the way things should be done. If the GAA is as democratic as it says it is, then members are entitled to know everything that goes on from management level down and not merely the carefully edited version which finds its way onto the official record.

Let me give an example. The GAA has not given a satisfactory explanation as to why the All-Ireland football championship had a sponsor in 1994 while the hurling championship did not. Nor has it told the ordinary members how much the sponsorship is worth. If we are all supposed to be equal in GAA land, what right has the top brass to keep such information to themselves?

I was very disappointed at the failure to secure a sponsor for the hurling championship, not just because of the money, but because of what it said about the game. It depicted it as a second class citizen, compared to football, a view held by many anyway. The GAA should have held off on sponsorship until such time as it had backers for both the hurling and football championships.

Some hurling people believe that it's time to split the association into two separate organisations, under the overall GAA banner. The argument is that the current system is heavily weighed in favour of football. Personally, I would not favour the two-organisation idea. It could prove very divisive in the long term and the last thing the GAA needs is internal friction. Having said that, I believe it's time that hurling was given more attention.

Basically, it's a summer game, yet most inter-county activity takes place between mid-October and mid-April. It's ludicrous that there are only six competitive inter-county games between July 1 and September 30. That's right, six games! The Munster, Leinster and Ulster hurling finals, the All-Ireland semi-finals and the All-Ireland final. It's ideal hurling weather, yet most of the top hurlers are idle, apart from club activity.

Several attempts have been made to devise a more streamlined fixtures' plan. All have been rejected. So we are left with the crazy situation where most county hurling teams are idle between May and October. The same happens in football. Meanwhile, your average club soccer and rugby players have a match every weekend during their season.

I don't accept that a better fixtures' structure cannot be devised. I know that the GAA is a multi-faceted and that it is difficult to fit in both hurling and football at inter-county and club level, but there has to be a better way than the current one. One possible method of helping to clear the log jam of fixtures is to ensure that every match produces a winner. In other words, play extra-time when a game finishes level, rather than going to a replay. Fixtures are often thrown into chaos because a few games finish level. That is wrong. If we were guaranteed a winner first time out, it would be much easier to streamline the programme.

It's time to look too at the National Leagues They tend to be treated as guinea pigs for rule experiments or whatever other innovation is in fashion at any particular time. Besides, they are not Leagues at all in the strictest sense, since counties are only guaranteed seven games. I would favour a real League of say, fourteen games, played on a home and away basis.

The League is seen as a second-class competition to fill the time between championships. That is unsatisfactory. In most other team sports, the League is on a par, if not actually enjoying a higher status, than the Cup (championship) competitions. The GAA will never achieve that while it keeps changing the League system every few years and while it makes provision for just seven games per division.

I would also favour the open draw in the championship. There is absolutely no logic in the current system and I have no doubt that is has contributed to certain counties getting others into a psychological grip and holding them there for years. In general, a big county will keep its smaller neighbour in check. At best it will be a three to one ratio in terms of wins. Extend that back to the foundation of the GAA and you have a situation where very definite trends have developed in all Provinces. Players from some counties come into hurling or football expecting to beat certain others while the 'victims' come into the games expecting to lose. An open draw would increase the options all round since counties would be meeting different opposition every year.

Hurling fans will claim that Galway would not have done nearly as well under the open draw. I don't agree. Certainly, we may not have played in as many finals but we would probably have won more. Our current situation is a joke. Going directly into the All-Ireland semi-final every second year gives us certain advantages but not as many as people seem to think. Yes, it guarantees us semi-final appearances but come 3.30 on the first Sunday in August we are invariably up against a team which has played two, or sometimes, three very competitive championship matches. Who has the advantage then?

If Galway were so happy with the current situation why should they favour an open draw? Yet, the vast bulk of hurling people in the county would support it. Why not try it on an experimental basis for even three years? If it was found to be less attractive than the current system, it could be scrapped and forgotten and those of us who called for it would be silenced for ever more.

Apart from the specifics of the competition structure, there are other areas which the GAA must carefully examine if it is to continue competing successfully with other sports. Television has flattened all barriers in relation to sport. The main events are beamed directly into people's homes from all over the world. Because they are confined solely to Ireland and to Irish communities living overseas, hurling and football have an exposure problem.

You won't find Galway v Tipperary shown on Italian TV, for instance, but you will see Juventus v AC Milan on RTE. English soccer games are shown on RTE virtually every Saturday throughout the winter. The games may not always be entertaining, but they are still creating an awareness among youngsters. Your average nine year-old can tell you who is reserve goalie at Manchester United and offer an enlightened opinion on the relative merits of Alan Shearer versus Eric Cantona. He can walk into his local shop and buy several glossy soccer magazines. By comparison, he would need a search party to locate any GAA publication. That creates an image in the lad's mind. Soccer is fashionable, colourful and vibrant. Hurling and football are great games to play but there is not a whole lot more to them. Long-term, the dangers of that thought process are obvious.

This country is very much part of a modern Europe so it will take very careful planning by the GAA to hold its games to the forefront. Corporate boxes or not, the GAA has shown itself to be progressive, courageous and far-seeing by redeveloping Croke Park but I would hope that the same sort of effort would also be devoted to games' promotion.

Television has to play a major part in that. The days when youngsters grew up thinking that GAA players were the only sporting heroes around are long gone, even in rural Ireland. The GAA now has to compete for attention. It seems to me that the only definite way of giving players a higher profile is to have more games on television, 'live' if possible. There are risks in doing that on Sundays as it would effect attendances at other matches, so the obvious answer is to play one major game every Saturday.

The Leinster Council have used Saturday as an 'over-flow' day quite successfully in recent years. Their games have been shown 'live' on TV, with the accompanying promotional benefits. If the National League's profile was improved, the same could happen for League games. After all, Gaelic Games make very good television and I'm sure that RTE would screen a National League game 'live' on a Saturday, if the fixture was sufficiently attractive. It is up to the GAA to provide such a fixture, week after week. As things stand, they concede Saturdays to every other sport, despite the fact that they have so many glamourous fixtures of their own, all crowded into Sunday afternoons.

The lack of an international dimension will always be a problem for the GAA but, rather than worry about it, the emphasis should be on more and more promotion here at home. Hurling, in particular, needs a massive push. It's a sad state of affairs that nine counties did not enter in the 1994 senior championship at all. Surely, it should be possible to broaden the base so that every county has a team capable of competing in the championship.

That is why it is so necessary to improve and develop coaching. I'm not talking here about big coaching manuals with colourful diagrams, showing how players should grip the hurley, but rather on-the-spot, practical coaching. That will cost money, of course, but it would be money well spent. There are literally dozens of former players who would be able, and willing, to do great work in weaker counties if the structures were in place to utilise them. Pay them for their time and effort. The long-term winner would be hurling.

No, I am not advocating professionalism. We can never have a situation where players are paid for playing. In a country of this size, the resources simply are not there. League of Ireland soccer proved that. Besides, there is no demand among GAA players for payment. All they seek is fair treatment, in relation to expenses. If they get the odd perk as well, so much the better.

But when it comes to coaching, then money should be spent. Lots of it. It should also be spent on subsidising the cost of equipment, such as hurleys and helmets. Hurling is far more expensive to play than football, rugby or soccer so inevitably, it starts from a disadvantage. That is a more serious consideration than many people think. It's up to the GAA to generate the resources to ensure that youngsters or their parents are not turned off hurling, purely because of the cost. If attention is not given to these practical areas, I have doubts as to whether or not hurling will be anywhere as popular in fifty years time. In fact, it could be on the way out.

That is why the GAA should undertake a fundamental overhaul of its entire structures and redefine its outlook. It drives me mad when I hear yearly debates over whether or not British Army or RUC officers should be allowed into the GAA. That has to be the most ridiculous rule ever imposed by a sporting organisation. Even if it had a relevance years ago, it has long since outlived its value. It is now no more than an embarrassing monument to intransigence and serves only to depict the GAA as divisive and sectarian. That is utterly unfair on ninety-nine per cent of the members. Believe me, there are just as many bigots in other sports, but the majority membership is not tarred with the same brush because they don't have a rule in place, proclaiming their prejudices. Does anybody seriously think that if the ban on the British Army and the RUC were lifted, there would be a mad rush to join the GAA? The rule, as it stands, alienates the GAA in the minds of a great many fair-minded people on both sides of the border. It also takes up a lot of valuable time at GAA Conventions every year, time which could be used far more profitably.

The GAA is a great organisation. Its contribution to Irish life is immense and it has much to be proud of. But it must be vigilant in an ever-changing world. It cannot be seen to devote time and energy to piffling little matters like whether or not Down and Dublin should be allowed to play a mid-winter challenge match at the same venue as a soccer game (remember the RDS affair in 1991?) or whether soccer is played at a brand new Croke Park.

Those are not the challenges facing the GAA. No, the real challenge is to make hurling and football so attractive in every way that enough youngsters will want to continue playing them. The games themselves are good enough to fight off the challenges being thrown down by other sports. Question is – are we in the GAA up to the task?

The dangers for hurling, which is weaker from a base viewpoint than football, are obvious. It will take more than lip-service to nourish it safely through the next century. It will take vision, commitment and, possibly most important of all, massive investment. Otherwise, the great art faces an uncertain 21st century.

EPILOGUE

Will I ever go back into team management? Frankly, I don't know. I was nominated by twenty-two clubs when the Galway managership fell vacant last autumn, but decided against letting my name go forward once it became apparent that there would be a contest for the position.

No, I wasn't afraid of being beaten in a vote. Team management thickens the skin to such a degree that losing an election would not have bothered me. What did concern me was the possible damage an election would have done to Galway hurling.

Ultimately, the health and welfare of the game come before any individuals. That applies to every county. I felt that the best contribution I could have made to Galway hurling last autumn was to stand back and let others challenge for the team manager's job.

Mattie Murphy, John Connolly and Monty Kerins, who did so well with Galway minors over the past few years, were eventually chosen and I'm sure they will do a fine job. They can certainly rely on my support. They are the men in charge and if they fail Galway hurling fails, so its in everbody's interest in the county to do all they can to help them.

Modern team management is a very onerous job, which takes over your entire life. It can either make or break an individual. But while it becomes an all-consuming passion, it has to be put in perspective. The capacity to be able to stand back and see it for what it is remains the only sure way of keeping your sanity.

It would be wrong to say that I enjoyed every minute of my managerial career. There were days when I thought to myself: 'What the hell am I doing here, why am I not outside the wire with all the other critics?' But, in any walk of life, there have to be people who are prepared to walk through the gate and put themselves on the spot.

I did that more than most and emerged to tell the tale. When I look back now I don't see the disappointments or the big games which we lost, but only the successes and the satisfaction of working with players and achieving at least some of our targets.

For me that is what sport is all about.

INDEX

B
Bailey, John F 51, 63
Barrett, Marty 137, 138
Bermingham, Brendan 106, 235, 235
Bernie, Dave 218
Best, George 27
Boylan, Sean 212
Bonnar, Colm 158, 164
Bonnar, Cormac 179, 197, 201
Brehony, Padraig 39
Brehony, Tony 32
Brennan, Kiernan 15, 17, 34, 236
Brennan, Mick 92
Bridges, Paul 66
Broderick, John Joe 39
Buckley, PJ 36
Burke, Frank 94, 104, 105, 107, 108, 110, 111, 121, 123, 137, 138, 173, 230
Burke, Gerry 62, 83, 160, 187, 210
Burke, Jarlath P 33, 44
Burke, Richie 203
Byrne, Mick 36

C
Callanan, Tom 200
Callinan, John 73
Callinan, Tom 86
Callnan, PJ 128
Carey, DJ 227, 234, 235
Carney, Jim 33
Carroll, Donal 111
Carroll, Jimmy 123
Carroll, Mossie 116
Cashman, Jim 194, 227
Cashman, Tom 234, 235
Clarke, Iggy 34, 94, 100, 105, 110, 111, 117, 121, 125, 131, 137, 138, 229, 231
Clarke, Joe 138
Cleary, Eamonn 217, 218
Cleary, Pat 45, 197
Clifford, Johnny 15, 208

Cloonan, Jarlath 197
Cody, Brian 233
Coen, Michael 129
Coen, Seamus 49, 62, 105, 110, 112, 125, 140, 230
Coleman, Michael 1, 6, 38, 62, 70, 75, 77, 151, 15-160, 164, 165, 179, 187, 192, 202, 207, 230, 231
Commins, John 9, 18, 38, 39, 59, 63, 66, 67, 77, 80, 164, 187, 199, 202, 203, 228, 229, 231
Conneely, Mike 102, 103, 107, 110, 114, 115, 138, 221, 228
Connolly, Gerry 103
Connolly, Joe 34, 97, 100, 103, 110, 111, 115-117, 123, 124, 125, 230
Connolly, John 92, 94, 97, 100, 103, 106, 107, 110, 117, 119, 120, 121, 138, 226, 230, 231
Connolly, Michael 38, 51, 62, 103, 110, 112, 125, 138, 230
Connolly, Padraig 103
Connollys, the 104, 117
Conroy, Sean 90
Cooney, Gerry 138
Cooney, Jimmy 100, 110, 112, 115, 125, 226, 228, 229, 231
Cooney, Joe 2, 9, 39, 49, 52, 56, 58, 60, 61, 66, 67, 69, 71, 80, 141, 144, 151, 154, 187, 194, 210, 226, 227, 228, 231, 235
Corbett, Gerry 132
Corrigan, Mark 106, 146
Corrigan, Paddy 45
Cosgrave, Brian 31
Cooney, Jimmy 88
Cooney, Joe 38-40, 46, 70, 79, 146, 164, 180, 193
Coughlan, Eamonn 193
Coughlan, Eugene 44, 151, 233, 235
Cregan, Eamonn 109, 123, 220
Crowley, John 62, 233
Cummins, Brendan 33

Cummins, Frank 33, 234, 235
Cummins, Ray 33, 101, 234
Cunningham, Anthony 12, 38-40, 51, 52, 56, 58, 60, 64, 66, 71, 80, 158, 187, 208, 210
Cunningham, Ger 50, 195, 233
Cunningham, Tom 64, 69
Curtin, Gerry 100
Cusack, JP 132

D

Darcy, Josie 31
Delaney, Pat 61, 151, 152
Delaney, Paul 166, 175, 233, 235
Dempsey, Tom 51, 66
Denton, John 179, 180, 181
Dervan, Colm 32
Dervan, Packie 39, 62
Dixon, Brendan 32
Dolan, Syl 187
Dolphin, Sean 187
Donnellys, the 104
Donoghue, Eddie 33
Dongohue, Frank 32
Donoghue, Miko 1, 3, 74, 78
Donoghue, Paddy 32, 33
Donoghue, Tom 137
Doran, Tony 234
Douglas, Mrs
Dowling, John 212
Downey, Paddy 110, 181
Doyle, Jimmy 78
Doyle, John 78
Doyle, Paddy 216
Duane, Ray 60, 178, 211
Duggan, Jimmy 7
Dunne, Liam 217

E

Earls, Michael 62, 68, 69, 140, 160, 202, 211
Egan, Paddy 90
English, Nicholas 48, 71, 79, 154-157, 163-167, 169, 170, 179, 191, 200, 222, 234

English, Theo 79
Enright, Leonard 115, 124, 233

F

Fahey, Frank 130
Fahy, Dermot 187, 192
Fahy, Mike 32
Fahy, Padraig 32, 138
Fahy, Sean 132
Fahy, Tom
Fennelly, Ger 9, 18, 52, 56
Fennelly, Kevin 9
Fennelly, Liam 3, 18, 52, 53, 58, 157, 234
Fenton, Andy 112, 129, 131, 137
Fenton, John 43, 63, 234
Finn, John 'Stack' 32
Finnerty, Peter 16, 38, 40, 42, 44, 46, 49, 56, 75, 77, 144, 157, 166, 179, 187, 192, 197, 203, 229, 231
Fitzgerald, Ciaran 129, 131
Flaherty, 'Inky' 82, 83, 95, 96, 97, 99, 117
Flaherty, Johnny 123
Fleury, Pat 34, 44, 233
Flynn, Colm 8, 73
Fogarty, Aidan 44
Fogarty, Declan 45
Fogarty, Mick 33, 197
Foley, Sean 111, 116, 123
Forde, Bernie 44, 52, 59, 106, 110, 115, 125, 140, 231
Fox, Pat 71, 79, 154, 166, 169, 170, 179, 234, 235
Francome, Johnny 169
Furey, John 132
Furlong, Dave 218

G

Gallagher, Pat 27
Gantley, Finbarr 100, 112, 123
Geraghty, Johnny 31
Gibson, Mike 23
Giles, Johnny 134
Glynn, Gerry 105, 110, 129, 137

Gohery, Larry 2
Goode, John 140
Grace, Paddy 132-134
Grealish, James 138
Greaney, Joe 140
Grimes, Michael 124
Guilfoyle, Michael 69
Guilfoyle, Tommy 68
Guiton, John 182

H
Halliday, Jimmy 173
Hanahoe, Tony 65
Hardiman, John 187
Harte, Eamonn 31
Hayes, Conor 1, 4, 34, 38, 58, 65, 68, 98, 100, 105, 108, 110, 111, 115, 116, 123, 125, 140, 143, 144, 152, 154, 156, 157, 163, 165, 166, 191-194, 199, 200-202, 211, 222, 228, 229, 231
Hayes, Joe 158, 164
Hayes, Liam 31, 211
Healy, Dermot 105, 121, 220, 232
Heffernan, Christy 52, 234
Heffernan, Kevin 95, 135
Helebert, Michael 170, 171, 185
Henderson, Ger 17, 61, 227, 233, 235
Henderson, John 48, 233
Henderson, Pat 60
Hennessy, Joe 99, 233
Hennessy, Kevin 63
Herbert, Pat 124
Hewitt, Dave 23
Higgins, Padraig 39
Higgins, Pat 187
Hogan, Conor 31
Hogan, Ken 166, 167
Holland, Gerry 131, 137, 197
Holohan, Jimmy 189, 215, 217
Horan, Padraig 106, 199, 220, 234
Hogan, Ken 79
Hogan, Vincent 181
Horgan, John 35

Holohan, Frank 12
Horan, Padraig 45
Horgan, John 33
Howley, Michael 90

J
Jennings, Declan 39

K
Keady, Tony 10, 34, 38, 40, 42, 44-46, 56, 154, 159, 164-166, 169-177, 182-185, 187, 195, 203, 204, 222, 229, 231
Keane, Gerry 196
Keane, Sean 39
Keating, 'Babs' 71, 78-80, 90, 91, 94, 96, 97, 120, 139, 154, 167, 216, 220, 232
Keenan, Donal 181
Keeshan, Brendan 45
Keher, Eddie 61, 133
Kelly, Joachim 193
Kelly, Paddy 32
Kelly, Sean 197
Kenny, Michael 187
Kilfeather, Sean 87
Kilkenny, Michael 100, 140
Kilkenny, Ollie 38, 40, 53, 125, 144, 149, 165, 166, 192, 202, 229, 230
Kilkenny, Tony 12, 40, 44, 56, 62, 75, 77, 158, 160, 166, 167, 202, 210
Killeen, Martin 39
Kirby, John 70
Kirwan, Gerry 69, 80, 167

L
Laly, Paddy 138
Landers, JJ 106
Lane, Noel 1, 6, 9, 10, 12, 13, 18, 32, 38, 44, 50, 52, 56, 58, 60, 62, 75, 76, 91, 92, 100, 106, 110, 112, 124, 125, 152, 157, 158, 160, 166, 167, 177, 178, 184, 187, 193, 195, 209, 210, 228, 231
Larkin, Alan 136

Larkin, Frank 102, 125, 133
Larkin, Tommy 8, 31
Leahy, John 156, 166, 180
Leahy, Mick 24
Lennon, Tommy 18
Linnane, Sylvie 1, 38, 49, 50, 58, 65, 66, 73, 99, 100, 105, 110, 112, 133, 143, 165, 179, 185, 192, 193, 198, 199, 200, 202, 228, 229, 231
Loughnane, Ger 73
Lynskey, Brendan 12, 40, 49, 51, 56, 58, 63, 80, 125, 141, 143, 151, 157-159, 171, 172, 183, 185, 193, 204, 205, 230, 231, 235

M

Madden, Pat 33
Mahon, Jack 94
Mahon, Steve 1, 9, 38, 56, 58, 60, 73, 77, 84, 100, 105, 110, 112, 124, 125, 140, 143, 144, 146, 149, 150, 151, 157, 185, 206, 207, 228, 230, 231
Malone, Pat 12, 13, 38, 39, 62, 66, 67, 83, 84, 151, 157, 158, 164, 165, 180, 192, 202, 207, 230
Martin, Damien 121, 123, 233
McCarthy, Liam 18, 235
McDonagh, Joe 34, 91, 94, 105, 110, 112, 131, 138, 173, 182, 222
McDonagh, Maitias 128
McGee, Eugene 220
McGloin, Michael 73
McGrath, 'Hopper' 12, 38, 62, 144, 180, 181, 183, 185, 210, 231
McGrath, Joe 94, 96, 139
McGrath, Martin 80, 90
McInerney, Dr Mary 74, 115
McInerney, Gerry 15, 17, 34, 38, 39, 56, 66, 68, 69, 72, 75, 77, 147, 151, 166, 177, 206, 208, 229
McInerney, Niall 91, 94, 99, 105, 107, 109-111, 121, 125, 138, 199, 229
McKenna, Joe 98, 111, 116, 235
McMahon, Mick 22

Molloy, PJ 18, 38, 44, 45, 51, 52, 62, 91, 94, 100, 110, 115, 121, 123, 125, 131, 137, 138, 139, 157, 210, 230, 231
Moloney, Tom
Monaghan, Tom 38, 39, 187, 192, 211
Moylan, Pat 33
Mulcahy, Denis 62
Mulcahy, Thomas 2, 63
Mullen, Frank 22, 121
Mulligan, Paddy 134
Mulvihill, Liam 174, 176, 182
Murphy, Bernie 83, 84, 85
Murphy, Brendan 132
Murphy, Dickie 188
Murphy, Eamonn 173
Murphy, Jimmy Barry 43, 221, 234, 235
Murphy, Noel 24
Murphy, Peter 59, 62, 69, 77, 159, 160, 199, 202, 211
Murphy, Phelim 6,7, 10, 38, 48, 53, 72, 75, 82, 83, 84, 85, 86, 87, 88, 139, 143, 144, 158, 159, 172, 174, 185, 214, 215, 222, 224, 225
Murphy, Sean 32, 138
Murphy, Ted 138
Murray, Alf 128
Murray, Donal 115
Murray, Larry 159
Murray, Terence 10, 17, 59, 188

N

Naughton, Martin 15, 16, 40, 52, 58, 79, 83, 152, 169, 177, 178, 184, 187, 192, 195, 205, 207, 230, 231
Nealon, Donie 78, 79
Nelson, Jim 186

O

O'Brien, Fr Michael 194
O'Conaire, Padraig 113
O'Connell, Donie 48, 80, 154
O'Connor, Bernie 6, 11, 38, 48, 82,

83, 90, 94, 108, 113, 143, 144, 158, 159, 172, 173, 185, 222, 224, 225
O'Connor, George 217
O'Connor, Ollie 109, 115
O'Dea, Canon 128
O'Donoghue, Liam 111, 233-235
O'Donovan, Conor 48, 154, 167, 180
O'Dwyer, Mick 95, 135, 140
O'Gorman, Larry 66
O'Hara, Dick 233, 235
O'Hara, Joe 59
O'Neill, Pa 156, 160
O'Rourke, Colm 211
O'Shea, John 142, 143
O'Shea, Ned 205
O'Sullivan, Jim 181
O'Sullivan, Tony 195, 234, 235

P
Patmore, Angela 107
Piggott, Pearse 56, 58, 60, 62, 75, 77, 125, 160, 211
Potterton, Pat 50
Prendergast, Paddy 61
Price, Brian 24
Punch, Dom 115, 124

Q
Quaid, Tommy 103, 233
Qualter, PJ 90, 138
Quigley, Martin 214, 218
Quigley, Pat 214
Quinn, Niall 39

R
Rabitte, Joe 193
Redmond, Charlie 36
Regan, Mick 29
Ringer, Paul 198
Roche, Dick 24
Ryan, Aidan 156, 165
Ryan, Bobby 48, 78, 79, 160
Ryan, Declan 166
Ryan, Eanna 9, 12, 38, 62, 70, 80, 164, 166, 178-180, 187, 195, 207, 208, 231
Ryan, Harry 59
Ryan, John 116, 140
Ryan, Paschal 105, 140
Ryan, Sonny 34

S
Salmon, Joe 7
Shaughnessy, Joe 214
Sheil, Jimmy 31
Shinnors, Seamus 100, 102, 112
Shinnors, Sean 92
Silke, Sean 34, 94, 100, 107, 110, 112, 121, 229
Skehan, Noel 92, 233, 235
Solan, Fr Jack 128
Stack, Sean 34, 73
Stakelum, Richard 3
Stanley, Cathal 33
Stanley, Sam 32, 34
Staunton, Aidan 170, 171, 185
Storey, Martin 217
Sweeney, Tim 7
Synnott, Eamonn 66

T
Tracey, Jim 133
Tracey, Noel 132
Treacy, Sean 38, 39, 177, 191, 192
Troy, Jim 2, 233
Twomey, John 36

W
Walsh, John 61
Walsh, Liam 12
Walsh, Ollie 216
Whelan, Jack 128